Carol,
  Parts of this were written
On that boat you slept on. Fond
memories. I hope you enjoy my
book!
        — Bill Raney 3/6/09

LETTERS TO ZERKY

A Father's Legacy
to a Lost Son
and a Road Trip
Around the World

•

Bill Raney and JoAnne Walker Raney

NICKELODEON
P R E S S

Nickelodeon Press
P.O. Box 3573
Santa Cruz, CA 95063-3573.

Printed in the United States of America

ISBN 978-0-9821384-0-3 First Hard Cover Edition 2009
ISBN 978-0-9821384-1-0 First Soft Cover Edition 2009

Publisher's Cataloging-in-Publication
(Provided by Quality Books, Inc.)

Raney, Bill.
   Letters to Zerky : a father's legacy to a lost son and a road trip around the world / Bill Raney and JoAnne Walker Raney. – 1st ed.
      p. cm.
   Includes index.
   ISBN-13: 978-0-9821384-0-3 (hardcover)
   ISBN-10: 0-9821384-0-7 (hardcover)
   ISBN-13: 978-0-9821384-1-0
   ISBN-10: 0-9821384-1-5
      1. Raney, Bill–Travel. 2. Raney, JoAnne Walker, 1933-1969–Travel.
   3. Raney, Eric Xerxes, 1966-1971–Travel. 4. Voyages and travels–Eurasia.
   5. Travelers–Eurasia–Biography. 6. Motion picture theater managers–
   California–Santa Cruz–Biography. 7. Fathers and sons–Biography.
   8. Eurasia–Description and travel.   I. Raney, JoAnne Walker, 1933-1969.
   II. Title.
   G490.R36 2009
   910.4   QBI08-600331

Library of Congress Control Number: 2008910400

Cover design by Kathi Dunn
Dunn+Associates Design, Hayward, WI

Interior layout and design by
Sue Knopf, Graffolio, La Crosse, WI

Printed and bound by Sheridan Books
Ann Arbor, MI

This book is dedicated to my wife Nancy,
who was JoAnne's friend and who has been
my coach and sounding board throughout the
long process of writing this book.

Nancy, who has had to live with the ghost
of my former wife.

Nancy, who put clothes in my closet
and love back into my life.

Contents

1967

1967 was the summer of love in a summer of death. As napalm rained down on the people of Vietnam and the first of the runaways began trickling into San Francisco, with flowers in their hair, JoAnne with her dachshund, her husband and their ten-month-old son, Eric Xerxes Raney, trickled out of San Francisco, wondering if they would ever return. JoAnne had just sold her little movie theatre and after all its debts were paid off, perhaps ten thousand dollars remained, which we decided to blow on a Volkswagen camper-van and a trip to Europe. The dollar was mighty back then and camping would keep us away from hotels and from restaurants; here was a formula to stay a long time. We would have no itinerary, just plenty of time to wander Europe as our fancies took us. That there might be a world beyond Europe, a world you could drive to, was something that never occurred to us until six months later when we met an elderly German couple on a lonely beach in Southern Greece, who were on their way back to Germany from Iran.

Gone missing from JoAnne's little menagerie was her parakeet, who would have come along too, just as he had on her previous trip to Europe, had not JoAnne's prematurely forgetful husband absentmindedly opened a window a few weeks earlier and allowed her free-flying flutterer to flap off to freedom. JoAnne was a great lover of birds, animals, absentminded husbands, and of author Gerald Durrell and all his many many-footed friends. When she was a young girl, a preacher once told her that her dog couldn't go to heaven with her, "because dogs don't have souls." She became an atheist on the spot. You didn't mess with JoAnne's animals.

In April of 1967, we flew from San Francisco to Munich, where we picked up a shiny new Volkswagen bus. What a shame our ten-month-old son would have no memory of his great adventure. Thus was born the idea of a series of letters to Zerky, letters for him to enjoy someday when he was old enough to wonder about all the places he'd been and the things he had seen. Four years ago, I came across these letters in the back of a file cabinet, where they had been languishing for thirty-six years. Should you enjoy them, you will have given them a new purpose.

The Adventures of Zerky

Zerky in Germany, looking cool

Zerky and Dad on Zerky's First Birthday, in Paris

Zerky at the Gas Chamber in Dachau

**Zerky in his new Lederhosen
in the Italian Alps (Dolomites)
Tarzan standing guard**

**JoAnne getting Zerky and Tarzan ready to climb
the Matterhorn**

**Zerky and Tarzan preparing their assault
on the notorious North Face of the Eiger.
JoAnne standing by.**

Zerky at the "Roman Baths"; Lake Ohrid, Macedonia

Zerky at the Acropolis in Greece

Zerky throwing rocks at the Black Sea

**Zerky at Persepolis, his namesake's
Seat of the Persian Empire**

**Zerky with Stephanie and Bill and Eddie
in the Great Sand Desert of Baluchistan,
trying to get water out of that well**

Zerky at the Taj Mahal, Agra, India

Zerky horsing around on an erotic temple at Khajuraho

**Zerky and his Sherpa about to climb 26,000-foot-high
Annapurna, in the Himalayas of Nepal**

Zerky Goes Riding on his Elephant in Assam

**Zerky with his Indian family in Assam
JoAnne and her Elephant Friends in background**

Zerky on the Burma Road

**Zerky Resting after a hard day's work at the
Temple of the Emerald Buddha, Bangkok, Thailand**

**Zerky Victorious coming home on the
USS *President Cleveland***

Main Street, Consumers, Utah, 1936
Library of Congress Photo by Dorothea Lange

Camels in the Snows of Persia

**Village of Potes in the Liébana
Northern Spain, Picos de Europa
Where Bill & Nancy later lived for six months**

Map 1
Eurasia

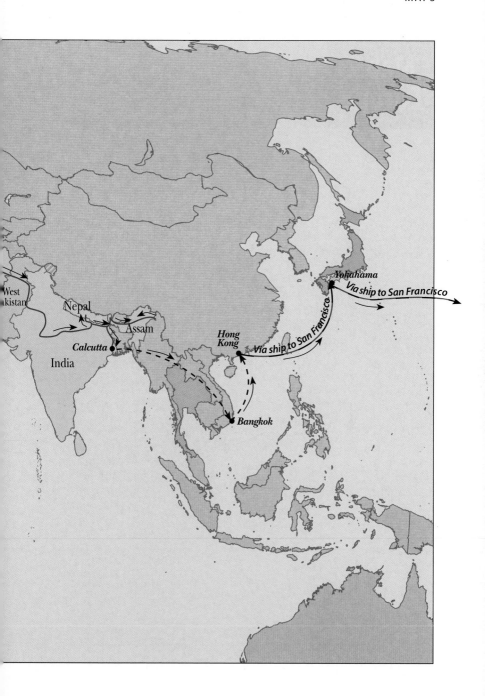

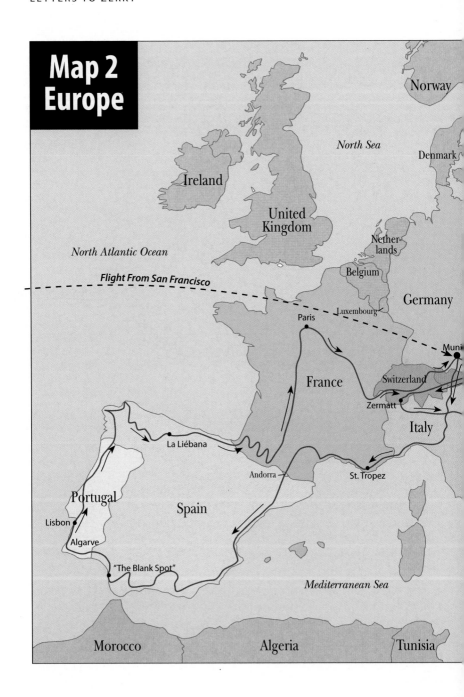

Map 2
Europe

Norway

North Sea

Denmark

Ireland

United Kingdom

North Atlantic Ocean

Nether-lands

Belgium

Flight From San Francisco

Germany

Luxembourg

Paris

Muni

France

Switzerland

Zermatt

Italy

La Liébana

Andorra

St. Tropez

Portugal

Spain

Lisbon

Algarve

"The Blank Spot"

Mediterranean Sea

Morocco

Algeria

Tunisia

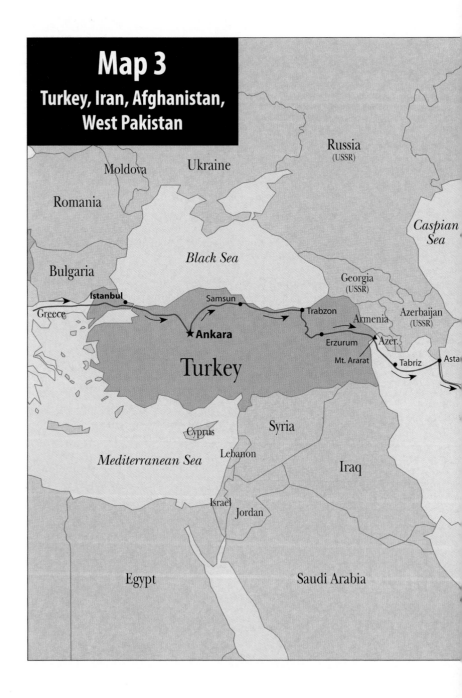

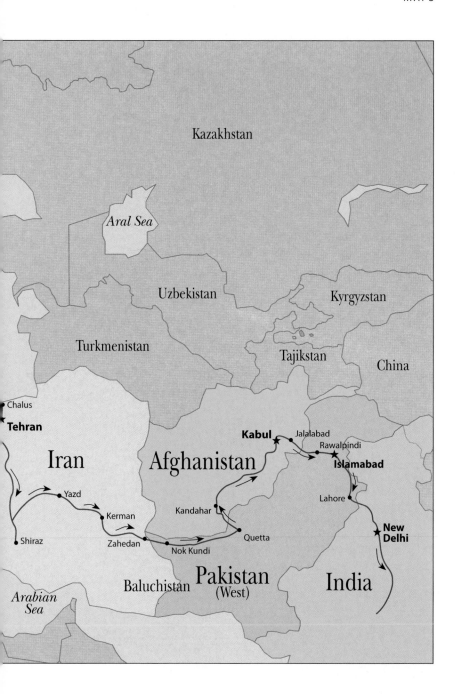

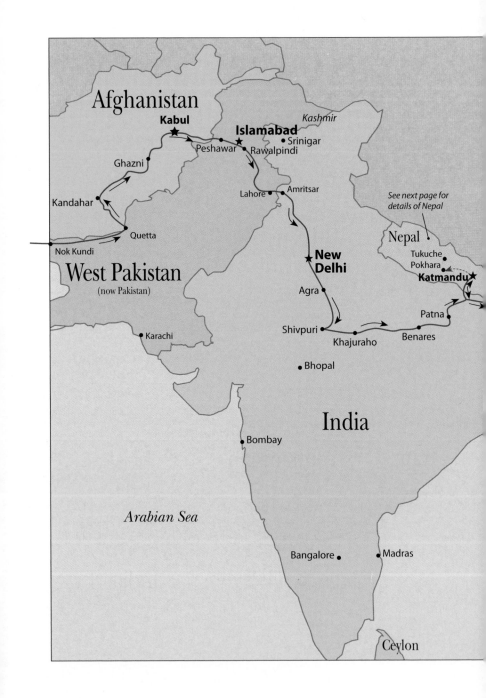

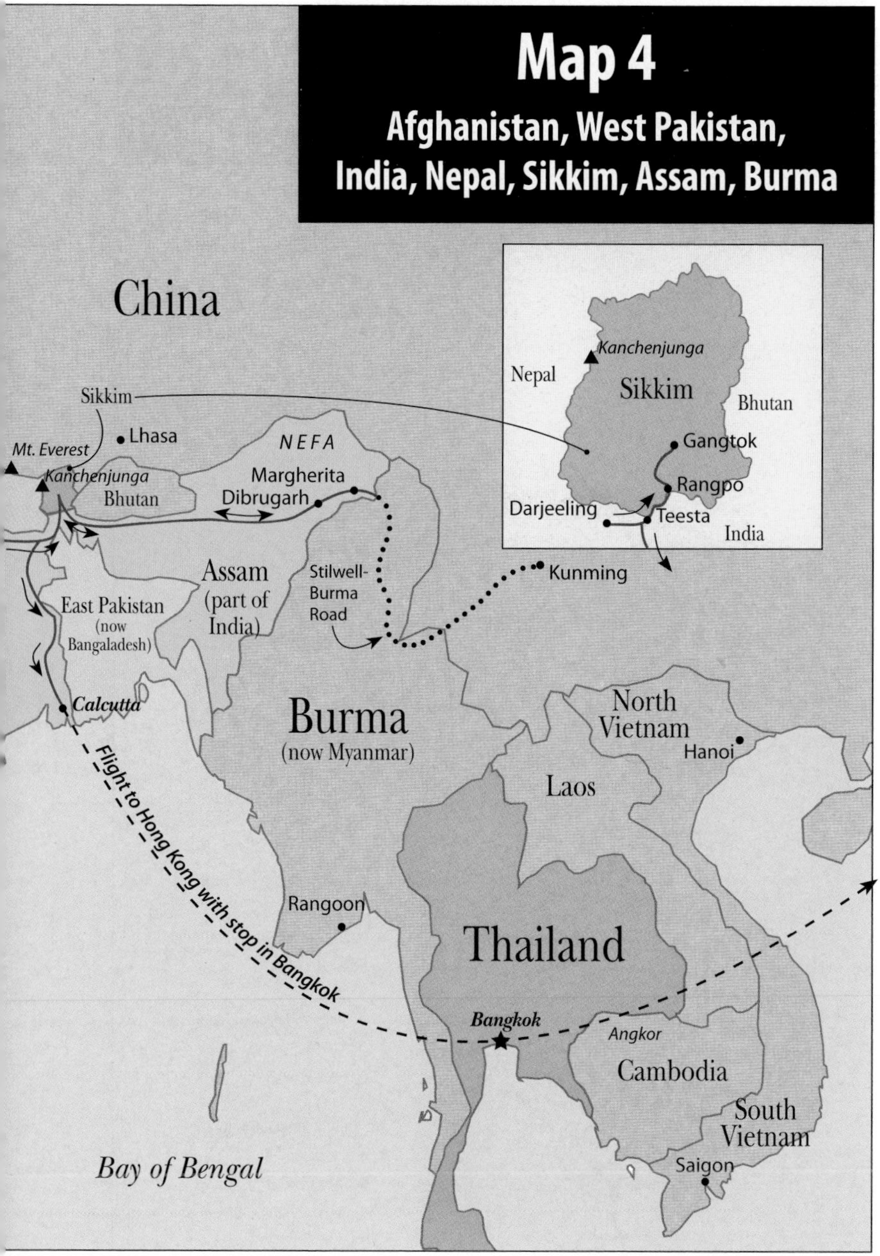

Map 4
Afghanistan, West Pakistan, India, Nepal, Sikkim, Assam, Burma

China

Sikkim

Mt. Everest • Lhasa

NEFA

Kanchenjunga

Bhutan

Margherita
Dibrugarh

Assam
(part of
India)

Stilwell-
Burma
Road

East Pakistan
(now
Bangaladesh)

Kunming

Calcutta

Burma
(now Myanmar)

North
Vietnam

Hanoi •

Laos

Flight to Hong Kong with stop in Bangkok

Rangoon

Thailand

Bangkok ★

Angkor

Cambodia

South
Vietnam

Saigon

Bay of Bengal

Inset (Sikkim)

Nepal

Kanchenjunga

Sikkim

Bhutan

Gangtok

Rangpo

Darjeeling

Teesta

India

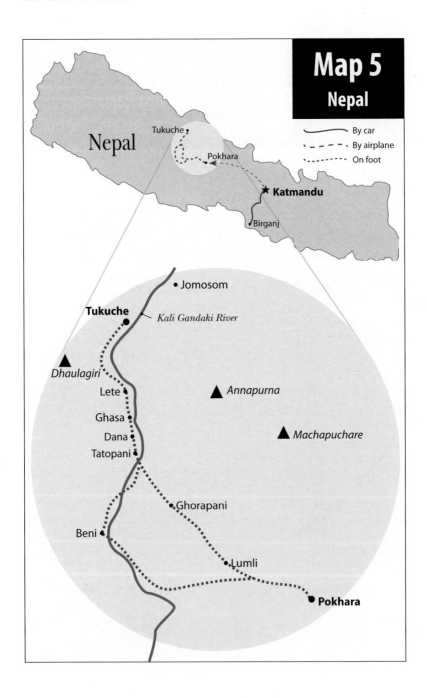

Mogrevo, a Village near Potes
Los Picos de Europa in the background
Northern Spain

Zerky in the Swiss Alps

**Machapuchare and Rhododendrons
Near Pokhara, Nepal**

Phewa Lake outside Pokhara

Bodnath Stupa in Katmandu
(Bill in the red shirt next to the man carrying a carpet)

**Temple of the Emerald Buddha,
Bangkok, Thailand**

Introduction

IN THE MID-SIXTIES, WHEN MY FIRST WIFE JOANNE AND I WERE getting to know each other in San Francisco's North Beach district, she told me about the time she'd been living in Paris and a friend had invited her to go to Morocco with him, to visit his family during the holy month of Ramadan. It was a time of fasting, he explained, but that didn't apply to non-Muslims such as JoAnne. She accepted the invitation and the two of them set off for the family house in Fez. I suspect this footloose young American would have been quite a catch for a young Berber man gone off to study at the University of Paris; his parents took them everywhere, "showing me off," JoAnne said, "I was the talk of the town."

Near the end of her stay, JoAnne was presented with a baby. "Please take her with you," the mother implored, and went on to explain that her daughter had no future in Morocco. But if JoAnne were to take her and raise her in America, she could have a better life. It was 1956. Yes, there once was a time when people in the Islamic world admired America.

This young would-be expatriate was of course stunned by the proposition and she agonized over it the remainder of her stay. The mother had simply assumed JoAnne would be returning to America, not realizing that she had gone off to Paris with the intention of living there more or less permanently. As the sensible young lady she was, on occasion, JoAnne declined this offer that would have changed her life. But by the tone in her voice when she told me this, and by the look in her eyes, I knew she regretted her decision. My future wife had just told me she wanted a child.

Zerky 1967

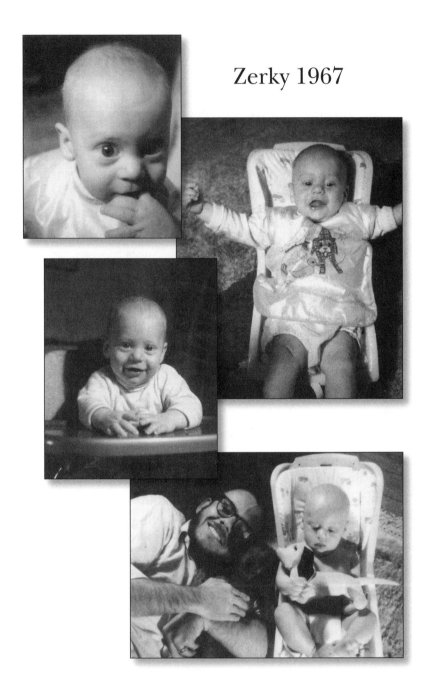

The sixties came early to San Francisco. Beatniks were in flower and Italians too when I landed there in 1957. Alan Ginsburg's *Howl* had just been published, Kerouac's *On the Road* was about to be. Disquietude was in the air as America was being undermined by racial murders in the South and by atrocities in a little-known far-off country known as Vietnam—that brand-new enemy most of us didn't even know was our enemy. This was the war in which we lost our innocence. The post-World War II era was over.

It didn't take long for me to discover that part of San Francisco where Chinatown and the old Italian neighborhood collided at the corner of Grant, Columbus and Broadway Avenues, in a place called North Beach, where there was no beach at all, only unruly outcroppings of Italians, poets, artists, and a new species of weirdo soon to become known as "beatniks." Somehow all of us had been attracted to this new vision of America. Here were people who ate garlic, people who yelled at each other, people who stayed up late, late, late, talking, talking, talking, forever talking about everything on earth and under the sun. Having been raised in the cold Scandinavian reticence of North Dakota's Great Plains, it was music to my ears.

I soon found a cheap room in the Montgomery Block Building, which by then had become known as the "Monkey Block." It had once been San Francisco's finest office building, having survived the 1906 earthquake, but by 1957 had declined to the point where it was being rented out as sub-standard housing to monkeys, poor people, drunks, eccentrics, beatniks, and disconsolate ne'er-do-wells like me. I remember the disembodied arm that used to live there. It had once belonged to someone no one had ever seen. Clad in a lacy white glove, it projected daily out into the corridor from a barely cracked door, snaking around blindly in search of the morning's newspaper. Nobody knew the arm's rightful owner, who was believed to be long dead and even more famous than Jack London, George Sterling, Frank Norris, Ambrose Bierce, Bret Harte, Joaquin Miller, Dashiell Hammett, Mark Twain, Mary Austin, Diego Rivera, Frieda Kahlo, Sun Yat-Sen, and all the other Monkey Block luminaries reputed to have once lived or worked in the hallowed Montgomery Block Building. Even today you can still find many of their names on a plaque in the lobby of the Transamerica Pyramid, which now stands on the site of the once grand Monkey Block.

Somehow my name got overlooked.

Not far from the Monkey Block was Miss Smith's Tearoom. It was really cool, it was always full of girls. I started hanging out there until late one night when proprietress Connie Smith tore into some poor bastard whose transgression I know not. At the top of her lungs she cursed him out in a stream of foul invective that made this poor North Dakota boy cringe. Wow! When it was finally over, the guy on the next barstool explained to me that Miss Smith wasn't really a lady at all, because her tearoom wasn't really a tearoom at all; it was a lesbian bar.

I moved on to the Black Cat, a legendary North Beach bar where I felt more at home. I liked the place because it was always full of guys. But it turned out to be a gay bar, so I just kept on going from bar to bar, looking for the right place. I finally found it. It was named *The Place.*

My biggest step down the road to fame was the time I got my name and pictures splashed all over the front pages of the San Francisco newspapers after having been busted for being in the wrong place at the wrong time in the middle of a vice-squad middle-of-the-night pot-bust operation. Down in the basement of the Hall of Justice, where I was being booked by the fuzz, I told the cop I was a musician; the next day's newspapers put me down as "unemployed."

From the San Francisco press, January 1960

One night in La Bodega, a Spanish bar across the street from Vesuvio's bar, I was brushed by an angel on the way to her seat at the end of the bar. I'd seen her before. She came in late before closing time. Someone told me her name was JoAnne, and that she ran *The Movie*, a North Beach movie theatre around the corner and on the other side of the block. Well now, I could talk movies! With a glass full of self-confidence and Louis Martini Mountain Red, I ambled on down to the end of the bar, looking cool. The angel explained that she came in late because that was when she got off work. "Movie theatres are open seven nights a week," she told me, as if I were some idiot. It wasn't getting off to a good start. But then she told me she'd liked my guitar playing when I'd been fooling around a few nights earlier, and that did it: she knew who I was! I soon discovered she had been to Spain too, as had I in order to further my budding career as the world's greatest flamenco guitarist,and to investigate the possibility of becoming a world-famous bullfighter.

It soon turned out that she had done more traveling than I had, and that Yugoslavia was her favorite country—even though she had once gone to Pamplona for the running of the bulls. She had even lived in Paris, and on the Left Bank, no less. Now how was a poor beatnik supposed to compete with this would-be member of the Lost Generation? But talk came easily that night and before long I found myself talking with an attractive, interesting, smart and good-hearted woman, who loved music, foreign films, and traveling—not to mention my guitar again.

A few nights later *I* was the one who came in late. There she was at the end of the bar. Waiting for me no doubt. So I bought her a drink and we talked until closing time, at which point

I invited her to an upcoming party at my pad up on Greenwich Street. And wouldn't you just know it? She showed up! Toward the end of the party, I realized I'd been ignoring my other guests most of the night; I'd been too busy listening to JoAnne's stories about Paris, and about Belgrade, and about the Hungarian Uprising, and about that time she went to Pamplona for the running of the bulls. Things were fast spiraling out of control. It was about time!

Jack was one of JoAnne's many projectionists. His main job was as head projectionist for one of San Francisco's premiere South-of-Market porno theatres. Jack was a prince of a man who thrived on helping people, and when he heard that JoAnne was thinking about getting married, he offered to drive us to Reno late one night after the theatre closed. Besides being JoAnne's projectionist, Jack became our chauffeur that night, and JoAnne's maid of honor, and my best man, and our witness, when we were married in Carson City, Nevada at 4:00 AM in a cute little neon Chapel of the Bells, right across the street from the Carson City Courthouse, which just happened to be open twenty-four hours a day for precisely such emergencies as ours.

At the conclusion of our five-minute ceremony, Jack stuffed us back in his car again and drove us to the nearest casino, where he treated us to a champagne breakfast, before stuffing us back in his car again for the long ride back to San Francisco. "Movie theatres are open seven nights a week," JoAnne had to remind her newly wedded husband. We had our honeymoon in Jack's back seat. He swore he never once looked in the rearview mirror. Next day I came in late at the insurance company, with a grin on my face, and an excuse nobody argued about.

Wedding Chapel Postcard

When we were first married, we screwed around with rubbers for a while, on the theory that it would be best to get our lives together first and then have kids in a couple of years. This half-baked theory lasted about a week, at which point we decided to screw the rubbers and figure it all out later. But as time went on and JoAnne didn't get pregnant, one day her doctor told her about a newborn baby soon to be available for adoption. And in June of 1966 we came home with the poster child for this book.

I plodded on at my job in the insurance company, which began looking less and less promising, probably because I was the one looking less and less promising. I got my big break when JoAnne's janitor left and I quit my insurance job. I started swamping out her theatre. Now I really was in show biz!

JoAnne's theatre had been up for sale when I met her. Along with my awesome janitorial skills, I brought her a large measure of renewed enthusiasm for the business. We worked hard togeth-

Six-week-old Zerky with JoAnne in the High Sierras

er for a year, but in the end were faced with an insoluble problem: general admission at that time was $1.75; students $1.25. But it cost $10.00 to park your car in a North Beach parking lot while you parked your fanny in one of JoAnne's seats. Parking was nearly nonexistent in North Beach at night—the streets were jammed full of cars filled with tourists come to gawk and get loaded in San Francisco's new cutting edge craze, the topless bars. They say, "location, location, location." We said, "parking, parking, parking." After a year of giving it our best, we finally gave it up. An offer was made, an offer accepted. Maybe someday I might find a theatre with lots and lots of parking lots.

And now for that journey around the world. I think it began in the Sierra Nevada Mountains of Eastern California where, in 1966, JoAnne and I baptized our little Zerky by taking him and our miniature dachshund, Tarzan, over eleven-thousand-foot-high Kearsarge Pass, into a basin of high lakes in the John Muir Wilderness. There, at Kearsarge Lakes, the four of us spent a week alone, exploring the area and discovering that babies are amazingly portable! You could almost say he was born in the saddle, this blond-haired little boy who crossed the High Sierras on horseback when he was six weeks old.

**JoAnne and Zerky at nearby Bullfrog Lake
on the John Muir Trail**

Tarzan and the Author at one of the Kearsarge Lakes

Germany

Letter From Munich

April 4, 1967
Munich, Germany
Map 2

Dear Zerky,

We made it to Europe! Your mother and I still don't quite believe it; we keep thinking it's time to go down and open the theatre. It's hard to get used to not having to go to work, not having to do much of anything, really, besides going to places we've dreamed about.

Poor Tarzan nearly didn't make it. When our plane touched down in Cologne before proceeding on to Munich, a German customs official dressed like a World War II Luftwaffe officer came on board and got all upset at seeing *der hund*. I smiled and told him we *nein sprecken zie deutsch*, at which point he stiffened up, wheeled around, stomped down the aisle in his black leather boots, and disappeared down the gangway in a huff. Your mother told me he was going for the Gestapo. While Tarzan and I were debating whether or not to make a break for it, the storm trooper marched back onto the plane with the gorgeous blonde stewardess who had previously served us drinks on the plane, and who proceeded to act as interpreter.

"No, we don't have any paper from the German government authorizing importation of *der hund*," I told him. His face remained cold and unresponsive, a trace of sneer curling up over his lips. I decided I'd best throw myself on the mercy of the lovely stewardess: "But of course we will be more than happy to obtain such a paper, once we are on the ground in Munich," I told her. There followed a debate in German. Then the stewardess gave me the loveliest of smiles and told me they would wire Munich to have a veterinarian meet us when we got off the plane. He would examine Tarzan and give us the necessary paper.

An hour later we landed in Munich, where nobody knew a thing about any veterinarian. All they knew was that Tarzan was supposed to have some kind of paper. An inspector at the gate called in his superior. They discussed the situation. *Der hund* must have der paper, he announced officiously. Then they called in the customs inspector, who agreed with them, no doubt on penalty of being shot. Then came the pilot. More arguments in German. Finally they called in some big wheel official who acted like he owned the airport. Here was a grand Teutonic specimen in full military uniform, complete with medals, stripes, and German officer's hat with traditional upswept brim. "*Vee müst hof der paper vor der hund,*" he told us in incomparable English. A crowd of similarly costumed aviators soon began to gather, all of them jabbering away in German about *der hund*. It was the German General Staff mapping strategy to defend the fatherland against the invasion of a ten-pound dog.

And then suddenly it came to me: "Eina dachshund, eina dachshund," I interrupted excitedly, jabbering away in my God knows what. "Eina Dachshund iss una German hund! Una German hund iss una German citizen!" They didn't think it was funny. Gradually it became clear to us that the regulations did, indeed, require some sort of paper, one that could only be obtained at a German consulate outside the country. And then— and only then—did it become clear to *them* that regardless of what their regulations might say, Tarzan was, as a matter of

Tarzan

demonstrable fact, on German soil. And the pilot made it clear to all concerned that, after having already flown us eight thousand miles, he was not about to turn around and fly us back to San Francisco. They say history repeats itself in times of crisis. They say all kinds of dumb things. But, as at Stalingrad, the immovable object had met the irresistible force. As we braced for the impending cataclysm, my beautiful blonde stewardess walked by again, looking a little jet-lagged after a hard day's work fending off lecherous male passengers asking for this and for that and the other thing, just to bask in her luminous glow. She smiled at me again and told me she had spotted Tarzan in the middle of the crowd and couldn't resist coming over to say goodbye to our "darling little dog." Crestfallen, I was happy to see her anyway. Noticing the consternation on the faces of the assembled throng, she cheerfully offered up that Tarzan wasn't really a very *big* dog, now was he? And since we were leaving Germany as soon as we picked up our car, well then—"This darling little German dog is only in transit now, isn't he?" *In transit.* Two words that shook the world. A collective sigh of relief began to settle over the Wehrmacht as a great storm began to subside. Flickers of smiles curled ramrod lips. They grew broader. The stewardess was right! Tarzan was indeed *a very little dog.* Soon he would be no dog at all, gone forever from the soil of the Fatherland. He would never have existed. Well then, why shouldn't everybody concerned do everything possible to help get this adorable nonexistent little dog out of the country? Everyone was happy. The logic was overwhelming. We must enjoy our stay, one of the officers insisted. "Are you aware that Bavarian beer is the best in the world?" he asked. We were. "Then you must visit a Bavarian *beer haus* before you leave Munich!

Such was our sweet welcome to Germany. By the time we found a hotel, we were exhausted, and after a beer and a breakfast we crashed. All those time zones really did a number on you, Zerky. You slept like the dead. It was your finest hour.

This morning we picked up our new Volkswagen campervan. It sure is a beauty! The rear seat makes into a bed, and it has a table, an icebox, and even some running water out of a tank. But it didn't have any heat when I turned the engine off, so I had to go scare up a small butane heater. On the way back I nearly smashed up the car. Driving is a terrifying thing to do in Munich, Zerky. I can't understand the traffic signs and everybody drives so fast! Attempting to find my way back to the hotel, I got caught up in a traffic roundabout that I feared

Zerky and Tarzan in Germany

I might never get out of. And then I got lost, and after half an hour of riding around Munich contemplating what they do with widows and orphans in Germany, I finally found my way back to the hotel, and now I'm afraid to leave.

Tomorrow we head for Austria. Then it's over the Brenner Pass into Italy, and down into the warm Mediterranean, provided I can muster up the courage to drive, and don't get munched in München. It's so damn cold in Germany, Zerky! We've rigged up a sleeping bag in a little hammock over the front seat, for you to sleep in at night. No matter how cold it might get, we promise to keep you warm.

Love,
Dad

ITALY

France

Letter From the French Riviera

April 9, 1967
St. Tropez, France
Map 2

Dear Zerky,

I think this camper thing is going to work out fine. Coming down the southern side of the Alps, we spent our first night camped on Lake Garda, the largest lake in Italy. Lake Garda is a popular summer resort area, but everything is closed now because it's not "tourist season"—whatever that means. "Good fortune" is what it means to me—we had the entire campground to ourselves for free. Your mother and I, and especially Tarzan, found our folding camper bed to be very comfortable. You liked your little hammock suspended over the front seat. You made nary a peep in the night. You are a happy camper, but then again we already knew that from the time we took you over Kearsarge Pass when you were six weeks old.

The following night—Alps behind us—we couldn't find a campground so we decided to try "camping wild" in the northern reaches of Italy's Apennine mountain chain. We just pulled off the road near a little Italian town called Bobbio, where we had an entire river canyon to ourselves. We have decided that "poaching it" is the best way to fly—provided you can find a place without lots of people around, which doesn't appear to be an easy thing to do. Europe is very crowded, as well as very cold. We flee southwards. Never before have I realized how far north Europe is. Even here in southern Europe, a hundred miles from the Mediterranean, we're on the same latitude as Maine. Brrr. We are thankful for our little heater.

The next day we hit the Mediterranean coast at Genoa, Italy, then followed it westward to the French border, and on down the Côte d'Azur, as they call this coast in France. We finally stopped across the bay from St. Tropez, where we are now camped for our second night. St. Tropez is part of the French Riviera, which is a kind of ritzy vacation spot where all the Parisians come each August to spend their month-long vacations, jammed together on a gigantic beach. I never had any desire to go to this place, but your mother, it turns out, is very fond of St. Tropez. She used to come here before I knew her. Today we went shopping and she told me she needed to buy some new clothes for France. When I reminded her that we don't have much room in the car for a new wardrobe, she cut me off abruptly by assuring me her new clothes would not take up much space. So we bought her a pair of tight, bright red pants and an even tighter yellow sweater.

And then she bought a bikini. When I questioned her about the wisdom of this purchase, she explained to me that she simply *assumed* I'd want her to wear *something* on the beach. She tells me she plans on doing a lot of "beaching it" in Southern Spain, where the weather is warmer. I tried to explain that Spain is a very conservative country, and that the people there don't much go for that "French look." Whereupon she told me I should be thankful she plans to wear *anything* on the beach.

And then she told me that while she'd been living in Paris she had spent several weeks one summer on a beach near here that is famous for being the biggest nude beach in the world. She'd had a job, she informed me, selling fruit to nudists. Then she told me how much she had enjoyed that summer, walking around in her suntan and her cute little basket of fruit. I'm not sure how it happened, Zerky, but it appears that your father has married a nudist.

Tonight we are camped on the side of a hill overlooking St. Tropez. It is warmer here than in Germany, but it is still pretty cold. No matter—our little stove is humming away and all is perfect. We just finished a wonderful meal consisting of a fresh baguette, a Camembert cheese, and a bottle of Rosé d'Anjou wine. With our own private woods, our own private ocean, and the incomparable French food, we are alive in the lap of luxury. And to top it all off, I just opened a bottle of cognac that we also bought in St. Tropez. Your mother insisted it be Remy Martin.

Now we have turned on the car's new FM radio and, strong and clear from a transmitter right across the bay, comes my favorite opera, *The Magic Flute,* by Mr. Mozart. We should have named you Wolfgang, Zerky. This is the life! You are getting into this French thing too. Your mother just fed you a jar of *Legume-Boeuf-Foie de Veau,* the French version of Gerber's baby food. Tomorrow we hope to show you some wild horses in the Camargue, the Rhone River delta. Along with wild horses, there are gypsies there too. When I was a little boy, people would tell me to stay away from gypsies because they steal little children. Don't worry, we will hold onto you tight. We might even hear some flamenco! I might even get out my guitar. And then it's up and over the Pyrenees and down into Spain. What more could a guy want?

Love,
Dad

Itty-bitty

Andorra

Letter From Andorra

April 14, 1967
Between France and Spain
Map 2

Dear Zerky,

Day before yesterday we visited a restored medieval walled city in southern France, known as Carcassonne. It is a shame you are only eleven months old, because Carcassonne is a storybook fortress straight out of King Arthur, or some such place. The tourist brochures tell us that the art of fortress architecture reached its zenith at Carcassonne, during the Middle Ages. They call it a "bastion," and it came under siege several times, but always remained impregnable. Until the invention of the cannon. The "citadel," as they call the village inside the walls, still functions today, even thought its only industry appears to be tourism. Your mother and I found Carcassonne to be a lot of fun. You fell asleep in your pack on my back.

The next day we began our climb into the Pyrenees, the mountains separating France from Spain. At their crest, we bumped into tiny Andorra. It is a postage-stamp-sized coun-

JoAnne and our new home in Andorra

try equivalent in area to a square eleven miles long by eleven miles wide. In Texas, we have farms bigger than that. We have taken a room here because it's so cold outside (below freezing at night) and we can't have our little heater on all the time. Besides, it's very cramped in the bus, what with all our gear. So we decided to get a room in this very rustic lodge near the little Andorran town of Arinsal. Our room is made out of stone, with doors and window frames of rough varnished wood. The lodge is planted in the bottom of a narrow, green valley with natural snow chutes that contain the avalanches rumbling down regularly from the glaciers above. Outside our window is a mountain stream. I began filling our water tank with the delicious water this morning, but it was so cold my hands froze before I could get the tank half full.

Andorra is a vestige of the Middle Ages, one that has somehow managed to survive into the twentieth century. Andorra is a living remnant of feudalism, the personal fife of two co-princes, the bishop of Urgel in Spain and the count of Foix in France. In ancient times, Andorra's strategic location on the crest of the Pyrenees made it a bone of contention between Spain and France. So to eliminate strife, in 1278 AD an agreement was worked out between the Count and the Bishop, whereby the two of them would act as co-sovereigns over Andorra. The rights and obligations of the Bishop of Urgel have continued on down to this day, while the rights and obligations of the Count of Foix defaulted to the President of France when the French Revolution abolished feudal holdings. The Andorrans are very fond of their two sovereigns, however; after the revolution they successfully petitioned Napoleon for reinstatement as loyal subjects. To this day, Andorrans pay tribute. Every other year a government representative, dressed in traditional cloak and Napoleonic hat, sets off down the Envalira River on foot, to the village of Urgel, in Spain, where he bestows upon the bishop there a tribute of nine hundred pesetas (about $13.00 US on today's market).

In addition, every Christmas, under the terms of the agreement, the bishop also receives six hams, twelve chickens and twenty-four cheeses of goat's milk. With characteristic French disdain for food not French, President de Gaulle forgoes his similar larder. The great man *does* accept the money, however, in return for which Andorra receives the protection of the French army, which is in token presence here for the purpose

Typical village in Andorra

of holding the Spanish army in check. A token detachment of Spanish soldiers is also present to keep the French army in check. For some nine hundred years now, this civilized arrangement has worked out well for all involved. Andorra is a prosperous, beautiful country, where your mother and I are talking about retiring someday.

Andorra has no army of its own; the country has not seen war for many centuries. Law and order is maintained among Andorra's twelve thousand citizens by a police force of twelve, plus one traffic cop. Andorra mints no currency, having designated both the peseta and the franc as currency of the realm. Similarly, the Andorran post office uses both French and Spanish stamps for mail outside the country. For mail inside the country, delivery is free. Andorra has no customs service; smuggling is the traditional enterprise of Andorrans. The expense of policing its borders is left to the French and the Spanish. Car registration is free, as is use of the roads, most of which were built by the French and the Spanish. Telephone service is also free; you pay for installation only. Electricity is next to free. Andorrans pay no taxes. What little government exists is supported by a 2 percent duty on imports and by a tax on gasoline.

If Andorra is utopia socially, so is it paradise scenically—endless green meadows with mountain streams coursing down from snowy peaks above. Outside Andorra's dozen or so villages, life goes on peacefully, much as it probably did in the Middle Ages. A Roman style architecture—large rocks fitted together with unmortared stones—completes the pastoral, medieval illusion. The stone construction makes buildings here cool in the summer and warm in the winter, when farm animals occupy the bottom floors of the houses, thereby making their contribution of body heat to the common welfare of the household.

We find it relatively easy to communicate with most of the people here. Andorra is trilingual. Almost everyone speaks Catalan, Spanish and French. Your mother's French sees us through with only an occasional problem, and I've been playing around with my pathetic Spanish. Soon it shall get a workout, once we pry ourselves loose from this fairytale land. All the roads are closed now because of a storm. They should reopen in a day or two, and then we will be heading at last for the warm beaches of Andalucia, where I promise to take you swimming in the warm Mediterranean Sea. Your mother wants to take you skiing. I keep telling her you first need to learn how to walk.

Love,

Dad

I hate to interrupt my little idyll of pristine beauty, but, should you be tempted to pull up stakes and move to Andorra like my wife Nancy and I did in 1992, I should warn you that much of Andorra has since been turned into a real estate developer's dream. The country's once-picturesque little capital, Andorra La Vella, is today a gigantic parking lot exceeding Wal-Mart's most hallucinogenic fantasies. After this letter from Andorra was written, back in 1967, some smart lawyer came up with the bright idea that since there were no taxes in Andorra, goods could be sold to the rest of Europe, tax-free. Now thousands of drivers from all over the continent, especially from nearby France and Spain, flock to tiny Andorra in cars and buses, in search of bargains made in China out of cheap dreams.

"Don't it always seem to be that you don't know what you've got till it's gone—they paved paradise and put up a parking lot."

–Joni Mitchell

Spain

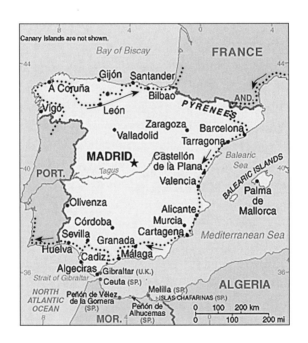

Letter From the Blank Spot on the Map (South of Seville)

May 3, 1967
Andalucia, Spain
Map 2

Dear Zerky,

Our journey from Andorra to southern Spain has been a pleasant one. We met the Mediterranean coast at Tarragona and have been more or less following the eastern edge of the Iberian Peninsula southward and westward ever since. Both your mother and I have been to Spain before. I first came here in 1959 to learn to play flamenco. Your mother was living in France that same year, and managed to come to Spain twice.

Spain has a special place in my heart because of its music and its unique history. It was an Islamic country for eight hundred years, until about 1492, the year Columbus discovered America. I had forgotten how poor parts of it are. The area along the southeast coast of Spain between Cartagena and Almeria is perhaps the poorest place I have ever seen. Most of it is very dry, heavily eroded near-desert partially covered with scrub. There is almost no water, and the peasant farmers have carefully laid out tiny fields along the bottoms of the dry watercourses that carry water only after the occasional rain. It seems to me that such inhospitable land is not fit for human habitation.

We took a side trip into Spain's Sierra Nevada Mountains, to visit Granada. Its Alhambra is an elaborate complex of Moorish gardens full of fountains, and palaces with lacy honeycombed vaults. Your mother was enthralled. Some people say the Alhambra is the finest piece of Moorish architecture in the world.

Lately, your life has been a succession of beaches, but you are not so fond of them as we had hoped. The waves keep knocking you down. In Malaga, we hooked up with Joe Vloemans, my old flamenco buddy from San Francisco. He and I were beatniks and bullshiteros together in North Beach. Joe is here on a three-week vacation, and has been with us for a week. We are on our way to Portugal.

A few days ago, we nearly lost poor Tarzan in the mountains near Ronda, that gypsy stronghold where Prosper Merimee set the novel that Georges Bizet later used for his opera, *Carmen*. We had stopped along the road and then started off again, without realizing poor Tarzan was still running around outside the car. Fifteen minutes later, when we discovered he wasn't with us, I turned the car around in a panic and started screeching back down the winding mountain road. Fortunately I had the presence of mind to stop every single oncoming car and ask if anyone had seen our *pero pequeño*. The third car I stopped produced our "little dog." The driver had seen him beside the road and was taking him to the police station, or so he said. Had I not decided to stop those oncoming cars, or had Tarzan been picked up by someone going in the opposite direction, we would never have seen him again!

Here on the Atlantic Ocean, on the southwest coast of Spain, we have discovered an immense, virtually uninhabited stretch of pristine beach. South of the highway between Sevilla and Huelva you will find a blank space on the map. Your father is a map junkie, and that blank spot has bothered him ever since he first came to Spain, back in 1959. We managed to locate a dirt road heading into the blank spot, which we followed southward into the delta of the Guadalquivir River. There we discovered a second primitive road, this one heading northwest toward Huelva, in the direction of the Portuguese border. Just to the south of this second road, stretching for dozens of miles, is a magnificent white-sand beach in a virtually undeveloped area—something very rare in Europe. We have been following this poorly marked road along the inside edge of the sand dunes for fifty or sixty miles now, through near-wilderness. Driving through sand makes me nervous, but so far we haven't gotten stuck. At that camping store in Munich I also bought a small shovel for precisely such situations as this. For most of the way we could sense that we were only a few hundred yards from the ocean. Always, there was an immense sand dune barring our approach.

Frustrated at being so near and yet so far from the ocean, we finally stopped the car and piled out. With you on my back and our lunch in my hands, we set out to conquer the dune and have lunch on the beach. After a difficult fifteen-minute climb through sliding sand, we finally reached the top of the dune. There on the other side, as far as the eye could see, was the most magnificent expanse of wild sand beach I have ever seen. Three hundred feet directly below us! The top of the giant sand dune we were standing on had been severely under-cut by the incessant pounding of the ocean below. I suddenly became afraid when I realized that the top of our dune could collapse from the weight of the five of us on top of it. We beat a quick retreat from the edge. There was no way to reach the seashore below.

This immense sand barrier guards almost this entire coast, effectively cutting it off from access by land. That is why it shows as the blank on the map, Zerky. It is empty, beautiful, and unapproachable, like many a beautiful woman. After several more miles of exploring by car, we managed to find a hole in the barrier where a stream had somehow managed to find its way to the sea. We followed some old tire tracks and finally made it into my "blank spot on the map." We are spending the night here, alone in one of the most memorable stretches of wilderness I have ever seen. We are being haunted by the remnants of an ancient Moorish castle. There will be no wading for you, Zerk! The giant waves would sweep you away. They roll in uninterrupted, all the way from South America. We are no longer on the peaceful Mediterranean. This remote section of the Atlantic Coast is wide open to the full force of the winter storms, which are what have created this formidable barrier.

Love,
Dad

Portugal

SPAIN

Viana do Castelo
Braga
Vila Real
Leixoes
Porto
NORTH
ATLANTIC
OCEAN
Aveiro
Viseu
Coimbra
Covilhã
Figueira da Foz
Castelo Branco
Leirla
Caldas da Rainha
Tagus
Santarém
SPAIN
LISBON
Barreiro
Évora
Setúbal
Sines
Beja
Cape San Vicente, the southeastern-most point in Europe.
Portimão
Faro
Golfo de Cádiz
Rio Guadiana
0   20   40 km
0   20   40 mi
Azores and Madeira Islands are not shown.

Letter From the Algarve

May 10, 1967
Southern Portugal
Map 2

Dear Zerky,

The Algarve, as they call this southern part of Portugal, is surprisingly different from the Andalucia of southern Spain. In contrast to stark, whitewashed villages, the houses here are painted in multi-hued pastels with brightly colored shutters and woodwork. Bright green fields interspersed with patches of red earth; we find it a pleasant change from the rigorous austerity of Andalucia.

After all the fine beaches we've been camping on lately, we have finally managed to work our way down to Cape San Vicente, the southwest tip of the European continent. Joe left us in Faro; he had to catch his plane back to San Francisco and go to work. Thus he shall no longer be with us to leadeth me into temptation. I shall have to find it on my own.

Joe's departure has driven home what we already knew: how incredibly fortunate we are to have the time and money to make such a wonderful trip. Oh, how we wish you were old enough to remember it all, little Zerky. These letters and photographs should help. Our trip is going marvelously. We keep asking ourselves, "where and when shall it end?"

Love,
Dad

Letter From Lisbon

May 12, 1967
Lisbon, Portugal
Map 2

Dear Zerky,

We are staying in a campground outside one of the most beautiful cities in the world. This campground just south of Lisbon is as elaborate as it is immense. It is virtually a town of its own, and can accommodate more than a thousand campers. It has its own restaurant, bar, store, laundry, barbershop, swimming pool, and even a post office. We spent our first hour here just driving around the campground, looking for a secluded spot with a little privacy. We finally found a place on a hill up in the far corner. Our spot is heavily wooded and a few minutes' walk from the nearest toilet. Why is it that people in campgrounds cluster around toilets like bees around honey?

When we pulled in here, there was but a single tent in the vicinity, a small mountain pup tent belonging to a young couple who also like privacy. Jean-Claude is French, and his wife, Anna, is Portuguese. She is finishing up at the university near here, and the two of them are living in their tent. We find them very likable. We have become friends. Anna is from Coimbra, a famous university town. We were delighted to learn that she is also a lover of *fado*; in short order she had us in a wonderful little restaurant named Caesaria, located in the Alcantara section of Lisbon. It has an authentic fado floorshow and most of the waiters and waitresses are musicians who both serve food and make music. The clientele last night appeared to be exclusively Portuguese.

Fado is a sort of Portuguese version of the Spanish flamenco. Both are distinctive folk musics heavily influenced by the Arab occupation, flamenco the more so. Fado is mellower, usually in a minor key, more haunting and melodic, and a little easier for most Western tastes to appreciate. The pop song "April in Portugal" is a fado melody. Fados have a bluesy, lamenting quality about them, and often speak of tragedies such as unrequited love, and death. A lone singer is accompanied by a Spanish guitar, plus a Portuguese guitar, which is a smaller mandolin-like stringed instrument unique to Portugal. The accompaniments are complex and imaginative, with the music of such caliber as to require substantial musical skills to perform. We had a wonderful evening!

Lisbon is a city of air, sunlight, and bright green hills nearly surrounded by water. It reminds us of San Francisco, although Lisbon is much larger. As soon as we arrived here, your mother, as is her way, immediately headed for the old section of town, where we spent a foot-sore day threading our way in and out of streets so narrow that the blue tile-covered walls of the tilting old buildings sometimes nearly touched overhead. You, comfortably seated backwards in your pack-seat on my back, were quite a sensation with the Portuguese women, who, apparently, had never seen a baby on a back before. One of them made her disapproval known very loudly when she stopped me and began to harangue me in a street full of people. She made it very clear to everyone around that I was abusing you and worse. I suspect you had fallen asleep in the pack, and been partially dangling out, as you often do when you are bored. In any event, you woke up and stuck up for me with your usual winning smile. Had you chosen to start crying at that point, I probably would have been stoned by the crowd.

Love,
Dad

Spain Again

**Village of Potes in La Liébana
in Cantabria, Northern Spain**

Letter From the Liébana

May 20, 1967
Potes, Spain
Map 2

Dear Zerky,

The best way to approach La Liébana is from the South, via the mountain pass at the head of the Valley of the Cherry Trees, and between the Gates of San Glorio and the Star of Liébana. The Liébana is a system of weather-protected valleys in northern Spain that lie in the shadows of the Picos de Europa, the highest mountains in the Cantabrian range. Because of its protection from cold winter storms off the North Atlantic, and from icy winds off the central Iberian plateau, La Liébana enjoys a moderate climate such as one might order up for an Eve and her Adam, should one be so inclined. It is a fairytale land from the Bible and its jewel is La Valle de la Cereceda, The Valley of the Cherry Trees. I like to call it heaven because it looks like an artist's rendering of the Garden of Eden. All lush and green, and sprinkled with multicolored flowers and red-roofed houses, it is an artist's vision. Cows, goats and sheep wander everywhere, in the green meadows, mountain passes, valleys, on the roads and on the highways. We don't drive at night because animals have the right of way.

The Peaks of Europe are among the most spectacular mountains in Europe, on a par with the Pyrenees and the Alps. Their more southern latitude and lower elevation, however, give them a special lushness that invites Garden of Eden comparisons. While not so heavily glaciated as their big brothers to the north, Los Picos are virtually as rugged. Over millenniums, raging rivers have dissolved the limestone formations into complex labyrinths of giant pinnacles and crags, which are a rock climber's paradise and a backpacker's paradise too.

Mogrovejo
A village near Potes in the Liébana

The seven-mile hike through the Cares Gorge is said to be "the finest walk in the world."

For over eight hundred years, Spain was the most glorious part of the far-flung Moorish Empire, and Cantabria marked the northern limit of Moorish expansion into Western Europe. On the Iberian Peninsula back then, the Peaks of Europe became the last stronghold of Christianity. Throughout Spain's eight-hundred-year-long occupation by Moslems, the Christians were never driven from these mountains.

At Covadonga, Zerky, you visited a shrine honoring Pelayo, the near-mythical hero who handed the Moors their first battlefield defeat. Thus began the *reconquista*, ending with the fall of Granada in 1492, the year Columbus discovered our "New World." You have seen history all around you in this little-known pocket of northern Spain: mini-cathedrals dating back to the sixth century, stone bridges built by the Romans, the prehistoric caves of Altamira; you even visited Guernica, the site of one of the most famous paintings in the world. Alas, you were asleep in your pack on my back at the time. It was only a reproduction anyway. Perhaps someday you will see the original in the Prado Museum in Madrid. If not, don't worry, museums put me to sleep too. Your mother loves them all. I shall endeavor to persevere.

Love,
Dad

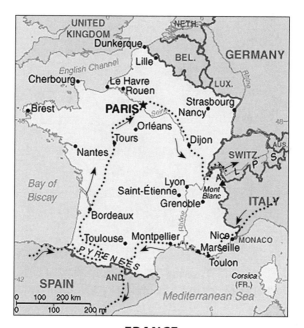

FRANCE

May 27, 1967
Dad and Zerky in Paris on Zerky's first birthday

SWITZERLAND

Germany Again

Letter From Dachau

June 15, 1967
Munich, Germany
Map 2

Dear Zerky,

We are back in Munich, this time for no particular reason other than that this is where the roads have led us, on our way to Prague. After my last letter to you from Northern Spain, we spent several days in Paris in the same cheap hotel that your mother used to live in during the year she lived on the Left Bank. We looked up a few of her old friends, but most of them were no longer around. We should have stayed longer, but frankly, I don't much like large cities and I found Paris almost impossible to drive in—let alone park in. Big cities make for a difficult life when you're living in your car.

When June arrived, I'm afraid I was much too anxious to get to the Alps and go backpacking. That was a big miscalculation, Switzerland is still clogged with snow. In the high country, at least. I still haven't learned to appreciate how far north Europe is. We decided to continue on to Prague, and then go back to Switzerland to go hiking in the Alps later on, in July. By then most of the snow on the trails will have melted. We hope!

Yesterday, quite by chance, we bumped into a small town called Dachau, a few miles outside of Munich. By the time you are old enough to read this, I wonder if that name will still sound as ominous as it does today? Yesterday was bright and sunny, the perfect day to take a drive into the beautiful Bavarian countryside. We followed a road out through the gradually thinning suburbs of Munich, a few miles beyond the grimy outer edge of the city, where the urban landscape gives way to the fresh green fields of Bavaria. We soon came across a small road sign informing us that we were entering the municipality of Dachau, which is about a half hour's drive from the center of Munich. Could this be the notorious death camp, we wondered? It seemed like a strange place to build such a thing, so close to one of Germany's largest cities, where all could see. Your mother and I came to the conclusion that, to the people who built them, at least, the death camps were probably not something to be ashamed of. We do tend to admire our own handiwork, now don't we?

We drove on into town. Surely there would be a sign telling us where the camp was. We found the Dachau Restaurant, the Dachau Cleaners, the Dachau Petrol Station, alas, no Dachau Concentration Camp. The obvious thing to do was to ask somebody, but somehow we couldn't bring ourselves to ask a stranger that question. How do you ask someone where he put his death camp? How do you tell them you came all the way from California to see it? Not long ago we played a movie about Dachau in your mother's little theatre. *Night and Fog* was about how millions of people disappeared into the night and the fog, in places like this. The film's defining images were the pictures of the crematorium here. People in Munich would have smelled the smoke of burning bodies drifting through their fair city, and through this little town only four miles from the camp. Its crematorium had an extremely tall smokestack, we remembered from the film. That smokestack would be visible from a long ways away. We decided to find Dachau on our own.

Eventually we spotted an American soldier. Yes, we were where we thought we were; the camp was a mile or so farther down the road. We started seeing signs reading "KZ," which stands for *Konzentration.* This symbol was apparently used as a signal to warn people all over Germany. A guy's got to keep track of his concentration camps. We first spotted the watchtowers and then a big concrete wall with barbed wire along the top. Then the visitors' center parking lot where we counted thirty-seven cars, virtually all of them with license plates from countries that had been occupied by the Germans during World War II. And then it hit us: most Dachau visitors are not tourists like us; they are pilgrims. Except for that big air-conditioned bus over there with the sign saying, "Unusual Tours, Inc., Los Angeles, California."

The first building we entered was the museum, which consists of a series of rooms filled with display boards covered with old posters, photographs, and newspaper clippings documenting the rise of anti-Semitism in Germany. Next were grisly pictures of the things that went on here during the war. The museum is very well organized and immaculately kept. The Germans are good at this sort of thing—scarcely a fingerprint has been allowed to smudge the countless square yards of stainless steel and glass that went into the museum's construction. There is little left of the original camp; most of the buildings that once housed the horrors have been torn down and have been replaced with squeaky-clean, freshly painted replicas. Why? They even built new concrete walls, with miles of shiny new barbed wire. Most striking of all are the grounds, which are as beautifully landscaped as the nicest of city parks. Freshly cut lawns are everywhere, interspersed with flowerbeds and immaculately trimmed hedges. Three very modern, semi-abstract shrines have been erected at one end of the compound. And finally, off in one far corner beyond the main section of the camp, the crematorium, which for some reason was never torn down. This is almost the only building that remains as it was.

This letter was never finished. I had wanted JoAnne to finish it because she was better at writing descriptions than I was. I guess she just never got around to it. I don't remember.

Zerky at the Gas Chamber, Dachau

Czechoslovakia

TODAY'S CZECH REPUBLIC

Letter From Prague

July 10, 1967
Prague, Czechoslovakia
[Now Czech Republic]
Map 2

Dear Zerky,

Crashing the Iron Curtain turned out to be a disappointment. We had been looking forward to an adventure, but where we were expecting barbed wire and machine-gun towers there was only a neatly mowed strip of grass separating the green hills of Bavaria from the green hills of Bohemia. A bored Czech border guard absentmindedly stamped our visas and motioned us through. He showed no interest in contraband, freedom fighters, dogs, animals, or wayward American children like you. Tarzan was delighted not to receive another welcome like the one when he arrived in Germany. We came all the way from America, only to be neglected.

The first thing we noticed as we drove through our first Czech town, Domazlice, was the seeming austerity of it all. Czechoslovakia is like going from technicolor into black and white—everything is grey. Later on I figured out that what creates that illusion is not so much the austerity as the total absence of advertising. Since no one is allowed to compete with the government in a communist state, there is no need for bright colors to attract customers. Never before had I realized how so much of the color we take for granted in the West is really just advertising. We are fish looking for a lure to bite on.

A couple of hours later we pulled over for lunch. It was a warm spring day and the fields and woodlands of Bohemia glittered in total disregard of government-mandated austerity. We stopped for lunch in front of a brewery, in the city of Plzen, and, with some help from her phrase book, your mother came up with a chunk of sausage, a fresh loaf of bread, and a couple bottles of Pilsner beer. The bread here is very unlike that found in Western Europe. Usually it is rye, seedless, heavy, dark, and full-bodied. The sausage was spiced, and the beer wasn't that bubbly stuff we think of as "Pilsner" in America, but rather a rich strong 12 percent brew you have to be careful with. Our project for tomorrow will be tracking down some Czechoslo-vakian cheese. These daily lunches in beautiful, ever-changing surroundings are becoming the highlight of our day.

We reached Prague the first evening and managed to find a campground on the banks of the Moldau River, a few miles from the city center. The campground turned out to be a hor-rible place with no shade at all, and badly overcrowded, with tents and vehicles packed so tightly there was scarcely room to walk between them. Somehow we managed to squeeze into our little *Kamping Platzle*. It was late and we were hot and tired. The campground had a sign advertising hot showers, which are a major attraction when you're not staying in hotels. The shower room was easy to find, you just had to look for the line. That's how you find everything in Czechoslovakia.

After half an hour in line, it was my turn. Jubilantly, I stepped into the pit and turned on the water. *Ka-wham*—the water heater exploded. As a layer of carbon soot settled onto my bare shoulders, one of the campground attendants rushed in. Even though he could not understand a word I was saying, my naked soot-covered body and the smoke billowing out of the heater told the tale. After admonishing me in Czech, he re-lit the heater and *KA-WHAAAM*—an even bigger blast shook the building, nearly knocking him down. Looking bewildered, he muttered something in Czech and disappeared for good. I doubt he intended to ever go near that heater again. I put my dirty clothes back on my dirty back and went back to our dirty bus, where I told JoAnne to forget about her shower. "You look like Al Jolson," she said, arms outstretched and falling to one leg. "Mammy, Mammy," she sang, "I'd walk a million miles, for one of your smiles, my Maa-a-a-a-mmy."

"We're getting the hell out of here first thing in the morning!" I said.

We spent the following morning hunting for another campground, and ended up in a place called "Camping-Sport," smack dab in the middle of a huge soccer stadium. These are difficult times in Czechoslovakia. The government is having serious economic problems. Foreign travelers bring hard currency. Tourists demand showers. Soccer players are smelly beasts. The team must not be doing well this season, the government is doubling up on use of its real estate. Camping-Sport has showers up the wazoo.

We find Prague to be a beautiful, dark, medieval city, full of blackened stone buildings, multispired steeples and cobblestone streets. As in other European cities old enough to have helped spawn the Industrial Revolution, the buildings here have been darkened by soot to the point where many of them are nearly black. But what buildings they are! Prague's city center is a showcase of eighteenth and nineteenth century architecture, and its buildings are in the process of being sandblasted. Beneath their grimy facades . . . JoAnne to continue:

Unfortunately JoAnne never did. Once again she was better at descriptions than I was, so I left this letter for her to finish off with a fuller description of perhaps the most beautiful city in Europe. Thirty-eight years later, I can't remember enough about Prague to make the attempt.

This letter was written during the "Prague Spring." A year later the Soviets invaded Czechoslovakia, Alexander Dubcek was driven from power, and darkness descended over Czechoslavakia once more.

Letter From Brno in Moravia
(Part of Today's Czech Republic)

July 19, 1967
Brno, Czechoslovakia
Map 2

Dear Zerky,

We had intended to spend more time in Prague. It's such a beautiful city—perhaps even more so than Paris—but it was much too hot. After spending three very uncomfortable nights there, we have decided to head east to the Tatra Mountains of Slovakia, the eastern third of Czechoslovakia. It should be cooler there. The heat, however, bodes well for the snowmelt in the Alps.

The day before yesterday as we were pulling out of the campground, a young Norwegian couple walked over with a present for Tarzan. They brought him an opened can of some sort of goulash made in Russia. It looked god-awful. They had been unable to eat it. Tarzan, gourmet that he is, found it delicious! The four of us watched in disgust as he wolfed down the entire can. Twenty miles outside of Prague, while riding on your mother's lap, Tarzan got sick. She quickly rolled down her window and held his head outside the car, but by the time I found a place to pull over, both the side of the car and your mother's lap were drenched in dog-digestive-juice-enriched Russian goulash. It was a stupendously sickening spectacle! We spent more than an hour trying to clean up the car, and your mother, without adding our own contribution to the mess. By then I was ready to give Tarzan away to a nearby farmer, but your mother intervened.

This morning we reached Brno, Czechoslovakia's second-largest city. We had read about a castle here that sounded interesting. At the top of a hill commanding the city, we found Spielberg Castle, built in the Middle Ages, and world-famous for its extensive network of dungeons, tunnels, and torture chambers. On display are the usual complements of thumbscrews, iron maidens, racks, etc. But there are also some other devices that were new to your increasingly jaded parents. Your mother was most impressed by the runway where they tied people down and stampeded rats back and forth over them. I was more impressed by the depressions built into the brick walls, in the shape of human bodies. The fronts of these depressions were designed to be bricked up around their upright victims, who were sealed in forever, except for their heads. Above the depressions, mounted on the wall overhead, were devices designed to drip water on heads, until their owners went insane. This particular torture was designed primarily for the chastisement of unfaithful wives.

After a trip through the catacombs of Spielberg Castle, it is difficult to emerge into the sunlight again without believing that the world, after all, has made some progress since the days when places like these were an acceptable method of treating antisocial behavior. And then again, it is questionable whether the napalm we are dumping on people in Vietnam is a step down the path to enlightenment. And it's also wrong to regard Spielberg Castle as an exclusive product of the Dark Ages. Scarcely twenty years ago, the Nazis made Spielberg a part of their KZ network. One can imagine the delight in their beady little eyes when they suddenly found themselves in possession of such an irresistible toy. According to the literature the Czech government hands out at Spielberg, the Germans wasted no time in getting their new torture chamber up and running.

Today, the Czech government has turned Spielberg Castle into a museum, but also into a memorial commemorating the betrayal of Czechoslovakia by the Western powers in 1938 at Munich. Unlike the museum at Dachau, this one tells the story of the concentration camps through the eyes of a postwar communist government still concerned with consolidating its power. The party line here is that the Munich Agreement proved that Hitler was an agent of the Western powers, who set out to destroy the Czech people's corrupt capitalist government, which then selfishly refused the protection of the Red Army. The United States is given no credit for the defeat of Hitler, even though during the closing days of World War II General Patton waited on the outskirts of Prague, in order to allow the capital to be liberated by the Russians in accordance with a deal worked out by their two high commands. I suspect there are as many versions of World War II as there are nations that were involved in it.

Here in Europe, World War II seems so much more immediate. Driving through the countryside, we often come upon old farmhouses, their outside walls chipped and spattered with bullet holes. In many places, destroyed buildings have yet to be rebuilt. Perhaps most thought-provoking of all are the countless monuments with the countless names on them. They stand in the town squares and parks of virtually every village or city. Two gigantic wars in the last half-century have redrawn the borders of central Europe.

These, then, are our pessimistic thoughts each time we cross one more border: that these arbitrary lines so scrupulously demarcated and defended because they define a sort of "motherland" that citizens seem to love, are but little more than the temporary products of the latest bloody cataclysm. which only ended because its combatants grew too tired to fight. Where are a nation's true borders, then? As far away as you are capable of keeping them. Your capacity to do so changes over time.

Love,
Your not always so pessimistic Dad

TODAY'S SLOVAKIA

Tatra Mountains (Carpathians)
Eastern Czechoslovakia (now Slovakia)
Near the Polish Border

AUSTRIA

Switzerland Again

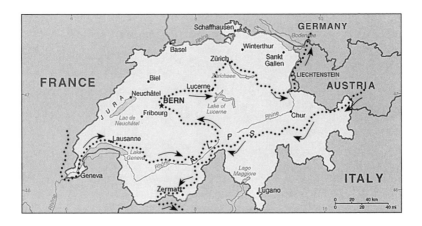

Zerky and Tarzan on guard in the Italian Dolomites

Zerky in the Swiss Alps

Letter From the Matterhorn

September 2, 1967
Zermatt, Switzerland
Map 2

Dear Zerky,

I have decided not to become a communist after all. On our way back to Switzerland, we tried going from Czechoslovakia into Hungary, but Hungary wouldn't let us in, so we had to go on to Bratislava and Vienna instead. At the Czech-Austrian border-crossing we found an iron curtain very different from what we had encountered upon entering Czechoslovakia. About an eighth of a mile wide, it's a no-man's land fortified with multiple barbed-wire fences and strategically located steel lookout towers, with guards and machine guns on top. I've always been comfortable around guns, but these made me very nervous. There is something extraordinarily sinister about that border. No doubt this has to do with the rebellion in Hungary eleven years ago. Our road to Austria is the road to the West. Recently we have been reading in the newspapers about more than one current incident along this border, in which would-be escapees from Eastern Europe have been gunned down on supposedly neutral Austrian soil. Borders are not so much for people as for the governments that control people. Borders are both our shelters and our prisons.

On a lighter note, we are in Switzerland again, in our tent beneath the Matterhorn, watching the snow coming down. JoAnne and I think it is fun; you and Tarzan do not. Since our

**JoAnne helping Zerky and Tarzan prepare their
Assault on the Matterhorn, Zermatt, Switzerland**

tent isn't large enough to move around in, you are suffering the agonies of having to sit still. Tarzan, who has more sense, has burrowed down into the foot of your mother's sleeping bag, and is now asleep. JoAnne says he's hibernating—he's been there most of the time since it started snowing four days ago. We've been talking about trying to put you into hibernation too. You are not a happy camper.

This summer has been immensely enjoyable. Ever since crossing the border from Czechoslovakia, we've been working our way westward through the Alps: first through Austria, then into Italy, and finally through Switzerland. We have been doing a lot of hiking this summer, if you can call it hiking. They do these things differently in Europe. Our first and most ambitious hike was into the Dolomites in Northern Italy—some people call them the Italian Alps. With you on your mother's back and the tent, sleeping bags, foam mattresses, food and diapers on mine, we took off into the Italian "wilderness," carrying everything but the kitchen stove. I carried a small butane cartridge stove instead. It weighs a pound, including the pot.

Before long, I began to confirm what I already suspected—that there isn't any wilderness in Europe, the pressures of population having been too incessant over too many centuries. Even the most remote valleys and passes have farms and shepherds' huts in them, and occasionally even a hotel and restaurant. Hiking is a popular recreational sport in Europe, and mountain inns have sprung up all over the place, in order to cater to the footsore traveler. First night out, we were camped in a beautiful meadow at about eight thousand feet when two hikers came down the trail. Seeing our bright little tent and our "darling little dog," not to mention our darling little boy dressed in his darling little new *lederhosen*, they couldn't resist

**Zerky and Tarzan getting ready to launch their
ascent of the notorious North Face of the Eiger
(in the background), near Grindelwald, Switzerland**

stopping and asking where we were from. They were amazed at
all the equipment we had managed to haul up into the mountains. "This is how we do it in America," I explained. "You mean
you carried all this stuff all the way from America?" one of them
asked incredulously. He thought we were mad. But interesting.
Never before had they encountered such a family—sleeping
alone in the mountains like wild animals. They, too, were on
vacation; they worked for a small-town newspaper and would
like to photograph us, if they might. Then they wanted to in-

terview us. They told us we would make a good story for their newspaper. We spent fifteen minutes answering questions. We no longer carry much in the way of supplies, Zerky, your mother carries a knapsack, I carry you. Maybe it's better this way. We find it much easier to take one-day hikes *down* from the tops of mountains, rather than *up* to them. Many of the peaks here are accessible by mountain railways, and by *teleferiques*, those suspended cable gondolas that carry people up into the most amazing places. You are quite happy with our newfound way of doing things. I hope your attitude doesn't change, once you've finished learning how to walk.

Your mother has gone nuts over the wildflowers. Everywhere they are in abundance in the Alpine meadows of Switzerland, Austria and Northern Italy. Your mother just bought a flower book and now she's trying to catalog them all. She is an interesting hiking partner, Zerky. She is usually terrified of high places, and sometimes nearly in tears when we go over safe, wide stretches of trail that have sheer exposures. But when she goes hunting for flowers she will crawl out onto steep cliffs, totally unconcerned that one misstep could mean the end of her. Oftentimes at the end of a long hard climb, when we stand on the top of some ridge or peak, looking out over a tangle of rocks, glaciers and valleys thousands of feet below, I understand why the Alps are said to be the most beautiful mountains of them all. At moments like these, which fill mountain climbers with awe, your mother can often be found marveling at the wildflowers. You and Tarzan are also delighted by them; I seem to be the only one who gets excited by the view. Sometimes I wonder why I'm hanging around with you guys, anyway.

All this pastoral living makes for a very quiet lifestyle. We often go into towns, to go shopping, but the towns are almost as quiet as the mountains themselves. Switzerland is the land of the bourgeoisie. A century of peace has given people here an excellent standard of living. Peaceful, industrious, and excessively capitalist, the Swiss appear so busy catering to us tourists that sometimes I wonder whether they have lost the ability to smile. Except for the mountains, I think life here must get very boring. Your mother and I have been talking about bringing a chapter of Hell's Angels over, to liven things up.

Since Zermatt is the most famous of all the Swiss Alpine resort areas, we have saved it for the end of summer; the later the season, the more the snow melt, the more accessible the high country. A few days ago we climbed up through the snow to the beginning of where the route for the final ascent of the Matterhorn takes off. We climbed no further. You loved walking in the snow for a time, but then quickly got tired of it. I carried you most of the way on my back. You are one very popular guy in the mountains, Zerky! Everyone stops to tell us what a lovely child you are. We meet a lot of people that way.

We hope to get out of here if the snow ever stops. We've hardly been able to leave the tent for the last three days. I think we waited too late in the season to return to this part of the Alps. Your mother says winter is here to stay. We've been living in our tent because it's not possible to drive our car into Zermatt. Even though there is a primitive road of sorts, they don't let us tourists use it. We had to take an electric train. Banning cars keeps things peaceful around here—just the way the Swiss like it. Meanwhile, our wonderful camper-van goes unused. Instead of its nifty little heater, we put on another layer of clothes. Every hour or so I go out and shake the snow off the roof. We are worried the tent might collapse if it snows too much in the night. If that happens, I don't know what we will do; we can't get Tarzan out of the sleeping bag long enough to fetch us a keg of brandy like all the St. Bernards around here are trained to do. Maybe next spring someone will find a little lump in the snow, kick it and say, "Jesus, what a terrible way for a one-year-old to die."

Love,
Dad

I don't know what it is about mountains, I've dreamed about them for as long as I can remember. Switzerland marked the fulfillment of that dream. But now that summer was over, where to next? Europe gets very cold in the winter. Where do people go when they don't have a house? The beaches of Greece seemed like a good idea. But then again someone told us Romania was the place to go. They told JoAnne the skiing there was good—and very cheap! JoAnne loved to ski as much as she loved Yugoslavia. What to do, what to do? We decided to take our cake and eat it too. Yugoslavia first, then maybe a dip into Greece to warm up, and then Romania! Things were looking up. Things were looking East!

ITALY AGAIN

Yugoslavia

CROATIA

JoAnne and Sarah
in Yugoslavia, 1956

*JoAnne had a bond with Yugoslavia. She had
been there before I met her and it was a forgone conclusion that we would go there, even though I had little
interest in that part of Europe. JoAnne was interested
in the politics and cultures of the world. At Stanford,
she had majored in International Relations, studied
Russian, and become an admirer of Milovan Djilas.
During World War II when the Nazis occupied Yugoslavia, Djilas and Tito had been comrades-in-arms.
Together they created the Partisans, the communist
anti-Nazi resistance movement that was to emerge in
control of Yugoslavia after the war. Djilas had once
been Tito's vice president and emissary to Joseph Stalin, with whom he had negotiated many of Tito's de-
partures from Communist orthodoxy. A few years later, Tito had Djilas expelled from the Communist Party
for criticizing Tito's increasingly authoritarian rule,
and by the time JoAnne and Sarah arrived in Yugoslavia, Djilas had become a rallying point for a more
liberal brand of communism, one with increased ties
to the West. Over the years, Tito's relationship with
Stalin had become very strained. Always looming in
the background was the Red Army.*

When JoAnne was in high school, she had a girl-friend I never met. "Sarah of the Silken Strings," I like to call her; she was a violinist in the Salt Lake City Symphony Orchestra. Shortly after JoAnne graduated from Stanford, the two of them went hitchhiking together through Yugoslavia.

The stamps in JoAnne's passport show her landing at Southampton on September 25, 1956, and moving on to London, Rotterdam, Munich, Vienna, and Bern, where she went nuts over the bears in the zoo. From there she traveled to Venice, where she was no doubt feeding the pigeons in San Marco Square on October 23, 1956, when the Hungarian uprising broke out in Budapest after a student demonstration demanding an end to the Soviet postwar occupation of Hungary. On this day when much of the world probably found itself contemplating the possibility of World War III, JoAnne set off for Yugoslavia, a communist country that shares a border with Hungary, to hook up with Sarah in Slovenia, which was then part of Yugoslavia. Three days later, on October 26, 1956, JoAnne's much-too-minimal notes tell us, she met Sarah in a café in Ljubljana, where our two young heroines "danced with army" into the AM.

In JoAnne's old photo album I came across an abbreviated, hand-written two-page itinerary of their trip (reproduced a few pages later). A careful reading between the lines will disclose another one of those classic "Girls Gone Wild During Spring Break Meet Joseph Stalin and his Six Thousand Tanks" scenarios.

On October 29, 1956, we find the two of them hitch-hiking together from Ljubljana to Rijeka, with "two drivers of a beer truck." The next day they continued on down the Dalmatian Coast, to the town of Split, where JoAnne makes the cryptic entry, "bad trip—Pepe—slept in sailor's quarters." So who was Pepe?

**"Pepe, Sarah, and the two sailors who wanted this taken on boat off coast,"
it says on the back of the photo.**

This picture was taken on the boat from Rijeka to Split (now in Croatia), on the Dalmatian Coast, but those "sailors' quarters?" JoAnne never told me about no sailor's quarters!

Wednesday, October 31, JoAnne goes on in her perfect perfunctory, she "slept, Suez, should have had a date." "Suez" is a reference to the Suez Crisis, the war the British, French and Israelis had recently launched against Egypt for control over Middle Eastern oil tanker routes. But I can't help wondering about who JoAnne had her eye on for that date!

Their next two days in Split included an "opera singer, the Mestrovic Gallery, a café," and another news broadcast, this one "at the home of Johnny." She never told me about no Johnny!

November 3 finds them on another boat, on their way to Hvar, an island in the Adriatic where they had a "wonderful room," and "ate fried sardines." Ho hum. But the following day they were on a much better boat, one where they met some more "sailors, a First Steward, and the Captain." After that there is something about "his home." Well at least they weren't running around with common ordinary sailors anymore. Or the Red Army. The next day, November 4, 1956, was the day Nikita Khrushchev sent his six thousand Russian tanks into Hungary, crushing the Hungarian Uprising.

Stalin and Tito had been on a collision course for a long time. JoAnne told me that all Yugoslavia was talking about were those six thousand tanks. Would they stop at the Hungary-Yugoslavia border, or would Nikita Krushchev now seize upon the opportunity to bring Tito to heel by sending his tanks all the way to Belgrade? Sarah and JoAnne were headed for Belgrade. But JoAnne's notes for the following day only tell us, oh so plaintively, that she "wandered the streets of Dubrovnik alone – slum – café – news – Swiss men." Pepe and Johnny must have been Swiss! Along with that First Mate, the Captain and all those other sailors. The entire Swiss Navy must have been in town—docked at Dubrovnik for a little R & R! That "news," however, would have been the Soviet invasion of Hungary.

The following day, JoAnne tells us wistfully, she went "alone to Gruz – cafe – musicians – concert," and then the day after that they were trying "to hitch-hike out" of Dubrovnik, to Sarajevo, where they found a "miserable room." The following day finds them back in stride, this time with Braco and Vojo.

Braco and Sarah in Sarajevo

Vojo and JoAnne in Sarajevo

"Hey, Mr. Braco man, play a song for me!" And tell Vojo to get his cotton-pickin' hands off my wife!

Sunday November 11: Sarah, JoAnne and Vojo are hitchhiking together to Belgrade, where JoAnne encounters a "horrible anglo-phobe," then, "Sarah's friend, private room." Hmmm. And then on Monday, November 12, they are still in Belgrade, where JoAnne "wandered, went to a concert," which was "bad." Looks like Sarah was getting all the guys! Three cheers for Sarah! And then on November 13, JoAnne tells us, she "drank." Hip-hip-hurray, for Sarah!

The next day, Joanne "met Misha for dinner, coffee, slipovica, and talk to 6:00 AM." Look out for that slivovitz, JoAnne, it's far too high octane for a sweet young thing from Utah! And finally, on November 15, 1956, JoAnne confesses, she "met Misha at Hotel Moscow – me & V." Dammit! I just knew this was going to happen! And then it's off to a "concert with Vojo."

The following day, JoAnne "took Sarah to meet Misha," after which she "met the US Ambassador." Her twenty-one day visa would have expired the previous day, meaning she was then in the country illegally. She had been very busy!

November 17th, she writes, another "concert, KAVA. M." "M" would be Misha, "V" for Vojo, but I have no idea who "K" was. Then she "moved to V's apartment house." And then there is something about a "medical club." Two days later, on November 19, the two of them went to a "movie," and the day after that, to another "concert – S. M. K. V. I." (Sarah, Misha, K, Vojo and I). And finally on the 23rd of November, 1956, JoAnne gets a new visa stamped into her passport, "from the Secretary of State of the Interior of the Republic of Serbia," and later that day she leaves Belgrade for Zagreb, now the capital of the independent country of Croatia. From there it was "Zagreb – Trieste (awful)," before being stamped out of Yugoslavia at the Sezana border crossing, "Trieste – Milan," on the 25th of November, 1956. From Trieste, she went back to Bern – to say goodbye to her beloved bears – before taking the train on to Paris, where she

JoAnne's Itinerary

SEPT.

Tues - 25 — Southhampton (arriv) - London (Mill. Cryms - found hotel - pub)
Weds - 26 — London (bus sites saw - bought sweater Old Vic's - Tale of woe)
Thurs - 27 — " (Westminster church & abbey - Tower - neighborhood play - religion talk)
Fri - 28 — " (Tower South Sea Bubble Piccadilly - Soho)
Sat - 29 — " to Hook of Holland (- guard - boat)
Sun - 30 — Hook - Rotterdam (train
Mon. - 1 — Rotterdam - Würzburg (train - arr. late)
Tues - 2 — Würzburg (dinner at jazz pl)
Weds - 3 — " (" - dinner)
Thurs - 4 — " (" " gasthaus)
Fri - 5 — " - Munich (train - Gif found me acc. - ate at std)
Sat - 6 — Munich (wandered)
Sun - 7 — " (beer fest with dull G)
Mon - 8 — " (shopped - bought slvr)
Tues. - 9 — " - Vienna (train - Milanese jaz salesman - almost lost bags - Pt priv car)
Weds - 10 — Vienna (wandered)
Thurs - 11 — " (
Fri - 12 — " (
Sat - 13 — " (
Sun - 14 — " (
Mon - 15 — " (
Tues - 16 — " (Grinzing - Schonbrun - Belvedere)
Weds - 17 — " to Bern (miserable - was fed by kind people)
Thurs - 18 — Bern
Fri - 19 — "
Sat - 20 — "
Sun - 21 — "
Mon - 22 — " (Marcel Hinterman)
Tues - 23 — " to Venice (9 US $i 2 Italian musicians & s art student)
Weds - 24 — "
Thurs - 25 — "
Fri - 26 — " to Lubljanje (
Sat. - 27 — Lubljanje (met Sylvia - Cafe danced with army til me pm)
Sun. - 28 — " (rem pm - art gallery - cafe)
Mon. - 29 — " to Rijeka (pop hotel hiked - 2 drops of beer - sobu priv)
Tues. - 30 — Rijeka - Split (boat trip - Pepe & slept in sailor's quarters

118

JoAnne's Itinerary

Weds - 31 - Split (wondered yl S. slept. Suse - should have had dates palace)
Thurs - 1 - " (opera singer
Fri - 2 - " (Meštrović Gallery - cafe - news broadcast at home of Johnny)
Sat. - 3 - " - Hvar (all day - wonderful swim - picked off streets - fried sardines)
Sun - 4 - Hvar   Dubrovnik (sailors. 1st S's stewed, 1st nf - bridge - Dub "captain
Mon - 5 - Dubrovnik (wandered viona - slum - cafe ★ news Swiss man)
Tues - 6 - "   alone to Gruz - cafe - musicians - concert in (Pizena)
Weds - 7 - "   ~~~~~~~~~~~~~ room tried to hitch hike out)
Thurs - 8 - S ~~~~~~~~~~~~~ Sarajevo (~~~~~~~~ visited miserable room)
Fri - 9 - Sarajevo (met Brac a V, ,,
Sat - 10 - " - Zenica (hitch hiked - village - filling station)   ~~~~~~~~
Sun - 11 - Zenica - Belgrade (horrible angle phopa U S's friend - priv. rm)
Mon - 12 - Belgrade (wandered ~~~~ concert (g) bad)
Tues - 13 - " (~~~~~~~~) drank -
Weds - 14 - " (met Miša - dnr, coffee, Sliporica Vd talk - 6am)
Thurs - 15 - " (" " at hotel Mosc. - met V. - concert with V ind K)
Fri - 16 - " (tk S. to met M: cont. Prozor - dance - mt US nmad
Sat. - 17 - " (concert. ★, K, V, M,)
Sun - 18 - " (moved to V's apt. house. ~~~~ - M - club) medical
Mon - 19 - " (movie)
Tues - 20 - " (concert - S M K V I)
Weds - 21 - " (caabua
Thurs - 22 - " (caabua for V.
Fri - 23 - " - Zagreb (2 uj o. - friendly!!Yugo
Sat - 24 - Zagreb - Trieste (awful
Sun - 25 - Trieste - Milan
Mon - 26 - Milan - Bern
Tues - 27 - Bern
Weds - 28 - " - Paris
Thurs - 29 - Paris
Fri - 30 - "
Sat. - 1 - "
Sun. - 2 - "

lived for the next fifteen months, before returning to the United States to start The Movie. Sarah seems to have lost her passion for traveling and appears to have remained in Belgrade. That is an even better story, too much of which I have forgotten, unfortunately.

When my two young heroines from Salt Lake City arrived in Belgrade, they started hanging around the university, where they met Misha, who introduced them to several of his friends, some of whom are in evidence in this itinerary. Misha had a lot of friends at the university. He was a student leader there and an up-and-coming member of the Communist Party. Sarah and Misha fell in love, JoAnne told me. And on Sunday, November 11, 1956, when she and Sarah plopped themselves down at the University of Belgrade, the students were in the streets debating the pros and cons of making common cause with their fellow students in Hungary, who had just touched off the Hungarian Uprising next door. At this point, Djilas had been arrested, the Cold War had become a hot war, and no one knew where the world was heading. Those would have been heady times for two young girls from Utah, as they were swept up in all the excitement of being young and idealistic in a time of war and revolution. From experiences such as these are indelible memories forged. And this is where JoAnne's bond with Yugoslavia came from, the bond that was to bring her back to Yugoslavia eleven years later, with her husband, her baby, and her dog. Sarajevo was the watershed from which the remainder of your journey flows.

I serendipitously came across this old woodcut recently, stashed away with a few of JoAnne's things. It is a scene of Belgrade, signed and dated by the artist. I suspect she probably bought it on the street from some "poor starving artist." That's how she was.

Bosnia-Herzegovina

Letter From Sarajevo

September 10, 1967
Bosnia-Herzegovina, Yugoslavia
Map 2

Dear Zerky,

I hope you have figured out by now that you did not perish in that snowstorm beneath the Matterhorn. You went south like the bird. The day we left Switzerland, we drove over San Gotthard pass in a blizzard and then, an hour later, and several thousand feet lower, we zipped eastward across Northern Italy in near-summer weather. We spent two nights camped on Lido Island, just outside of Venice, from where we took the boat into the city. You had a good time chasing pigeons in San Marco Square, and you liked your gondola ride too. But we didn't stay very long—your mother had been there before and I found Venice too much of a tourist trap.

After three nights on Lido Island, we crossed into Yugoslavia, near Trieste, and followed the Adriatic Coast southward through the rocky hills that plunge into the sea all along that coast. We were then on the scenic Dalmatian Coast, which is Yugoslavia's biggest tourist attraction. It is very popular with East European vacationers, who love warm beaches. Halfway down the coast, at the town of Split, your mother became impatient with "this Yugoslavian Riviera," as she called it. She suggested we "split from Split." So we left the coast and cut inland. Eleven years ago, she had hitchhiked through this part of Yugoslavia and she remembered the Yugoslavian interior to be very different from the Dalmatian Coast.

Climbing into the mountains known as the Dinaric Alps, we followed an asphalt road northeast for about ten miles. We expected no difficulty, as our map shows the road to be a major thoroughfare to Belgrade, the capital. At the first village, the road virtually disappeared. Bewildered, we got out our Serbo-Croatian phrase book and tried asking some nearby villagers about the road to Livno, which, according to the map, was the next town along our route. Always with a laugh, the villagers would wave us on. What's so funny about a road to Livno, we wondered? All we could find was a dry streambed.

Very slowly and carefully, we inched ahead, creeping ever so slowly over so many stones and boulders that I had to stop and let the clutch cool down three times. What happened to our highway, we wondered? A flood must have washed it away. But surely it would not have disappeared all the way to Livno, about thirty miles away? An hour later our road had not yet improved. We stopped for a conference—we were making no more progress than we could have on foot. VW buses have high clearances, fortunately, but at the rate we were going it would have taken us days, or weeks, to reach Sarajevo. Assuming we didn't break an axle. Or burn up the clutch.

The sensible thing to do, we finally decided, was to turn back. But we were having too much fun. So we continued on, yard by yard, picking our way up and over and in between the rocks, ever higher into the mountains. Ta dah, te dah! "These damp barren hills strewn with gray boulders and patches of brush," JoAnne writes, "are among the most desolate I have ever seen." Pregnant with meaning, such boulders are the metaphorical building blocks of modern Yugoslavia.

We stopped to look at a small stone monument, the first of many we were to see. Beneath its faded red star, your mother could read just enough Serbo-Croatian to understand that it commemorated a band of Partisans who had been killed on this spot by the Nazis. During World War II, when Yugoslavia was occupied by the Nazis, Marshal Tito and his guerrilla band waged highly effective guerrilla warfare from these same Dinaric Alps. Since the Germans could afford neither the time nor the troops to crush Tito's resistance fighters, Germany adopted a policy of terrorism through blind retribution. Often with the help of sympathetic townspeople, the Partisans would swoop down upon some vulnerable German train, convoy, or barracks, and blow it up. Then they would quickly disappear back into the mountains. In retaliation, the Germans would then go into the nearest village, systematically pick out an arbitrary number of its inhabitants, and have them shot.

Afterward, many of the able-bodied men and boys who survived such massacres headed up into the mountains to join Tito's ever-growing guerrilla army. This is how World War II was fought in Yugoslavia: a vicious circle of bloody defiance and blind reprisal in which most of the casualties were civilians. By the time World War II ended, Tito's Partisans were heroes, and Tito was the new leader of Yugoslavia. These mountains we have been driving through are peppered with such monuments.

Still climbing upward, the road began to improve. A wind came up and it turned cold. We crawled along in low gear for two more hours. At the top of the pass, a weather-beaten sign announced that we were leaving Croatia and entering Bosnia-Herzegovina. The sign denoted only a change of province. Little did we know we were entering a whole new world. Asia may begin at the Bosporus, geographically. Culturally it begins at Bosnia-Herzegovina.

The most stunning change was in people's dress: women's skirts became billowing pantaloons turned under at the bottoms and drawn up tightly around their calves, as in pictures from the *Arabian Nights*. These garments seem to us to be the ultimate in Puritanism; by closing off the bottoms of skirts, any chance of catching a glimpse of a woman's legs is automatically forestalled. The women we passed along the road drew shawls up over their faces, in the manner of a veil. Any doubts as to which culture we were in were soon dispelled when we began seeing men wearing the fez.

Passing through our first Bosnian village, we found a central square commanded by a tall minaret. Soon minarets began popping up all over the place. Towns of any size have several of them, and often a mosque. We had read that Bosnia was once under the heel of the Turks, but we had never expected to see so much Turkish influence surviving on down to this day. In other parts of Yugoslavia—in Macedonia for example—this might be understandable. Many of the people there are of Turkish descent. But here in Bosnia-Herzegovina, most of the people are Moslems and Slavs, which means that they are indigenous Europeans. Who ever heard of indigenous European Moslems? I suppose they converted from Christianity after the Turks conquered this southeast corner of Europe. I suppose it was convert or die. People sometimes say the mountain came to Mohammed. Here in Bosnia-Herzegovina, a good-sized chunk of the European continent came to Mohammed.

Our biggest surprise upon entering Bosnia-Herzegovina was the road. We soon found ourselves zipping along at thirty miles an hour and we reached Sarajevo by nightfall.

Sarajevo is by far the most interesting city we have yet seen. It is a city full of mosques, minarets, country people in Turkish costumes and city people in western coats and ties. Parts of it are very modern. We spied a supermarket. They seem to be popular in communist countries. Good capitalists that we are, we rushed in, to replenish our supplies. We spied canned goods, breads, cheeses, sausages, wines, and slivovitz. A major part of Yugoslavia is devoted to this fiery plum brandy, the Yugoslavian version of central heating.

You found Tito in that supermarket, Zerky. Your mother quickly named him after her favorite bear in the zoo at Bern. I wanted to call him Ferdinand, in honor of the Archduke, but she insisted "Tito" would be easier for you to say. It was love at first sight. Unfortunately Tarzan doesn't love Tito at all. When you showed him your new teddy bear, Tarzan grabbed him away from you and tried to shake all his stuffing out! Your mother charged to the rescue. But now you need to be careful to keep Tito away from Tarzan. I think Tarzan is jealous.

It is raining heavily now. Tomorrow we plan to head into Montenegro and take back roads southward toward the coast. It should be sunny there, which will be a relief—most of the time it's been raining ever since we left the Adriatic Coast. Let's hope we don't get stuck!

Love,
Dad

Montenegro

Letter From Montenegro

September 19, 1967
Ulcinj, Yugoslavia
Map 2

Dear Zerky,

After more than a week of bad weather and terrible roads, we have at last reached the Adriatic again, a few miles south of Titograd (now Podgorica). It was a struggle because the roads in the interior are a disaster. Most of the villages are so hard to get to that the people there don't seem to know what tourists are. Life in those villages must be very difficult, although their names are very beautiful. The j's in Serbo-Croatian seem to be pronounced softly, like the j's in French—as in "Jean" and "Jacques." We went through Gorozde (go-roj-day), Pljevlja (plyev-lia), and Zabljak (tsab-lyek) near Mount Durmitor, which, at 8,196 feet, is Yugoslavia's highest peak. We love the way they pronounce these silken sounds, which peacefully co-exist along with their impossible spellings.

When we finally got back to the Adriatic we continued down the coast as far we could go. We've had to stop a few miles north of the Albanian border. Albania is closed to foreigners. Here at Ulcinj, there is a delightful campground on a peaceful beach. The weather is perfect and the water so warm that we've not been able to tear ourselves away, and have ended up spending more than a week here. Like most Yugoslavian children at the beach, you have been going nude. Do not fear, your mother isn't trying to make a nudist out of you, although you do have a beautiful suntan. All over. Your mother does not. Fortunately. Unfortunately, you don't seem to care for this Adriatic much more than you cared for most of the Mediterranean beaches— the waves are still knocking you down, much to your mother's dismay. Here's the choice, Zerky: either you learn to stand up to the waves or you learn how to swim.

Ulcinj is the quintessential Mediterranean fishing village, bathed in sunlight and warm sea breezes. The townspeople here are the most colorfully dressed we have ever seen. They wear bright traditional costumes such as you only see on holidays in the rest of Europe. The women wear many varieties of brightly colored skirts, blouses, shawls and head dressings, all of them generously covered with hand-embroidery. Both Christians and Moslems are easy to distinguish by their dress, although it's hard to decide which are the most colorful. One day on the road between Ulcinj and our campground we saw a wedding procession. At its head, seated on a donkey, was a bearded patriarch whom we decided was the bride's father, or maybe the priest. Behind him, on separate donkeys, came three elaborately gowned bridesmaids, and then, on the most heavily decorated donkey of all, the bride, draped in flowing robes. Over her head she wore an immense vermilion veil covering her to the waist. Behind came a string of donkeys loaded with household goods: bedding, furniture, cooking utensils, clothing—the dowry, no doubt.

We've been doing our reading again. So let's see now: Yugoslavia's geographical location makes it a hub of diverse influences that have pulled the Balkan Peninsula in conflicting directions for many centuries—it says here. During much of this time, most of Yugoslavia was under the sway of the Ottoman Turks to the East. And, also in the East, both the Yugoslavian and Greek Macedonias have age-old conflicts with Bulgaria, which has a large Macedonian minority, while in the West, Yugoslavia's Dalmatian Coast has been Italian for many, many years. Now in the North—the richest part of Yugoslavia—the allure of Austrian affluence even farther to the North has become a political problem for Yugoslavia's central government. And—oh yes, I almost forgot—while in the South, Yugoslavia's portion of Macedonia has been embroiled in conflicts with the Hellenic civilizations of Greece for as long as anyone can remember. And then, also, in the southwestern part of Yugoslavia, where we are now, there is a huge Albanian minority believed to have descended from the Illyrians, who are the only people native to the Balkan Peninsula. Got it? Now you know how World War I got started, Zerky.

Along religious lines, Yugoslavia is equally confusing. In keeping with the tenets of communism, Yugoslavia is officially atheistic, even though its constitution grants freedom of religion to all, thereby allowing the Orthodox Church to flourish. Except in the West, where the Italians brought Catholicism to Dalmatia, while in the North, Protestantism crept in. And, sort of in the middle, Bosnia-Herzegovina became Moslem.

Even the Serbo-Croatian language is an amalgam of the languages of the Russian-leaning Serbs in the East and the European-leaning Croats in the West. In Serbo-Croatian, two alphabets coexist. When driving, we pray for road signs written in the Roman alphabet, which we can sometimes decipher. Unfortunately, as we get closer to Belgrade, more and more of them are written in the Cyrillic alphabet, at which point the Russian your mother studied in college oftentimes saves the day.

All this diversity, we have decided, seems to have engendered a peculiarly liberal outlook on life here in Yugoslavia. Your mother and I find this very refreshing. For example, most Yugoslavs we've met show considerable interest in the oval identification sticker on the back of our car. It says "USA." People are anxious to talk to us about politics, and they don't take dogmatic positions on the cold war either. We met a Croatian on the beach yesterday. He is an economist from Zagreb, on vacation with his mother. He told us how proud he is of all the progress Yugoslavia is making. Nevertheless, there's an egg crisis here in Ulcinj. It seems there was recently a local draft call-up, and all the eggs were used up by all the going-away parties. The economist's mother volunteered to go off with your mother to help find you some eggs, Zerky. Your mother thanked her and tried to explain that you still have a few eggs left, and that, in any event, we are not going to be here much longer. So take it easy on them eggs!

Love,
Dad

SERBIA

Macedonia

Letter From Macedonia

September 25, 1967
Yugoslavia, at the Corner of
Albania and Greece
Map 2

Dear Zerky,

When we left Ulcinj, we doubled back to Titograd and continued eastward and southward through Montenegro and Macedonia, along the Yugoslavian side of the Albanian border. Albania fascinates us. We want to go there, but so far have been unable to come up with a workable scheme. Your passport states that it is:

> NOT VALID FOR TRAVEL TO OR IN COMMUNIST CONTROLLED PORTIONS OF CHINA, KOREA, VIETNAM OR TO OR IN ALBANIA, CUBA. A PERSON WHO TRAVELS TO OR IN THE LISTED COUNTRIES OR AREAS MAY BE LIABLE FOR PROSECUTION UNDER SECTION 1185, TITLE 8, U. S. CODE, AND SECTION 1544, TITLE 18, U. S. CODE.

We want to go anyway. And you do too, dammit! Whether you want to or not. A man in Titograd, at Putnik, the Yugoslavian government tourist office, told us this would probably be possible if we went with one of their government-sponsored tours out of Lake Ohrid. That way we would be in Albania under the auspices of the Yugoslavian government. He didn't think our American passports would pose a problem. Albania is desperate for hard currency and both governments have apparently worked out an arrangement to cooperate with each other on tourism. Unfortunately, by the time we arrived at Lake Ohrid it was too late in the season; all their tours have been discontinued until next spring. So now it looks like we are going to have to settle for views of Albania from across the border, and for Radio Tirana, the "Voice of Albania," which we've been listening to for several days now. Radio Tirana is the strongest station on the dial and broadcasts an exotic mixture of Chinese and Albanian folk music, interspersed with long harangues, of which we can pick out a few words such as "Americane," "Criminale," "Aggressione," "Vietname," and—our favorite—"Gangster."

Once a day Radio Tirana has a broadcast in English, a broadcast that scarcely resembles "news" as we know it. Mostly it's about the heroic advances of "our Chinese brothers under the enlightened leadership of Chairman Mao." The rest is relentless diatribe more or less equally divided between the USSR and the USA. This is a tragic situation, really. For years now, Albania has been completely isolated from its neighbors and natural trading partners, and has become almost completely dependent upon China, an alien society halfway around the globe. Aside from the Putnik tour, it is impossible to enter Albania, as far as we've been able to figure out. The Albanian government doesn't allow foreigners to travel freely and, besides, there are almost no roads in Albania.

On our way to Lake Ohrid we traveled through a region tucked in between southern Montenegro and western Macedonia, known as Kosovo, which is the poorest place we have yet seen on this trip, including Andalucia. The Yugoslavian government is currently pouring large sums of money into Kosovo, building roads, dams and communications, in an attempt to bring the standard of living up to par with the rest

Zerky at Lake Ohrid, Albania in background

of Yugoslavia. It still has far to go. This whole section of Yugo-slavia seems to us to be an isolated pocket that somehow got bypassed by the rest of Europe. I doubt life has changed much here since the days of Alexander the Great.

While driving through a town about thirty miles north of Lake Ohrid, we had another close-up view of poverty, this time in an Albanian village in the Yugoslavian province of Macedo-nia, which is part of neither Albania nor Bulgaria. However, there are nearly as many Albanians living in Yugoslavia as there are in Albania. This village was composed exclusively of mud houses with straw roofs and dirt streets filled with cows, pigs, chickens, and children, all of them mingling freely together— sometimes inside the houses. It reminded me of pictures I have seen of villages in Africa.

Lake Ohrid, where we are now, is a popular destination for Yugoslavs and other Eastern Europeans looking for a cheap vacation. Its cool shores and warm waters have made it fashionable since ancient times, when the Greeks and the Romans used to vacation here. Lake Ohrid is a very large lake located in a remote rolling mountainous area, at an elevation of about four thousand feet, where Yugoslavia, Albania, and Greece all come together. All three countries share its waters.

Camping season is over now and the campground we are currently in is virtually deserted. This is all very luxurious, really. We have the beach all to ourselves, and you find Lake Ohrid's gentle, tideless, waveless water to be a lot friendlier than the rambunctious ocean surf. The lake is your bathtub.

In a couple of days we will be going on down into Greece. Although our destination is Bucharest, we are so close to Greece that we can't resist its attractive forces. Going there now will allow us to spend more time in Romania later on. In Athens, we should be able to stock up on disposable diapers and the other necessities of life. But we've got to hurry; it will be turning cold in the Transylvanian Alps and we want to get you to Transylvania before Count Dracula flies south for the winter with those birds. Let's hope he waits for you.

Love,
Dad

Greece

Letter From Athens

October 13, 1967
Athens, Greece
Map 2

Dear Zerky,

When we crossed into northern Greece just south of Lake Ohrid, the Greek border official there became very interested in your passport. After studying it intently, he informed us that Xerxes was defeated by the Greeks in 490 BC, at the Battle of Marathon. As always when approaching a new country, we had been reading some history prior to our arrival. I wanted to correct the guy by telling him it wasn't Xerxes who had been defeated at Marathon, but rather Xerxes' father, King Darius the Great. I also wanted to explain to him, in excruciating detail, how Xerxes came back to Greece ten years later and kicked the shit out of the Greeks at the Battle of Thermopylae. But I decided it best to hold my piece and not challenge him on the history of his own country. People like to think their history belongs to them, so they can make it up as they go along. But, unfortunately, that guy *was* the government. A bunch of Greek colonels recently staged a coup d'état here and Greece is now under military rule.

I think I've been corrupted by travel. Here I am in one of the most interesting countries in Europe, and I'm bored! The most exciting thing about Greece is our decision to leave it. Although the beaches in Peloponnesia really are wonderful, Zerky, I'm tired of beaches and you are too. The waves are still knocking you down and you seem to have lost your appetite for eating sand. Tarzan still likes to dig in it, however, probably because his legs are too short for swimming. I told him dachshunds are built that way so they can go down holes and catch rabbits, but Tarzan says he doesn't want to go down holes and catch rabbits, he says he *likes* rabbits and doesn't want to chase them either. He just wants to dig in the sand.

Tarzan heard Elvis on the radio the other day, belittling him. Elvis told Tarzan "You ain't nothin' but a hound dog. You ain't never caught a rabbit and you ain't no friend of mine." Well, naturally, your mother jumped to the rescue. She told Tarzan that Elvis ain't never caught no rabbit neither. And then of course I had to get into the act, so I told Tarzan that Elvis is so fat he'd get stuck in the hole if he ever tried to catch a rabbit. And then all the rabbits would eat him! Tarzan seemed to like this idea but still seems diminished by it all. It must be hard on a guy to hear someone belittling you on the radio, especially when you are only a miniature to start with. Thus it was on a beach of the Peloponnesus, where Athens lost an empire two and a half thousand years ago, that Elvis finally got his comeuppance. He should have knowed better than to mess with your mother's dog!

A week ago, we visited Olympia, a ruined city with an old coliseum where the ancient Greeks held their original Olympic Games, more than twenty-five centuries ago. Usually you are not fond of excursions to historical places, Zerky, you don't like being dragged around by the hand. But Olympia was different. Its ancient amphitheatre is in surprisingly good condition, and of considerable interest to your mother and me, because it is the oldest theatre in the world. Its seats are still in amazingly good condition. In the movie business, you're lucky

**Zerky at the Acropolis
Athens, Greece**

to have seats last twenty years. People cut the upholstery with jackknives and carve their initials into the armrests, things we were never able to keep them from doing in your mother's theatre.

The ancient Greeks, however, came up with an ingenious solution to this vexing problem; they made their seats out of marble and didn't provide any armrests at all. At Olympia, immense elongated square blocks of stone have been stacked one row upon the other so as to create theatre seats far more durable than the finest in modern stadium seating. Greek seating holds up well under tough conditions, requires minimal maintenance, and endures for centuries if kept clean with wind, rain and mild detergent. You were very impressed by Olympia, Zerky. It was the perfect gymnasium in which to practice your rock climbing. With a little help from your friends, you started at the bottom and just kept climbing and climbing until you pooped out. You never did quite make it to the top, but then who ever makes it to the top when they are only one year old? Tell your friends you won two Olympic events: gold from your parents for outstanding behavior and you silvered in rock climbing.

Your mother and I have been stricken by an infectious malady we caught on a beach a few days ago from an elderly German couple traveling in a Volkswagen bus similar to ours. They were winding up a two-year trip from Germany that started when they took the ferry across the Strait of Gibraltar, to Tangiers, in Africa. From Morocco they drove all the way down to South Africa and then back up to Kenya, on the other side of the African continent, where they put their car on a boat from Mombasa to the Persian Gulf. From there they drove back to Europe through Iran, Turkey and Greece, and are now on their way back to Germany. We spent most of the day with them, listening to their stories and asking them questions. They assured us that driving through Africa really is possible. "All kinds of people do it," they said. That is why we are bored with Athens, Zerky, and why Romania is out. Maybe we can catch it on the way back. We are now heading for Tehran, and then on to the Persian Gulf, where we hope to catch a boat to Kenya. Then we will drive back to Spain via South Africa. We shall see lions and tigers and elephants, little Zerk! Well, maybe not tigers, but we will still have a lot of fun.

Athens is a big, smoggy, traffic-clogged city, and the staging ground for "our expedition." It seems like all we've been doing since we got here is getting shots. Cholera shots, typhoid shots, typhus shots, yellow fever shots, smallpox shots. Some of them require an entire "course," meaning they shoot you again and again and again. Our arms are still sore. Yours are the sorest of all. At first you took the needles better than we did, but then you caught on to how the system works: shot after shot after shot. Tarzan was the lucky one. All he needed was the rabies shot we had already got him before we left San Francisco.

In addition to getting shot, this past week we have been expending a huge amount of energy running around Athens trying to get a *carnet du passage* for the car. Everybody needs one of these things in order to drive a car into Asia. A carnet is a document—a sort of insurance policy—guaranteeing that you will not sell your car in the country you are bringing it into. At first, everybody told us that in order to get a carnet we would have to go back to the place where we bought the "vehicle," in Germany. But thanks to the generous help of some very nice people at the German Embassy, who sent multiple wires to Germany on our behalf, for free, *we now have our carnet!* And we also got you a visa for Turkey. You had to go to the Turkish Embassy for it. When we gave the nice lady there a picture of you, which she needed in order to issue you your visa, she told your mother and me that you were "so cute." I told her Tarzan is cute, too, but she told me Tarzan doesn't need a visa. I don't think she much cares for dogs. Oh, well.

Then we went to the Iranian Embassy to pick up visas for the next country down the line. Some Iranian guy there was all grumpy and told us we would have to pick up our Iranian visas in Ankara, the capital of Turkey. Maybe I should have offered him one of your pictures too.

We also bought two new tires. After only twelve thousand miles, the tread had disappeared off both our rear ones. Those "roads" in Yugoslavia sure took their toll. We've been so busy getting this kind of junk done that we haven't had time for much sightseeing. We did make it to the Acropolis, and to the National Museum. You liked the former better: you could climb around on the Acropolis. That seems to be your *modus operandi* these days. Time for you to start learning Latin.

Our bus is now loaded to the gunwales with baby food and diapers crammed into every cubic inch of space there is in and on top of a Volkswagen bus. You have over two hundred jars of German baby food, and close to a thousand bulky disposable paper diapers. Once we leave Athens, we don't expect to be able to buy you either of these things. So take it easy. This stuff has got to last!

The recent takeover of the government here by the military junta is much in evidence. The army is everywhere, and not just idealistic young soldiers, either, but ill-tempered old career officers standing on all the street corners. We will be glad to be out of here next week, as soon as we finish off our shots. After our taste of Yugoslavia, Asia has us chomping at the bit. Tarzan chomps on bones. You chomp on *Legume-Boeuf-Foie de Veau* out of a jar. We see many such jars in your future.

Love,
Dad

Turkey

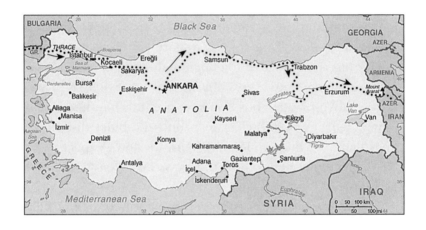

Letter From Istanbul

October 28, 1967
Istanbul, Turkey
Maps 2 & 3

Dear Zerky,

We finally reached the end of Europe. The ride was worth it. This city is like nothing we have ever seen. Istanbul is an oriental puzzle of twisting, climbing, cobblestone streets laid out in no pattern at all but what has been bestowed upon them by two thousand years of blind evolution. Its gutters feed an army of dogs, cats and rats, and the air is heavy with the household smells of a million and a half inhabitants. Seen close up, Istanbul is probably the dirtiest city in Europe, but it is also the most beautiful. Seen from a distance—from the Galeta Bridge spanning the Bosporus, for example—Istanbul is a breathtaking mixture of green hills, blue waters and exotic white buildings shimmering in the sunlight, with a skyline as spectacular as Manhattan's. And instead of skyscrapers, there is a profile of hills, jumbled rooftops, barbed minarets and soaring domes. This is a city of mosques, dozens of them. It was the seat of Islam when the Ottoman Empire ruled much of Asia, Africa, and parts of Europe.

Today we visited Santa Sophia, perhaps the most spectacular of Istanbul's many mosques. Santa Sophia is an immense hemispherical vault supported by 107 columns. Originally it was a Byzantine cathedral built by the Christians when Constantinople was the seat of the Holy Roman Empire. But when

147

the Ottoman Turks captured the city in 1453, changed its name to Istanbul, and made it the seat of their Islamic empire, they too loved the magnificence of their newly acquired Christian cathedral. So instead of tearing it down, they just added some minarets, rechristened it a mosque, and kept its Christian name, Santa Sophia. Its counterpart would be the Great Mosque of Cordoba in Spain, which you just may remember, Zerky—we had to keep you from running around in it and trying to climb all the marble columns. When the Christians drove the Moors out of Cordoba, a few years after the Muslims drove the Christians out of Istanbul, Christianity in turn paid homage to Islam when it built a brand new cathedral, right in the center of that newly captured Cordoba mosque.

We took you to Santa Sophia today and, like a plant to the sun, you were drawn up the long spiral ramp-way that ascends to the gallery beneath the dome at the top. There beneath the elaborately painted ceiling, your mother and I were entranced by the incomparable frescos. How brilliantly their colors had survived the centuries! It came as a shock to suddenly realize we were not looking at frescos at all, but at mosaics constructed out of fine aggregate.

We've been in Istanbul for three days now, Zerky. The most magical time of all is early morning when the first glimmer of dawn begins to wash out the stars and the muezzins call the faithful to prayer. Each morning from our campground on the European shore of the Sea of Marmara, I hear three of them at once, their quavering voices piercing the silence like twisting silver shafts. Half awake, I lie there in my sleeping bag, my sleep-sopped brain awash in three separate rivers of sound. Five minutes, ten minutes…they finally stop. I lie there savoring the sounds of this new world awaiting us on the other side of the bridge over the Bosporus. And then I pull up my eider-down bag and drift happily back to sleep. What a place! Unfortunately, we can't stay here much longer. Autumn is in the air and we are becoming apprehensive lest a sudden snowfall close the mountain passes into Northern Iran. We are now on the only overland route to the East.

Love,
Dad

Zerky at the Black Sea

Letter From Somewhere in Anatolia

October 31, 1967
Eastern Turkey
Map 3

Dear Zerky,

Turkey is a country astride two continents; only about 5 percent of it is in Europe. We were surprised by how similar the European part is to Greece. As soon as we crossed into Asia, however, that similarity faded rapidly. Asia has a flavor all its own. Heading east, we went through the capital of Ankara and then northeast as far as Sansum, on the Black Sea. From there we traveled due east along the coast, as far as Trabzon. Before we got there, however, you spent one very happy morning on a very black Black Sea beach near Sansum, where in spite of the advanced season and the cold we had encountered in the interior, it was like summer. The Black Sea was a mirror framed with black sand, and there was no surf to knock you down. You are growing up, dear boy.

We spent the following night in a campground on the Black Sea near Trabzon, where we met a Land Rover full of Englishmen on their way back from India. Now we are on our way to India too! If you can catch a boat to Africa from the Persian Gulf, then why not from Bombay?

Leaving the Black Sea at Trabzon, we began the steep climb up and over a range of mountains as high as the Pyrenees, onto the rocky, often mountainous plain of Turkey's interior. As fertile seacoast crumbled into arid desert, Third World poverty began to assert itself. Mud villages similar to the ones we saw along the Kosovo-Macedonia-Albania border are the rule here. Fields are smaller and poorer, and inevitably plowed by a man with a lone ox pulling a single-bladed wooden plow. The verdant vegetation and productive fields of the coast have now disappeared, to be replaced by the semi-barren rocky highlands known as Asia Minor's Anatolian Plain. Here we find an almost completely agricultural society, one in which no one grows very much and only the hardy grow anything at all. Perhaps it is because I grew up in a farm state that I find this so shocking—people digging livings out of land so poor that North Dakota Red River Valley farmers would consider it uninhabitable.

We are now traveling at an elevation of 5,000 to 6,000 feet, and it is miserably cold. Let's hope it doesn't snow. This afternoon it started to rain, and now our land of rocks and dirt is turning into a land of mud. There is little in the way of natural vegetation around here to protect this poor, unhappy crust of earth. Increasingly, we are passing women along the road carrying large loads of agricultural produce on their backs. Only the well-off farmers, it appears, can afford a donkey. For everyone else there is the wife. The men, as seems to be the custom, are too busy to be beasts of burden; we see them seated outside the cafés in the villages, laughing and talking over cups of thick black Turkish coffee. And perhaps a little *raki*, a sort of anise-flavored brandy that—as in Yugoslavia—keeps everybody warm. After all, how can a guy talk business out in the cold?

Coming into the city of Erzerum this afternoon, we saw our first real Asian city. Even the remote areas of Yugoslavia look tame in comparison. The buildings of Erzerum are mostly of mud construction, with a few wooden beams supporting their roofs. There must be trees growing in these mountains somewhere, but so far we've not seen enough of them to make lumber. We stopped in Erzerum this morning to go shopping and replenish our food supply. The main street was a morass of mud being constantly churned by horses, ox-carts, trucks, and buses. The men wore heavy, more-or-less western-style shirts and trousers, the women long, heavy dresses reaching all the way down to their ankles. Over their heads, they wore heavy shawls, and over their faces some of them wore veils. And not flimsy, Moroccan-style peek-a-boo veils, either, but veils like scarves drawn up over the lower halves of their faces. Even though for many years now it has been official government policy to do away with the veil, the custom is still in wide use here in eastern Turkey.

Your mother has been learning a few words of Turkish in the car, and today when we went shopping she had an opportunity to try them out on a veiled woman. Your mother discovered that it is very hard to talk to, and to understand, a woman whose mouth you cannot see. After a spirited struggle, we did manage to find most of what we needed, however. Bread, cheese, eggs, sardines, some canned goods, a bottle of raki.

It is still raining on and off, and getting colder by the mile. About a thousand feet above us there is snow on the hills, and it is making us nervous about the passes we need to climb in the vicinity of Mount Ararat, near the Iranian border.

Today we pushed on after nightfall. We try not to do this because you can never be sure what you might run into on such lonely roads at night. Furthermore, driving after dark makes it hard to find a decent camping spot. You never know where you really are until next morning. Tonight we are in a turnout at the end of a switchback. Right before the road turned, we caught sight of a nice little flat spot lit up in our headlights, where we are now camped for the night. Tarzan doesn't want to go out and run around—it's too cold and windy out there. So here we are, the four of us, snug in our little tin house on wheels, with our little propane heater singing its little heart out, god bless it, and with raindrops drumming on our roof. Your mother is cooking dehydrated soup for supper and the windows are all fogged up. Tomorrow we shall be in Iran!

Love,
Dad

Boy beside the road in Anatolia, Eastern Turkey

This boy still haunts me. We were stopped by the road when he wandered up, and I got the feeling he wanted to get out of his bleak little village. He reminded me of me. I wished he might come along, too.

Letter From Near Mount Ararat

November 1, 1967
Dogubayazit
Eastern Turkey
Map 3

Dear Zerky,

Last night you wouldn't wake up and you missed all the excitement. Your mother and I were awakened in the middle of the night by a torrent of shouting and pounding on the side of the bus. Still groggy, I pulled on my pants and stepped out into the cold. It was snowing lightly. There I found eight very angry Turks dressed in a variety of uniforms. They all had guns, and most of them appeared to be soldiers. The others, your mother and I have decided, were probably police. They were all yelling at me and I could not understand a word they said. When they finally figured this out, they tried to solve their language problem in the age-old way, by yelling at me louder.

So there I was in the middle of the night, half-dressed, in the middle of nowhere, with the snow coming down and an angry gang of men all pointing guns at me. One guy, who appeared to be their leader, soon grew impatient and took two steps back, put his rifle to his shoulder, and aimed it at my chest from six feet away. My entire life did not pass before my eyes in an instant, I am happy to report, but I did do a quick run-through on how Turks have a reputation for violence, and on how our wonderful camper is unobtainable in Turkey, except by extraordinary means. In other words, I was scared.

Not having the slightest idea what to do, I proffered my idiot smile, which must have been the right thing to do, because pretty soon the guy lowered his rifle and started gesturing with it wildly towards the hills. Then he would point it back at me, take aim at my heart again, lower it again, point it towards the hills again, and then back at me, all the while yelling at me like he was crazy. "Maybe what he is doing," your mother finally ventured, "is pantomime. Maybe what he's trying to tell you is something in sign language—perhaps that it's not safe to stay here because bandits will come down from the hills and shoot you?"

It still wasn't clear. Not to me at least! What *was* clear, however, was that we were supposed to get the hell out of there. So I said to myself, I said, "Bill," I said, "you'd better get the hell out of here! Just because it's middle of the night and dark and snowing out is no reason not to get an early start and beat all the rush-hour traffic." But it's not so easy just to drive away once we've set up camp for the night. First, all the curtains need to be drawn back and refastened individually. Then all the gear we stow beneath you on the front seat each night needs to be retransferred into the back of the bus and stowed away there. This was a challenge I was up to.

In order to show my cooperation and demonstrate my need for a slight delay, I opened the front door of the bus on the passenger side, and there you were, still sleeping peacefully for all the world to see, your little blond head poking out of your sleeping bag like the head of an angel with golden hair.

Last night at the end of the earth, a miracle occurred. Peace fell upon the land of Anatolia. The soldiers were stunned. Their angry faces melted instantly, to be replaced by smiles. As I reached to pull you out of your bag and transfer you to your mother in the back of the bus, a soldier grabbed my arm gently with one hand, while waving the index finger of his other hand back and forth across his face, and shaking his head silently. "Do not awaken the angel," he was telling me, with all the clarity his previous orders had lacked. I was to close the door quickly before the angel caught cold. This child must go back to sleep now, he gestured, holding his palms together against the side of his cocked head. We were safe, he assured us, patting his rifle. All the voices were soft and reassuring now. You are the universal language, Zerky.

Your mother and I climbed back into our sleeping bags and talked for a while. As we were finally drifting off to sleep, we could still hear a few sounds outside. They were the sounds of people trying to be quiet. We spent the remainder of last night under the protection of the Turkish army. When we awoke this morning, all was quiet, the soldiers were gone. A thin blanket of fresh snow had erased all traces of the night before. All was peaceful as in a dream. An angel had saved us in the night. Thank you, Guardian Angel.

His Dad

Letter From Mount Ararat

November 2, 1967
Dogubayazit,
Eastern Turkey
Map 3

Dear Zerky,

We had planned on crossing into Iran today, but we are still all hopped up over that run-in with the army last night and we've stumbled across some new information which has delayed us. This morning after driving for about an hour, we spotted a gas station at Dogubayazit, the last Turkish town before the Iranian border. There we stopped to fill up our tank. Off to the left was nearby Mount Ararat, an immense 16,695-foot volcanic cone that dominates the horizon for miles in all directions. Our eyes followed it upward to the snow line, perhaps a thousand feet above us. In another thousand feet, its upper half disappeared into the clouds.

We are disappointed. We had been looking forward to taking your picture in front of this fabled mountain, which is the highest in Asia Minor, and, for Christians, at least, the highest mountain in the world, as demonstrated by a really olden guy named Noah who once landed a boat full of animals on top of Mount Ararat when it became the first dry spot of land to emerge from a great big flood that drowned all the other animals and everybody else in the whole wide world. To this day, in newspapers around the world, stories keep popping up about shepherds and mountain climbers coming down off the summit with a piece of wood from the remains of Noah's Ark.

At the gas station—or "petrol pump," as we are attempting to learn to call them—we came across eight or nine British teenagers in a big Land Rover pulling a trailer. They had spent the previous night camped near the pump. As soon as we pulled in, one of the older guys, a scout leader type, came over as we were fueling up and began telling us their sad story:

The day before yesterday they were driving by on their way to India, when they could no longer resist the lure of Mount Ararat. The urge to climb it is almost irresistible. Like the Abominable Snowman and his friend, the Loch Ness Monster, "you just never know what you might find." Finding Noah's ark has been an age-old dream of Christians for many centuries. They view its periodic discovery as proof of the Bible. For many of them, this would be seen as the ultimate triumph of Christianity over Islam.

Our teenagers drove their four-wheel-drive vehicle straight up the mountain as far as it could go, nearly to the snowline. There they left it on the side of the mountain and continued upward on foot. None of them got anywhere near the summit, but they did have a good time in the snow, throwing snowballs at each other and horsing around as teenagers are wont to do. Upon their return to the car, they discovered that someone had heaved a rock through the Land Rover's windshield and made off with two of the girls' suitcases. Inside these suitcases, along with their clothes, were the girls' travelers' checks, passports, inoculation certificates, visas for Iran, and all their other identification. Fortunately the Land Rover was still drivable. They managed to get it back down the mountain to the petrol pump, before dark. There they've been stuck for the last three days. After talking with them for an hour or more, we have decided to spend one last night in Turkey.

The Brits reported the theft to the police, who immediately called in the army. The next morning they all went up to the scene of the crime, where the army spent the rest of the day rounding up shepherds and all the other usual suspects, whom they interrogated at the end of a gun. At first the soldiers were friendly and helpful, the "scout leader" explained. He told us the soldiers seemed very happy to show off their authority to foreigners. But as a grueling day wore on and it became increasingly unlikely they were going to find the culprits, the soldiers' dispositions changed into frustration, resentment, and finally into outright hostility. The scout leader's opinion is that the soldiers believe that the youngsters are not sufficiently appreciative of their efforts, and that they are also embarrassed at having come up empty-handed.

By the end of the day, the soldiers had become quite nasty. "If these rich foreigners would just stay home where they belong, with all their fancy automobiles, fancy clothes, and fancy money, none of this would have happened." This seems to be their thinking, the scout leader told us. By the time the Brits returned to Dogubayazit, this attitude had infected the entire village. Virtually everyone here is now hostile to the Brits, and even we are beginning to have second thoughts about being associated with them.

Although we are only a few miles from Iran, there is no reason for the Brits to go on. The girls don't have papers for crossing the border and neither are they welcome to stay here. No one wants anything to do with them. Someone said something to someone, and now only the owner of the petrol pump is the least bit friendly toward these poor kids. And probably he's only allowing them to stay here because they are his new profit center. We have become friends with the bunch, probably because we, too, are lonesome for English voices. We find something very "plucky" about a gang of kids trying to climb a major mountain on a whim. They must be lonely too. They are anxious to pour out their tale of woe.

Earlier today, at some sort of small government office in the village, one of the Brits was allowed to use a telephone in order to place a call to the British Embassy, in Ankara. But they couldn't get through—the telephones don't work very well in this part of the world—and he was not allowed to try to place a second call. Then they had to go to the chief of police in hopes that he might issue them an affidavit stating that their car had been broken into and their passports stolen. The chief of police would have nothing to do with them. Shortly before we rolled in, they had gone into town one last time to try to buy food, but the shop owners wouldn't sell them any. Finally, the girls, virtually in tears, managed to talk the petrol pump owner into letting them stay here one more night. After two days of spinning their wheels going nowhere, they have now decided to make the long drive back to Erzerum, where they plan to put the girls on a train all the way back to Ankara. There they should be able to have new passports issued at the British Embassy. After that, their plan is for the girls to fly on to Tehran and hook up with the Land Rover again. They are heading out in the morning. "Watch out for the army," I told them. "We had a run-in with some soldiers last night. They patrol the road. They're looking for robbers…"

"Looking for robbers…Watch out for the Army…We had a run-in with them last night…They patrol the road." My words stuck in my mouth. And then it dawned on me: could our soldiers last night and their soldiers the day before have been one and the same soldiers? Both incidents involved soldiers and police together, in the same general area. Might not it be both their jobs to fight crime out in the remote reaches of the country? This would seem to make sense. We hadn't seen enough police around to fight much of anything. Might not soldiers be stationed here, at least in part, in order to provide the police with muscle? A long day's search on Mount Ararat had just ended in a Turkish defeat.

After World War I, when the victorious western allies were busy carving up the Ottoman Empire, and even before that war, when Lawrence of Arabia was harassing the Ottoman Turks, there was another war going on in Turkey—the Turkish War of Independence. It was the Turks against the Western powers, who considered Turkey their rightful spoils of war. Kemal Ataturk emerged from this Turkish revolution as the new nation's savior and first president. Ataturk is Turkey's George Washington. Every Turk knows this. They are taught it in the schools. Soldiers know it too. So do the police. And the villagers. Now, a half-century later, here comes a bunch of Westerners causing trouble again and making the army look bad. They want to inform their embassy—the embassy of Turkey's former oppressor—that they are having problems with Turkish legal authorities. Those soldiers who stumbled upon us in the dark last night, Zerky—listen to me—might not they be the very same soldiers who had been humiliated earlier in the day by a bunch of Westerner kids, when they had not even been able to catch a common, ordinary thief? They had probably been out all night looking for the culprit, when they stumbled across another foreign vehicle. I'll bet you, Zerky, that's what last night was all about!

Love,
Dad

Iran

**Camels in the Snows of Persia
Near Tabriz, Iran**

Letter From the Caspian Sea

November 7, 1967
Chalus
Iranian Azerbaijan
Map 3

Dear Zerky,

After hundreds of miles of interminable earth-colored roads, landscapes, and houses, the Iranian border came as colorful relief. The Shah of Iran is restaging his coronation and all the government buildings along the border are decorated up like Christmas trees, in the colors of the Iranian flag, red, white and green. Some of the villages are similarly festooned.

Upon crossing into Iran, to our great surprise we discovered that we were in *Azerbaijan*. We thought Azerbaijan was in the Soviet Union. We never intended to go there, and even if we had, this is not how we would have expected it to look. Instead of green fields and orange groves, we find only barren dry land and an occasional irrigation project. As was the case in eastern Turkey, Iranian Azerbaijan strikes us as an awful place to live. All was redeemed, however, by our first camel—a whole caravan of them in fact—ambling on down the road in their long-legged, deceptively slow gaits. They were a tonic to our rain-soaked souls, our first taste of the romantic Persia of childhood fantasies. Your namesake, Xerxes, used to own this place!

A few hours later we arrived in Tabriz, Iran's second largest city, where we spent the day getting our car serviced. It provided us with a welcome opportunity to go exploring on foot. In contrast to eastern Turkey, where the men wear more or less Western-style clothes, in Tabriz I found the younger women to be quite striking and exotic. As part of his coronation, the Shah has issued a decree banning the veil, which decree doesn't appear to be having much effect. Most of the women of Tabriz still appear in public in large flowing shawls of high-grade dark blue and brown material, which they coquettishly—and belatedly—pull up over the lower parts of their faces, in the presence of men.

Beneath their shawls, you often catch glimpses of expensive western-style dresses. But they don't fool me! These Iranian women like to tease! I think they're sexy: a pair of dark almond eyes and a pair of spiked heels, peeking out at you from opposite ends of a lovely Persian shawl—my imagination runs riot even though Mother Nature may not have endowed the in-between so generously as she endowed my prurient interest. Such a blending of Middle Eastern tradition with a little Western kicker would seem to be a reasonable compromise for a modern Iran.

Driving around Tabriz trying to find our way out of this huge city, we were pulled over by a police officer on a bicycle. He demanded that I follow him to the police station. Must have violated some traffic law, I figured. That's easy to do when you can't read traffic signs written in Farsi. On the other hand, exactly *why* ignoring traffic signs should be a problem here isn't clear to me. Everyone else ignores traffic signs. My guess was that once again I was the rich foreigner about to pay his dues.

For nearly an hour we cooled our heels in the police station. I spent much of that time contemplating the unfairness of law enforcement authorities who use otherwise unenforced laws to harass people they don't like. Finally a translator was brought in. He told us to go with some officers and unload the top of the bus. "Everything?" I groaned. After eight months of living in it, the bus was no longer an automobile, it was a household on wheels. *"Everything!"*

We still don't know why that cop stopped us; we hadn't been searched the entire trip. As the police officers started picking through our things, we began to get the picture. They were especially interested in our food compartment. "What is this?" Their translator picked up a box of your baby food, sifting a little white-powdered Cream of Wheat through his fingers. "And this?" A bottle of aspirin tablets. Then finally, way down deep, they came across the first of more than a hundred little glass containers. Here was pay dirt. They studied the little jars with great interest. "For the baby," I smiled, pointing to the picture of the little baby on the label, a baby whom, I might add, is not nearly as cute as you are, Zerky.

It soon became apparent they were looking for drugs. Opium is grown extensively in Turkey and Iran. Then one of them came across several boxes of dried brown pellets, a few of which he poured out into his hand and squeezed between his thumb and forefinger. They looked like hashish. "Kibbled dog food," I said, pointing to the picture of the happy little dog on the side of the box, who is not nearly as cute as Tarzan. Then they tasted the salt in one of the many little saltshaker boxes we stocked up on in Athens. Then our powdered milk in cardboard cans. Even our cornflakes. They finally arrived at our first-aid kit, which contained everything from sore-throat spray to perianal ointment. By then it was obvious they had never before seen most of these things. The contents were printed on the packaging, but nearly always in German, French, Italian or English, all of them as incomprehensible to the law enforcement officers as are their traffic signs to us. In most of Asia, packaged foods and drugs such as we take for granted in the West are virtually unknown.

Gradually JoAnne and I began feeling sorry for our captors. We watched them as their authoritarian attitude at the beginning of the search gave way to surprise and wonderment as the search progressed. Towards the end, they appeared to have lost all interest in finding anything illegal; they were simply taking advantage of an opportunity to muck around in our wonderful, magical stuff. We Westerners are now the ones out of the *Arabian Nights*. We are the ones with the latest improvements on their magic carpets; they were the Keystone Cops. When one of them came across a box of tampons and held one up inquisitively, your mother and I cracked up. Later, when they were gone, we laughed some more about how they probably thought they had nabbed a couple of arms smugglers smuggling in some new kind of high-powered American ammunition.

They finally signaled for us to pack up our stuff and come back to the office when we were finished. An hour later, when we finally got the car back together, we went to retrieve our passports. It had all been a mistake, the commissioner offered, politely. If we would just sign a sworn statement they had prepared, we could go. We had to swear we were who we were; and that you were who you were; and that Tarzan was who he was. "Tarr-saan"—the commissioner sounded it out phonetically, his pen tracing beautiful Arabic script backwards from right to left. "What good is this dog?" he demanded suddenly. "What good?" I asked, confused. "This dog must be good for something," he prodded. "What is his purpose?" I'd never thought about it before. "He *must* be good for something!" the commissioner pressed on, sensing my befuddlement. "Can this dog hunt? What does he hunt? Does he herd sheep? He is very small!"

"He belongs to the baby," I finally ventured, passing the buck on to you, Zerky. "He protects us from robbers, he barks and scares them away," I said with a triumphant nod. He wrote it all down, and then made each of us sign a series of statements swearing that each and every one of the statements, individually and collectively, was the truth. Then, as soon as JoAnne and I had finished initialing every item on the list, all the officers stood up together and said, as if on cue, "Welcome to Iran! You are free to go."

Alone again, we talked about what our interrogators, jailors, hosts, or whatever they were, must have been thinking: "Those policemen in America, they must have it pretty easy chasing robbers who are afraid of little dogs." And by the way, Zerky, just what is your purpose?

Leaving Tabriz, the countryside remained dry and largely barren as we climbed over the Talish mountain range separating the arid interior from the Caspian coast. After reaching the pass, the scenery began to change rapidly as we started our descent to the sea. Soon we were engulfed in clouds. It started to rain. In the space of fifteen miles we went from mountain-desert, to alpine, and then into a subtropical climate and landscape. By the time we reached the Caspian Sea at Astara, on the Soviet border, that monochrome earth-toned world we have been living in for so long had changed into sunshine and green.

This fertile strip along the southern shore of the Caspian Sea is Iran's breadbasket, a vast agricultural area generously watered by wet winds off the Caspian Sea colliding with the east-west-running mountain range. What a relief to see color again. And farmers living on hospitable land. Here was the Azerbaijan of our imaginations, or rather *there* it was, right across the border in the Soviet Union. It turned out that Azerbaijan lies in two countries, some of it in the Soviet Union, some in Iran. We have been reading our history again: After World War II, in the early days of the Cold War, Stalin set up a puppet government here in Iranian Azerbaijan. Back then, where we are now parked was behind the Iron Curtain. A few years later Stalin's puppet government collapsed, Iran took back the south shore of the Caspian, and Azerbaijan was split between the two countries.

Heading east along the Caspian, we discovered that this coast is fast becoming a vacationland for Tehran's growing middle class. It's an easy day's drive from the capital, and its beaches are a welcome relief from the torrid summers of the interior.

Resorts are springing up all over the place and we have found a delightful place to camp near a motel, on a large beach. The motel charges us fifty cents a night, so we are "recuperating" for a few days. "Rejuvenating." Lying on a waveless beach eating cheaply priced Iranian caviar. And drinking even-cheaper Russian vodka. I had never tasted caviar before. Mmmm! You don't seem to care for it—it's too salty—gimme. Mmmm! Nevertheless, you are having a very good time splashing around in the warm water and throwing sand at Tarzan, who is happy too. He loves scampering around on the beach. That is his purpose!

Love,
Dad

Zerky at the Caspian Sea

Letter From Tehran

November 14, 1967
Tehran, Iran
Map 3

Dear Zerky,

We are in Tehran at last. A month ago we were in Europe, talking about how hard it would be to drive here. Persia, to me, was always one of those legendary places people love to write about but never really go to. Surprisingly, it was not all that hard to get here; anyone with a reasonably dependable vehicle and a sense of adventure could do so. In the campground where we are staying, on the southwest edge of the city, there are several groups of foreigners traveling together in vehicles that few people would characterize as being "reasonably dependable." Several of them are hippies who pooled their money, bought a junker and are now driving it east until it breaks down, irreparably. Then they will sell it for a song and go hitchhiking, or otherwise improvise their way down the "Road to Katmandu."

So far the most dangerous part of our trip has been driving in Tehran. The drivers here are crazy. When we go into town, we feel like kamikazes on their final mission. Somehow I had imagined Tehran to be the center of Persian culture: ancient mosques, magic carpets, Omar Khayyams sitting around under their palm trees, sipping mint tea and eating their dates, loaves of bread, thou—or whatever. But, to our surprise, Tehran has turned out to be a very modern city that appears to have little to do with those kinds of images. It is a Western-style city with over six million inhabitants, most of whom at any given moment are careening around in cars. No narrow twisting streets full of carts and donkeys here—instead there are wide landscaped boulevards filled with steel projectiles whizzing by. I doubt there are any traffic laws at all in Tehran, only a few token traffic signs now and then, which nobody pays any attention to, other than traumatized foreigners who can't read Farsi. Two of our fellow campers have already had accidents. After talking with one of them, we rushed on down to an automobile club and took out a special insurance policy. I suspect we are the only ones in all of Iran who have car insurance. The auto club was very happy to take our money.

Money. We went to the bank yesterday to exchange some American Express traveler's checks for Iranian rials. While we were there, we thought we would take advantage of an opportunity to pick up a few Pakistani rupees and some Afghan afghanis. We always try to have a small amount of local currency on hand when we enter a new country. We had no problem getting the Iranian rials, but then the teller told us that in order to get Pakistani rupees and Afghan afghanis we would have to go see one of the moneychangers hanging out on the sidewalk across the street.

Normally we try to steer clear of these street hustlers, but since this time it was a bank sending us there, we decided to give it a try. It turned out to be a harrowing experience. For half an hour we went round and round in circles trying to get the moneychanger, who could speak English only when it served his purpose, to answer one simple question: "What *rate* will you give us on afghanis—and on Pakistani rupees—for dollars?" The guy had a bottomless bag of tricks. We never did get an answer. If we would give him so many dollars he might give us so many Pakistani rupees, provided of course that we also took a large number of afghanis, plus a vague and uncertain number of *Indian* rupees. "But we don't *want* any Indian rupees," I told him, "and only a *few* afghanis, just enough to hold us until we can get to a bank in Afghanistan." Well then: if we didn't want that many afghanis, then we could still buy some Pakistani rupees, provided of course we were to buy even more of those same Indian rupees that we didn't want any of in the first place.

"No?" Well then. How about some rubles? He could give us a *very* good deal on rubles. In Russia we could exchange them for Pakistani rupees, which we could take into Pakistan and spend as we liked. Then we could take what was left of them back out of Pakistan and into India, where we could exchange our leftover for mucho, mucho more of those same old Indian rupees we didn't want any of in the first place. That we were not going to Russia was of no consequence. You will *love* Russia, he insisted.

Calculator in hand, he kept coming at us with a bewildering array of scenarios, all of them designed to separate us from our American dollars. Luckily your mother once worked in a bank and is good at handling money. It was only her cool head and agility with numbers that saved us from impending disaster. And then, for no apparent reason, the guy just rolled over and died, telling us that our original proposal was fine. By the time your mother okayed the deal, I was on the brink of giving him anything he wanted, just to get away. Exhausted, we left with a strange assortment of very large, very beat-up funny-looking crumpled bills. When we got back to the car, one of the tires was flat.

A half-inch slit in the casing told me someone had been up to monkey business. Cursing, I got out the jack and started to put on the spare. Immediately some juvenile delinquent darted onto the scene and started falling all over me in an attempt to help change the tire. I took him to be just another street hustler making a living off foreign tourists. He spoke a little English, so I taught him a good American expression: "Shove off!" Americans might seem stupid to him; I would show him we are not so stupid as to be incapable of changing our own tires. Only after I finally got rid of the guy and finished changing the tire myself, did it occur to me that he was probably the very same guy who had stuck the knife in it in the first place. Here was a budding entrepreneur with a novel business model: when demand is slow, you just go take a walk and create some demand.

Yesterday we had a bad experience at the petrol pump. I told the attendant there to "fill 'er up," an ungrammatical statement in English that every gas station attendant in the world understands. Per usual, I got out of the car to make sure the pump was zeroed out before the attendant started pumping. A bit slow on the draw, by the time I got to the pump it was already running. Even worse, I couldn't read the numerals, as they clicked on by—they were in Arabic cursive-style script, as was all the other writing on the pump.

I began to get that clammy, paranoid feeling that tells me I'm in trouble. Sure enough, when the tank was full, the attendant handed me a piece of paper with an exorbitant number written on it. We argued for a while, each of us in a language the other didn't understand. My message was loud and clear: "I'M NOT GOING TO PAY!"

"How many liters are you charging me for?" I demanded. "How many liters—litres—litros"—I tried them all. To my surprise, he wrote down a number in western-style numerals. It was much too large. I got out my Volkswagen service manual from the glove compartment. Under "Specifications" is listed "Total Tank Capacity in Liters." The number was much smaller than the one he had written down. And the gas gauge wasn't even on empty when I pulled in. You never pass up a gas station in this part of the world.

So I showed him the manual, pointed to "Tank Capacity," and started yelling and acting very upset. "You're trying to *cheat me, cheat me, cheat me*," I yelled. *"Cheat, cheat, cheat! Thief, thief, thief!"* I had the bastard flat-footed! Problem was, I still couldn't read the damn pump and had no idea of how much I owed him, in real life, for my now-full tank of gas. I owed him something. He got all sullen. Now he wouldn't respond—he just shrugged, which really pissed me off! I contemplated driving away without paying him a thing, but thought better of it. Peeling off a few of those same crinkled old bills your mother and I had already been screwed on by the moneychanger, I stuffed a few of them into his hand, and he shrugged again. So what the hell does that mean?

Your mother and I find business transactions to be very trying in Iran. We are getting used to being pestered by people trying to sell us things, but not to people pestering us by trying to buy things from us. For some reason, Tarzan is very popular here. We don't know why this is. People keep asking us how much we want for him. We always tell them, "No, he's not for sale, he's part of our family." Which inevitably leads to a higher offer. "No" appears to mean "yes" here: "Yes, we are negotiating."

Everything seems to be for sale. For example: lots of people are interested in our van. Most of them appear to have never before seen a magical car you can live in. At first we would sometimes show off its interior to people who seemed interested, just to be polite and to strike up a conversation. We don't do that anymore. It always elicits the question: "How much are you asking for it?" What do they think I am? A damn car salesman?

More people want to sell us things than buy things from us, however. "We have no use for your Persian carpet," I told a guy. "We live in our car; we don't have a floor big enough to put a carpet on." "Why would you want to put such a beautiful carpet on your floor?" he replied. "You would wear it out! You must hang it on your wall so you can look at it, and then, when you are in one of the many countries you are traveling to, you will be able to sell it for much more than you must pay me for it."

"But I'm not in the carpet-selling business!" I told him, exasperated. He didn't believe me. What kind of a man would pass up an opportunity to sell something at a profit? Buying and selling don't appear to be ends in themselves here, only intermediate steps in an eternal process of buying and selling. No doubt that's why things in stores here don't have price tags on them—with everything for sale, a fixed price would be an impediment to reselling. But with everyone here so versed in the art of buying and selling, what chance does a poor Westerner have?

Dear Zerky: The notion of "fair price" is one of those truly big ideas the likes of which I hope you will someday want to try to get your mind around. This is an issue that has plagued Western civilization for centuries. The "fair price," the asking price, the selling price, the buying price, the fixed price, the right price, the real price: what do they really mean? How do you know what they are? Catholicism, Capitalism, Communism—they all had their own ideas about this thorny subject. Wars, crusades, famines, the Holocaust"—they, too, were part of it.

In medieval Europe, the Catholic Church believed it its duty to regulate the moral behavior of its flock, including economic behavior and commercial and financial transactions. Back then, the reach of the church extended into areas we think of today as being within the province of the state. In 1515 AD, the Catholic Church, at the Council of Letran, in conjunction with a church-mandated ban on usury, issued an edict known as the *fair price doctrine*, which declared all prices other than those set by the church to be illegal. This idea was an outgrowth of a statement in the Bible that said bread is to be made "by sweat of the brow." Unsweated-for profits were looked upon in the same way they were looked upon later by Karl Marx: as a perversion of the law of nature akin to incest, which if left unchecked would ultimately destroy the society in which it was allowed to flourish.

As with incest, the damage unleashed by interest was seen to compound over time, leading slowly but surely to a feeding frenzy of economic cannibalism. Today's multinational corporations come to mind. Under the fair price doctrine, the only price you could charge was the price the Church had previously determined to be fair. Presumably, this was a well-meaning attempt to shield unsophisticated and desperate people from being taken advantage of—perhaps in the same way your father was taken advantage of today, Zerky. A price that is fair is a nice idea, the idea of protecting people from being victimized by the unscrupulous, but unfortunately the church was soon to realize that it had bitten off more than it could chew. As it became increasingly clear that greed was a more powerful motivator in the short run than were hell and damnation in the long run, the fair price doctrine began to require continual modifications in order to accommodate special interests.

This is where my sense of outrage at the gas pump came from today, Zerky—my idea that the price of a tank of gas needed to be "fair." Under our system of capitalism, the fair price is any price at all that a willing buyer and a willing seller can agree upon. The sky is the limit. "If you don't like the price, you can always walk away," they say, but that doesn't work very well when it's a two-hundred-mile walk to the next gas pump, and two hundred miles back again, carrying a full can of gas.

I should hasten not to make too big an issue out of "thievery" in the Middle East, Zerky. We Americans are quick to blame others who do not share our values. Here on Middle Eastern turf, rich Westerners like ourselves do, I am sure, have dollars stolen from them from time to time, but this pales in comparison with what we stole from the Iranians. We stole their entire country, or, more precisely, we stole the *government* of their country.

Here's a good word to work on when you get older, Zerky: *conspiracy*. It comes from the Latin *con*, meaning "with," plus *spirare*, meaning "to breathe," as in respiration. "To breathe with, to breathe together, to breathe in concert," is how *conspirare* is variously expressed in dictionaries. In 1953, our government got very upset with Iran because its prime minister, Mohammed Mossadegh, tried to nationalize the Iranian oil industry, which had been formerly controlled by the British Petroleum Company. Mr. Mossadegh believed Iran's oil industry belonged to Iran. Our president back then was a general named Eisenhower, who didn't like Mr. Mossadegh's idea. Eisenhower believed the Iranian oil industry belonged to our British friends, and potentially to us. So the general and the CIA had a concert together, to which they invited the British and some of *their* good friends, who just happened to be generals in the Iranian military. Then they all breathed together and pretty soon the democratically elected government of Iran was no more.

Conspiracies are like magic, Zerky, a certain sleight of hand that goes quicker than the eye can see. Some people call it a *coup d'état*, like that one we ran into in Greece. But when General Eisenhower's concert was over, the musicians went out and found a new guy to run things for them, an Iranian guy who liked us a whole big bunch for making him so special and so much richer than he already was. This new guy's name is Shah Mohammed Reza Pahlevi, the shah of Iran. He's the guy who owns all those beautiful crown jewels you saw yesterday in the National Museum. Remember all those pretty diamonds in that great big beautiful crown? The shah loves to wear that crown—that's what all those Christmas decorations we've been seeing are all about. The shah loves to play with his toys, just like you. And he loves to restage his coronation. It gives him an opportunity to wear all his pretty jewels and play with all his beautiful diamonds. This shah guy, Zerky, is the richest guy in all of Iran, and, thanks to us Americans, he is also the strongest guy in Iran. He loves to play coronation because that's how he tells people he's in charge. He has to do it a lot because lots of people don't think he's in charge at all. They think he's a puppet. You know what puppets are, don't you, Zerky? Remember all those funny little wooden guys in Switzerland, coming out of clocks?

So you see, Zerky, Iran doesn't just belong to the Iranians anymore, it also belongs to you and to me, and to all our fellow Americans who benefit from the world's cheapest gasoline prices every time they pull up to the gas pump and say, "Fill 'er up." Our tax money financed the overthrow of Iran's government. It was done in our name. It is to us the benefits flow. "We stole it fair and square."

So when you grow up, Zerky, please try to be thoughtful before passing judgment on people from foreign countries whose histories and cultures you don't understand. And when you go traveling on your own someday, please try to remember that you are often the beneficiary of your government's foreign policies, most of which you are probably unaware of. Someday you, too, will have dirt on your hands.

With love,
Your pissed-off Dad

Many of our problems today in the Middle East stem from what Eisenhower and the CIA did to Iran back in 1953, when they toppled a democratically elected government and had it replaced by a dictator. History is a collective memory that fades very slowly when you are the victim of major injustice. Iranians still remember how much they hated the shah, while most Americans have conveniently forgotten—or remain oblivious to—this shameful episode in our history. Iranians have not forgotten.

Nor have they forgotten our good British allies, who, along with their oil company, BP (British Petroleum), exploited Iran's oil reserves for too many years. Iran has the oil we hunger for because we have chosen a lifestyle that requires us to drive long distances to and from work, on a daily basis. This is

what our troubles with Iran are all about. Oil and the
angry collective memory of the democratically elected
government our government toppled—and replaced
with a dictatorship.

**Persepolis: Seat of the Persian Empire under
King Xerxes, 486-485 BC, with JoAnne, and
Zerky very small under the scaffolding**

Letter From Shiraz

November 19, 1967
Persia (Iran)
Map 3

Dear Zerky,

These last few days have taken us into the most exotic places we have ever seen. We have found storybook Persia—that fabled land where camel caravans wind their way through deserts, linking together cities of shining emerald mosques. In southern Iran, the city of Isfahan is especially wondrous. With its bulbous domes and many minarets, its honeycombed ceilings and all its delicate painted tiles, the mosque at Isfahan is surely one of the most beautiful buildings in the world. A *quanat* system brings water to its gardens, making them nearly as spectacular as the mosque itself. You cannot truly appreciate the beauty of gardens, Zerky, until you have seen them in the context of the desert. Together, the overall effect is of total luxury. It is natural to expect beautiful gardens in bountiful Western Europe, and in North America, where nature has endowed us with so much generosity. But when you see green luxury bursting forth in a sun-parched desert, the effect is truly magical.

There really is magic in Persia, Zerky: mirages, whirling dervishes, exquisite carpets reputed to fly. This is the birthplace of Zoroaster and of the religion that bears his name. Zoroastrianism still flourishes in some Persian cities, with magical names like Yazd, Bam, and Zahedan. Persia is the birthplace of Cyrus the Great and of Darius the Great, whose son, Xerxes, once ruled a Persian empire stretching all the way from India to Egypt, Greece, and Romania. The capital of King Xerxes' empire was a place called Persepolis, which was built by his father, Darius the Great, who ruled Persia from 522 to 486 BC. Some say he and Zoroaster were friends. At Persepolis, you visited the Giant Gate of Xerxes, guarded by two immense stone bulls. You also visited what is left of Xerxes' Hall of the One Hundred Columns. Unfortunately, after two and a half thousand years, the ruins are not in good shape. Some wood was used in the original construction, before Alexander the Great sacked and burned Persepolis in 331 BC. Most of the statuary has sat out in the weather for many centuries. When you were there, there was no one around to keep an eye on us during our visit. The place is a mess, and much of Iran's historical treasures have been carted off to foreign museums all over the world. Especially to London.

Driving through the desert, we have become interested in *quanats*. Quanats are the ancient watering systems on which life in southern Persia has long been based. Just like the Roman aqueduct that you saw in Segovia, Zerky, in Andalucia, quanats are still in use today. They do under ground what aqueducts do over ground. Quanats are what made Persian civilization possible in this desert. We see them often from our car—long, straight rows of truncated cones in the distance, one to two hundred feet apart, stretching as far as the eye can see. Most of them are still in use. They run to the nearest underground water, usually at the base of the nearest mountains or hills. From a distance they look like giant strings of anthills. What they really are, though, are long series of manmade wells, connected by a single horizontal tunnel near their bottoms.

Those "anthill" cones you see on the desert floor are really "people hills," detritus from the shafts and tunnels below. The horizontal connecting tunnels lie as much as three hundred feet below the surface of the desert, hooking the succession of wells together to create the subterranean rivers that carry water to many of the towns and villages of southern and central Iran. Most of the population here owes its existence to these ingenious survival devices, dug by hand over hundreds or thousands of years, without benefit of modern engineering. No pipes, culverts, or timbers are used to shore up the shafts and tunnels. Quanats are simply burrows, burrows traditionally dug by children—take note—children who are better able to work in the narrow confines of dark tunnels. So be good. Or you, too, of the blond hair, could meet such a fate.

We bought a book about quanats that was written by an amateur English scientist who descended into a quanat and went swimming in the dark. There he discovered a previously undiscovered species of freshwater fish—a species that has evolved in the dark over many centuries—a fish without eyes in a place without light; a fish even whiter than you are, Zerky. Without light there can be no color. The book is titled *Blind White Fish in Persia.*

We have been making some friends lately. Not Iranians, alas—the language and cultural barriers make that very difficult—but fellow travelers like ourselves. First and foremost are "The Swedes," Lars and Ula, whom we met in the campground outside Tehran. They bought an old VW bus for two hundred dollars and are now driving it eastward until it breaks down. Ever since Tehran, we have been playing leapfrog along the road. They are younger than we are, but are very interesting nevertheless. We are beginning to think of them as "family."

We have also met four young Americans traveling in another beat-up old VW bus, some hippie types from LA. We first saw them at the mosque in Isfahan, after which we passed them, and were passed by them in turn, several times on the road to Shiraz. We also ran into them at Persepolis, and then once more when we woke up early yesterday morning and spotted the silhouette of a van parked a mile or two away on the flat floor of the desert. Today when we came across their van again, parked far off the road, we couldn't resist the temptation to go see what was up. It was about 10:00 AM and they were just waking up.

They told us they had been stopped there for two days. A few days back, they had purchased a water pipe in a village bazaar. Then, when they passed the spot where we found them, they decided that, with all its weird eroded rock formations, that was the perfect place to break in their new water pipe and try out their latest purchase of hashish. It was "some real good stuff," they told us enthusiastically. It got them so stoned they hadn't been able to move for two days. They were hoping to get back on the road before too much longer, they told us.

Two of them turned out to be a nice young couple, Mike and Fiona, on their way to spend Christmas in Katmandu. They are sharing the gas with Frank and Ben, whom they met at a pot party in Istanbul and don't know very well. Mike and Fiona have an extensive medicine kit, which, among its more pedestrian drugs, contains Aralen, a common anti-malaria pill. Aralen is made out of quinine, and is the most incredibly bitter substance on earth. As you will no doubt testify. Once you learn how to talk. Prior to Mike and Fiona and their fancy coated little tablets, you had successfully thwarted virtually every attempt your mother and I had made to get our own *uncoated* tablets down you. You are small but mighty. Even when your mother and I overpowered you and forcibly stuffed Aralen down your darling little throat, you managed to have the last say. In one or two minutes, up came the Aralen, along with what remained of your last meal. Mike and Fiona's coated little pills are a godsend. For you and us. Fiona says you are too cute to get malaria. So she gave us a generous supply. Our daily struggle to get those old uncoated tablets down you had become a serious problem. Now you are holding up well. As is Tarzan, who loves it out here in the desert. It is such a good place to dig!

Love,
Dad

Letter From Iran's Great Sand Desert
(The Dasht-e-Lut)

November 22, 1967
Between Yazd and Kerman
Map 3

Dear Zerky,

This morning you gave us quite a scare. We were camped near the road at the base of a rocky ridge four or five hundred feet above us. I was standing there outside the bus, finishing the breakfast dishes, and you were wandering about. Tarzan was underneath the car, in the shade. Suddenly this exotic-looking tribesman rides up on a beautiful black Arabian horse—a tribesman in flowing white robes with a wild floppy turban straight out of *National Geographic* magazine. Your mother poked her head out of the bus to see what was going on. Soon all four of us were standing outside, smiling at each other and admiring his horse. He was most polite and friendly, and seemed as interested in us and our conveyance as we were in him and his. We tried talking with him in a mixture of pantomime, gestures, and body language. That seems to be our primary means of communication these days.

But, besides our bus, he was also interested in you, as well as in Tarzan. Babies and dogs. That's how you get elected. Before long he had our vote of confidence. You fell in love with the horse. After a little attempted chitchat, he climbed back onto his horse and then gestured down at you. He was offering you a ride. What an opportunity! You were as excited as I was. Your mother and I found his manner very pleasant and friendly, and pretty soon I found myself hoisting you up onto his horse, into his outstretched arms. I assumed he was simply going to trot you around the car, but instead, wrapping one arm around you and pressing you back into the crook of his saddle, he slapped his horse on the rump and the three of you took off down the road at full gallop.

After a few hundred feet he made a turn to the right and started climbing up the ridge, at an angle. As the grade grew steeper, the horse began to struggle, setting off small rockslides as you climbed ever higher and higher. You were heading for the top of the ridge, a quarter mile away. Your mother and I watched with increasing horror as you grew smaller and smaller. How could I ever have been so stupid! He had seemed so friendly, so gentle. And then the unthinkable: Middle-Eastern people seem to have a thing about blond children. That run-in with the Turkish soldiers flashed through my mind, and I started thinking about how people can't seem to keep their hands off your blond little head. How much might such a boy fetch in some Arab bazaar? I wondered. Paranoia ran rampant!

How would we ever find you? Even though the horse's hooves were leaving a few intermittent marks on the rock-strewn slope, such scattered markings would be insufficient to track you. That would take bloodhounds. Do they even *have* bloodhounds in Iran? I should call the police. What is their telephone number? Where is there a phone? Why would there even be such a thing—or any police—out here in this godforsaken desert? There wasn't a town within seventy-five miles. And even if I could find some police, would they be willing and able to find you? What had they accomplished that day up on the slopes of Mount Ararat? Would they even care? How angry are they still at us Americans? Who stole their country. Such were the thoughts that raged through my mind as you grew smaller and smaller. Your mother remained mute and petrified.

Gradually the horse began to slow, growing tired from the climb. As you approached the top of the ridge, I prayed you not disappear down the other side. If your horse didn't stop, by the time I could climb up to you, you'd be long gone. Please God, or Allah, or whatever…I was ready to convert on the spot to anyone or anything that would answer my prayer.

At the top of the ridge, the horse slowed to a walk, and then stopped. Silhouetted against a fluffy white cloud in a pale blue sky, was an angel in the arms of a man in flowing white robes, on a jet-black Arabian horse. You were a biblical vision, Zerky. In a minute or two, the horse began turning counterclockwise, very slowly. Half-way around, you were finally facing back in our direction. I waved to you, and then—lest a wave be misconstrued as a goodbye—I raised my other arm and moved it toward you in a hooking, come-back-lit-tle-Zerky sort of motion. He picked up your arm and waved back to me. His horse continued swinging. Full circle. Until you were once again facing that valley on the other side of the ridge. We stood there, terrified. You kept on swinging. You finally stopped when you were facing us once again. "Maybe he's just showing him the view," I ventured, feeling hopeful and stupid at the very same time. After an eternal minute, the horse started slip-sliding back down the hill, in a rush of rocks and gravel, and soon you were back at the car. Beaming. This had been no pony ride at the zoo. You were Zerky of Arabia! By the time our now-gallant tribesman handed you back down to me, your mother and I were on the verge of tears. He had returned you safely to us, from a wonderful ride.

Who was he, this mysterious stranger on horseback? Where had he come from? Where was he going? Why had he given us such a scare? Like all good cowboys in the ends of all good cowboy shows, our apparition smiled. And rode off.

Loving you more than ever,
Your dumb Dad

Letter From Zahedan

November 24, 1967
Southeast Iran
Map 3

Dear Zerky,

Ever since Yazd we have been skirting the southern edge of the *Dasht-e Lut,* Iran's Great Sand Desert. Most of this area is uninhabited, except for the oasis towns of Kerman and Bam. We are enjoying the desert immensely. Camping alone at night has turned out to be a wonderful experience. All day long we look forward to the cool and the peacefulness that come with the setting sun, bringing relief from the relentless dust boiling up from beneath our tires, and seeping into everything.

In the middle of southern Iran, beyond the city of Kerman, the Anatolian Plain begins to fall off gradually. By the time you reach Bam, you have dropped over four thousand feet. You soon enter the Iranian province of Baluchestan (as they spell it in Iran), where the desert begins to assert itself with ever-increasing grandeur. Often we will drive for an hour or more seeing no one. Sometimes the road is little more than a path through the desert marked by a small mound of earth pushed up on each side by the road grader at the time of construction. In truth, there was never much to construct; the desert is flat and often hard enough to drive on without benefit of a road. Our problem here is *corrugation.* In America we call it *washboarding.* As we drive through the desert, a drama is playing itself out beneath our wheels, as our rear tires perform a dance of death in accordance with the laws of physics. I shall whimsically entitle it:

Where the Rubber Meets the Road
ACT I: A Pebble on the Road

As one of our rear tires begins its ascent of a lowly pebble, its revolutions slow in response to the increased demand placed on the engine by the need for additional horsepower to lift the car vertically to the top of the pebble. Once up on top, however, the tire's slowed rotation receives a quick burst of energy from the engine as the now descending vehicle is released from the load gravity had imposed upon it during its brief climb to the top of the heap.

ACT II: A Puff of Sand

As our now fast-spinning rear tire falls from its momentary state of grace, it collides with a graveled roadbed, whose sole desire is to remain forever flat. At the precise moment of impact, our excessively rotating rear tire has a tire-tantrum as, against its will, gravity forcibly reengages it with the surface of the road. In a fit of pique, the tire releases its excess energy by spitting a puff of sand backward. Now, adding insult to injury, the displaced puff of sand lands atop the hapless pebble, as our now decelerated, reengaged rear tire races madly away with nary a thought to the destructive process it has just unleashed upon the road. A few inches in front of that pebble, where our overly exuberant tire just landed after its brief flight of fancy, there is now a slight depression in that very same spot that ejected puff of sand once called "home." How often as we speed through life do we go back to examine all the damage we have done?

ACT III: Malignancy Marches Forward

Our little alternately decelerating-accelerating tire has just created a height differential between the top of the sand it kicked backward and the bottom of a depression where our oblivious tire landed. In time, this will prove fatal to the road.

A second motor vehicle approaches. The little pebble who once stood so proud never gave much thought to its impending burial. The tires of oncoming trucks, however, are wise in the ways of the road. Like trained ski jumpers, one after another they launch themselves off the top of the poor pebble, on an upward trajectory, soon to come crashing down onto the road, on that very same spot where our pebble once stood so proud. Again and again, bursts of energy are released, and each time we have a mound a little higher, a depression a little deeper.

Enter stage left an immense diesel truck barreling along, its huge dual rear tires accelerating-decelerating, spinning and spitting at frightful speed, as it careens down the road just like all the other crazy trucks in Iran. This behemoth is barely lifted at all as it squashes our little pebble into the mound of sand, driving it ever downward into what will eventually prove to be no useless sacrifice.

For just beneath the surface, the solidity of that poor pebble has just added more stability to an incipient mound, a mound that is destined to grow and to grow until it becomes a *ridge*. For while the Great Diesel gained only the tiniest of loft upon takeoff, when its great dual tires came crashing down in the very same spot as its predecessors, it spit backward a mighty blast of sand and gravel, thereby increasing the height of the mound.

Should an educated eye now peer intently into the ever-deepening depression, it will be horrified to discern the unmistakable beginnings of a *pothole*. In the future, each oncoming vehicle will try to dodge that pothole, but an increasing number will fail, and their tires will accidentally run over the edge of that pothole, which shall widen and widen until that same educated eye discerns the now unmistakable beginnings of a *trench!*

Hammered by tire after tire, our one-time, small-time pothole will continue to expand sideways until it runs from one side of the road to the other. And with it, marching along in lockstep, will be the pothole's loyal traveling companion, a parallel ridge built from the trench's expelled debris. In months and years to come, hundreds and thousands of cars and trucks will launch themselves in turn from that mound that never aspired to become a ridge. And their rear tires, too, spinning and spitting, will methodically carve series after series of parallel ridges and trenches onto that one-time, once upon a time, small time, freshly graded road.

ACT IV: The Domino Effect

Ridge upon trench together continue their assault on the road. In tandem, their cumulative effect propels the process forward. Each newly made ridge and trench in turn become both ammunition and launching pad for each and every oncoming set of rear tires. Upon their violent deceleration, the system is added to relentlessly, as ridge by ridge, trench by trench, mile by mile, the impoverished roadbed is eaten alive by that evil runaway phenomenon known as *The Cancer of the Corrugated Road*. When you drive too fast in Iran, you are sure to run into this cancer. It can knock your front-end alignment silly and even break your axle. Corrugated roads rattle your teeth, destroy your shock absorbers, and reduce even the most red-blooded motorist to a humiliating crawl.

CODA: The Cancer Spreads

Inevitably, some enterprising corrugation-wise driver sees another shuddering ordeal ahead and wonders why he should drive on such a terrible road when the surface of the desert seems so much more friendly. What the hell, give it a try! The next driver sees his tracks and opts for the newer, smoother route. Because it was never compacted by heavy road-building equipment, this new route will become corrugated much sooner than did the original road. Thus the need for a third track through the desert, and a fourth, and a fifth, until before long everybody is involved in their own freestyle do-it-yourself road building project. It's really fun!

The feeling of freedom and power you get when you are unshackled from the confines of the road is addictive. On our long road to Zahedan, we find many such expressions of human frustration and creativity—multiple diverging-converging paths through the desert, in bewildering combinations. Sometimes we come upon so many nonsigned roads that we can only guess at the correct one. Sometimes we find ourselves intentionally zigzagging across all these roads, at right angles, trying to compare each with the other in order to find the one true path. At times like this, we pray for the deliverance that resides only between those two parallel mounds of sand so long ago created by the one true god of the desert, *The Road Grader.* Sometimes you got to travel on faith.

The true test of faith comes with the realization that the maker of any particular set of tracks might not necessarily have been going where *you* are going. After all, not everyone is going to Zahedan. So when you drive at right angles, you need to pay attention, lest ye cross that last road to Zahedan. Because when you do, you need to recognize it as, indeed, that last road to Zahedan, or sooner or later you will discover, to your shock and dismay, that there is no road at all in sight, other than the one you have just created.

Having tried to play God, you will have found yourself lost in an ocean of sand. Remember to turn around very carefully then. Do not get stuck. Remember to partially deflate your tires should they start to dig in. In the face of calamity you must have faith in yourself. Your road to salvation now resides in your ability to follow your tracks back to where you came from—to return to the womb, so to speak. Now, should you sense your vehicle bogging down, whatever you do, don't slow down! Gun the engine no matter how counterintuitive that may feel. The book of wisdom requires you to carry a shovel for hard times such as this. A collapsible shovel shall set ye free!

Curtain
Coke bottles
Boos!

Our rough and occasionally nearly indiscernible road through the desert is sometimes more visible on the map than on the desert floor. We are now at the southernmost tip of the two east-west-running roads through Iran, linking Europe and the Indian subcontinent. The northern route goes through the city of Mashad, in northeastern Iran, and then directly on into Afghanistan. That is the more direct route of the two, and is the one most people take. Unfortunately, we have been hearing bad things about the Iranian border officials near Mashad. Our hippie sources have communicated to us the fact that Mashad is a center of Islamic fervor, and that some of the border guards there are making it rough on Westerners. This is probably an exaggeration—this kind of talk usually is—but then again how can you know anything for sure? So we have decided to outflank the enemy by taking the southern route, thereby making an end run around all the mullahs and going directly into West Pakistan. Once inside, we plan to continue eastward as far as the city of Quetta, and then north into Afghanistan from the border crossing south of the city of Kandahar. That way we will be able to enjoy more wonderful desert and less cold interior plateau.

I am writing this from inside the city of Zahedan. We have been seeing our first sand dunes nearby. Your mother and I are talking of becoming Bedouins, and trading in our bus for a camel and a tent. About fifty miles before Zahedan, we suffered our first casualty: a broken shock absorber. Don't blame the shock absorber—we all have our limits. All four shock absorbers have been taking a vicious beating ever since we left the asphalt north of Shiraz. Slowly, we managed to limp our way into Zahedan, at five to ten miles an hour. Upon entering the city, a vision appeared: Allah be praised, an "Authorized Volkswagen Garage"! I told you there was magic in Persia, Zerky!

Love,
Dad

West Pakistan

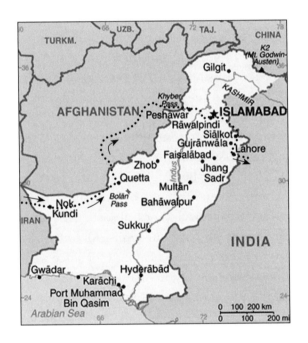

Letter From Baluchistan

November 25, 1967
Near Nok Kundi, West Pakistan
Map 3

Dear Zerky,

Yesterday morning in Zahedan we had our broken shock absorber replaced. The garage had a big inventory of them. It went like a charm. They even steam-cleaned the bottom of the bus. On our way to the West Pakistan border, we were stopped by an Iranian who told us he was in charge of the local tourist office. This came as a surprise; it's hard to imagine tourists coming to such a place. I doubt the "facilities" in Zahedan have been improved much since Marco Polo came through here on his way to China. The tourism guy spoke passable English and told us he had a couple of American hitchhikers in his office. Would we please give them a ride? But I didn't like the way he was acting as their intermediary—if I'm going to pick up people I want to get a look at them first. "But they are Americans like you," he reassured me, unreassuringly. I wanted to tell him that it was perhaps precisely because they were Americans that I didn't want to pick them up. But this gets hard to explain sometimes, so I just told him, "No," they would have to find a ride with somebody else. Then he became agitated and began to explain that they had been living in his office for the last five days. They had no money; he had been feeding them and looking after them personally. Not long ago I read something about Middle Eastern hospitality, and about how it is forbidden by the Koran to turn away the poor from your door. Perhaps a little light should have dawned about then.

Would I please give his guests a ride, just across the border, he begged; I could drop them off immediately once we were on the other side. "One of them is an American just like you," he told me. It soon became apparent he was desperate and wanted to get these two foreigners off his hands. By dumping them on me! "No," I told him forcefully—the guy was beginning to make me mad! I told him I wanted nothing to do with his hitchhikers, and now would he please stop trying to shove them down my throat. "Please get out of the way." Sometimes you've got to be firm with people, Zerky!

After my mini-tirade, the guy got all upset and kept repeating that they were Americans, "just like you." He went on to explain that he was a poor man, not a rich man like me, and that he could no longer afford to take care of them. In the last five days only three vehicles had passed through Zahedan on their way into Pakistan. All three of them had turned him down. If we didn't take his Americans off his hands, he didn't know what to do. Almost in tears, he then went on to tell me how he had been running the Zahedan tourist office for more than ten years now, and that during that time much of his efforts had been spent helping westerners like ourselves. Now, for the first time, he was asking a westerner to help *him*, and what was he getting in return? Ingratitude. Then he went on to tell me, "I do not understand westerners. I do not think they are good people."

By then he had me feeling like the ugly American I sometimes am. "Yes," I said, "we'll be happy to take your guests off your hands," whereupon he broke into a grin and began thanking me profusely, and went on to assure me how much everybody in Iran loves Americans, "because they are so generous." Then he dashed off to get our "guests." Hmmm. Had it all been a negotiation? I wasn't sure. I would have plenty of time to reflect on that in the car.

Your mother and I value our privacy, Zerky. When you are out in the middle of nowhere, it's not easy to get rid of people once they've become dependent on you. Our hitchhikers sounded too needy. In a few minutes they showed up in backpacks and ratty-looking hiking boots. Eddie was completely unshaven, with a scraggly beard, and Stephanie's scruffy hair made it clear she'd been sleeping in straw. She was from New York City, she said; Eddie was her husband. Eddie was Dutch, and spoke a little English. They were hitchhiking from Holland to India, on their way to work with Christian missionaries there. Yeah, right! I told Eddie we were going to take them only as far as Nok Kundi, the first town inside West Pakistan. He assured me that would be fine, and we were off, your mother and I not without reservations.

We soon arrived at the West Pakistan border. In order to make the crossing we had to wake up the Iranian customs officer to get our passports stamped, and our *carnet* stamped. Showing no interest in us whatsoever, he stamped us out of the country and went back to sleep. Except for a few mud huts, the border area appeared deserted. At this point we were confused about which country we were in. Driving around for a few minutes, we finally found a chain across the road. We stopped and honked. In a few minutes three men emerged from a tent down the road, which appeared to be part of a multi-tent compound. One of them seemed to be some kind of a soldier. Your mother dubbed him "the leftenant." Another uniformed soldier carried a Khyber rifle over his shoulder—those guns with the long

wooden stocks going all the way down to the ends of their bar-
rels. Our "leftenant" referred to this second soldier as "his constable." A third man, this one not in uniform, was younger than
the other two. In her notes JoAnne dubs him "the dreamy-eyed
Afghan border boy in green." We never did figure out what he
was all about. The following morning we had our suspicions.

The constable dropped the chain and motioned us to drive
on through, and to pull over alongside the first tent. We went
inside. The leftenant was waiting for us. In short order we were
answering questions about where we wanted to go in West Pakistan, and why. The leftenant spoke eight languages, he told
us: "English, Farsi, Urdu, Pashto" and some other languages
we had never even heard of. His English was not so good, he
admitted, but he appeared to enjoy making small talk, so we
seized on the opportunity to have our first conversation with a
real live Pakistani—and an army officer no less. He asked us,
would we take tea with him? "We would be delighted." He sum-
moned his constable and gave him an order in one of those sev-
en languages we did not understand. The constable marched
off, rifle over his shoulder, like Gunga Din. Our leftenant was
now acting more the gracious host and less the officious army
officer. Living in a van has a tendency to isolate us from contact
with "the natives," we have found. It appeared that our host was
as isolated as we are; he was probably starved for conversation.
Westerners, he told us, were a rarity at this remote border post.
"Mostly it's trucks and camels," he said.

After half an hour of chitchat, he informed us that we were
free to go. But it was getting late, he said, and "It's a six-hour
drive to Nok Kundi, the next town." Then he pointed out
that the road permit he had just issued us did not allow us to
stop and camp along the road. Rather than drive all night, he

suggested, why not spend the night in his compound, where we would be safe? We could pull our car up beside his tent. That way, Stephanie and Eddie could sleep inside the tent rather than outside on the ground. Sounded like a winner! We gratefully accepted. Off we went to move the car and to unload Eddie and Stephanie's smelly bedrolls.

By now it was getting dark outside, and JoAnne and I decided to take you on a walk around the compound, Zerky. Along the way the fullness of the evening began to well within me. Here we were in a land most people have never even heard of, at a remote border post where an important government office consists of nothing more than a tent in the sand in the middle of a desert stretching from the Mediterranean to the Arabian Sea, and with a herd of camels tethered barely a hundred yards away. To top it all off, we were about to be dined by a Pakistani army officer straight out of Rudyard Kipling, and by his sidekick, Gunga Din. How much better does it get?

Gazing back to where we had just come from, the cluster of mud huts on the other side of the border suddenly burst into flame. Red, white, and green. Just like when we *entered* Iran. The Shah was still celebrating his "coronation." Someone had hauled an electric power generator all the way from Tehran, just to light up a few red, white, and green Christmas tree bulbs. For the Shah.

When we got back to the car, Eddie and Stephanie had moved their gear into the tent and JoAnne was about to prepare supper in the bus. Then the army officer appeared. "Would you please be so generous as to share my evening meal?" he inquired. We told him we would be honored. However, since our host appeared to be interested in the inside of our bus, "Why not eat here?" JoAnne suggested. He seemed pleased, and disappeared back into his tent in order to tell the constable to bring us dinner in the bus. Soon he returned with a bottle of arak, a clear, vodka-like spirit Moslems are forbidden to drink. We, too, had a small bottle of *arak*, which we quickly produced as our contribution to good fellowship. "To peace and understanding between nations!" I toasted grandiosely. Then it was but a matter of time—and arak—until I toasted again: "To our good fortune at having ended up together under such improbable circumstances!" I said even more grandiosely. JoAnne told me not to get carried away. Soon the constable arrived with his rifle strapped over his shoulder, dinner in hand. It turned out to be a large bowl of very tough curried lamb stew, plus a stack of *chapattis*, those coarse, dark flatbreads that are a staple in the Middle East, and in India. We used the bread and our fingers to eat from the common bowl. It felt like the right thing to do.

As we were eating away, we asked the leftenant many questions. Yes, he did find it lonely way out there in the desert at his remote post. Pakistani army officers must be thirty-five to marry, he told us. He was looking forward to it—"only two more years to go." Although he had been wounded in the 1965 war in Kashmir, he assured us he was happy with his career in the army, even though he did find a few of his duties "unpleasant." When I pushed him as to what these duties were, he explained he had had to kill six men in the past month. "They were smugglers." He did not enjoy killing, he went on, "but it is my duty, Allah forgive." Much of his time was spent leading patrols out into the desert, looking for smugglers. As we talked, he told us he currently had fifty captured camels and seventeen boys in the stockade out back. This explained all the camels we had seen earlier. But those seventeen boys?

As the evening wore on and conviviality increased in inverse proportion to the amount of arak left in the bottle, the leftenant's talk started wandering increasingly back to the still ongoing political hostilities between Pakistan and India. He had been wounded in a tank battle, he said, and afterwards had spent several months in a hospital staffed by American nurses. That experience proved to be quite an eye-opener for a young Moslem man unaccustomed to seeing the faces of women not part of his family. More and more as the evening wore on he kept returning to these "wonderful American nurses." Who had saved his life. How much he respected them. Those wonderful American nurses who saved his life. And who never covered their faces. I should have seen it coming. I was too full of good cheer. We emptied his bottle and opened ours.

Soon the leftenant began losing control of his English, and started slipping into Urdu, intermittently. We began to notice that the subject of every conversation eventually seemed to lead back to one of the two recurring subjects that appeared to obsess this man: his hatred for Indians who had wounded him in the war, and his love for American nurses who had saved him in the war. Soon he started giving us variations on the theme of respect: It wasn't *just* his American nurses he respected, it was also me and your mother and, yes, little Zerky, you too. Over and over he reassured us how much he respected us all. He never once mentioned Tarzan. Your mother still holds that against him, perhaps even more than what was to follow.

The leftenant finally got around to telling us how honored he would be if we were to spend the night in his tent. By then he was very drunk, and began reassuring us that his constable would soon arrive to take him home. Then he veered off onto a new tack and started telling me I was his brother. By now, he was making me very uneasy. How was I going to get rid of him? Come on, Constable. Hurry up!

In an attempt to get the conversation out of its anti-India, how-much-I-respect-you, you-are-my-brother rut, I seized upon some interest he had shown earlier in my guitar. "Would you like to hear me play some flamenco?" I asked. "Flamenco is a Spanish music and Spain was once ruled by Arabs. Flamenco's roots are in the Middle East," I told him, trying to deflect him onto another topic. A little music might soothe the savage beast. Or at least get his mind off those nurses. In any event, it would buy time for the constable's return, I figured.

I began to play, you and I and the guitar on one side of the table, Tarzan, your mother and the leftenant on the other. I strummed a few chords to get warmed up. Then I launched into my *Soleares*. Your mother kicked me under the table. I thought she *liked* Soleares! So I switched to some livelier *Alegrias*, even though I wasn't yet warmed up. It's hard to get your fingers up to speed for all those fast alegrias arpeggios.

Before I could get them really rolling, your mother kicked me under the table again. I noticed the leftenant's hand was no longer fingering his glass, which sat alone on the table. Then I figured out he was fingering JoAnne's leg! Oh shit, now what? What am I supposed to do—play outraged husband and punch him out? I thought about those six men he said he'd killed, "because it is my duty." He was the law out here in this remote corner of Pakistan. I quickly realized that if I didn't handle things right, I, too, could become one of his "smugglers." And you, little Zerky, you could have become one of those boys in his stockade! What might happen to JoAnne, I didn't even want to think about. No punch in the nose.

Not knowing what to do, I cut off my obviously under-appreciated recital and informed our host, guest, asshole, or whatever the hell he was, that it was late, and that we had to get an early start next morning. There followed an awkward silence. Then, to my great relief, his hand emerged once more from beneath the table. He told me how much he enjoyed my music. Same way he enjoyed those nurses, I'll bet! I stood up and began putting my guitar back in the case. Again I informed him that it was late, and that our delightful evening was over; he replied by telling me I was his brother and JoAnne was his sister. By now, he had turned into a grammarless incoherent jumble of something or other mixed in with virtually incomprehensible English. He was also ill at ease. Fortunately he agreed with me that, yes, it was late, and soon he was gone. We locked the door behind him and looked at each other. We were in over our heads.

Next morning the leftenant slept late. After gathering up Stephanie and Eddie and their few belongings, we had to awaken the leftenant in order to get him to put our papers in order. He did so without comment, and obviously in pain, which pleased me immensely. Soon we were off into West Pakistan. Driving along, we began to hear about Stephanie and Eddie's unusual night, which began upon the officer's return to their tent. It had been a rough night. Their host had kept both of them awake most of the night, by trying to seduce Eddie! He had offered them liquor, hashish, and—when that didn't work— opium. Eddie had defended his honor, Stephanie assured us. "God damn pervert!" she exclaimed in a most unmissionary way. The leftenant had shown no interest in her, and she was no dog. "Hell hath no fury like a woman scorned."

As we were exchanging stories about our adventures the night before, your mother and I began to feel a bond with our two hitchhikers. We had been through the war together. Of course we weren't going to drop them off at Nok Kundi. "You must come all the way to Quetta with us!" Besides, how would you hitchhike a camel?

By the time we finally hit Pakistan passport control at Nok Kundi, I was beginning to wonder about all the English-language signs I'd been passing while we'd been busy talking. "Keep to the Left," they said. They'd obviously been talking about passing, or going around curves, or something. You don't keep to the left, and besides, there aren't any curves out in the desert. These Third World countries really get screwed up! I'd not been giving weird signs much thought.

Upon entering Nok Kundi, all the cars were driving on the wrong side of the road. Pretty weird place, this Pakistan! In a panic, I pulled over to the side of the road, to contemplate this dangerous new situation. Thinking back on it, I must have passed a few cars between Nok Kundi and the Iranian border, you would think; unfortunately I didn't remember seeing any. Surely I would have noticed had they been driving on the wrong side of the road. Strange indeed. Inside Nok Kundi, cars were coming at me now from all directions. Pakistan had been a British colony until World War II. Unfortunately, nobody in the car had ever driven a car in England. It's not easy learning how to drive on the wrong side of the road; your instincts are all backward. We didn't get killed.

This poorly maintained, frequently unpaved road we are traveling on is the main highway linking southern Iran and West Pakistan. Since it hasn't been adequately maintained for many years, if ever, why hasn't it been totally abandoned? I wondered. With virtually no traffic at all, and with railroad tracks paralleling it most of the way, the road didn't seem important. I suspect the answer is that we are in Baluchistan, home of the fierce Baluchi tribesmen whom the Pakistani government has never been able to bring under its control. There are many such "Stans" in this part of the world, sometimes semiautonomous political entities coexisting inside another country. My theory here is that this road is largely a symbol of the central government's authority—a reminder to the Baluchi tribes that Islamabad can come get them any time it wants to.

At last the desert is beginning to fulfill our expectations of what deserts are supposed to be. There are sand dunes stretching for miles, furrowed like waves upon the ocean and breaking onto mountains miles away. We have run into several government road crews laboriously removing sand from the road, with shovels. It blows right back. Sand is everywhere. It has permeated our car, our sleeping bags, our clothes, and our hair. It is drifted across the road in many places. Again I am very happy I bought that small collapsible shovel.

We are camped tonight on a salt flat a few miles south of the Afghanistan border. We have been driving through dunes most of the day. A short while ago as we were setting up camp alongside the road a camel caravan passed by, probably on its way from somewhere in Iran to the city of Quetta, where we should arrive tomorrow. Our first big city since Tehran.

Love,
Dad

When I tell people about trying to drive a car around the world, especially through the deserts of the Middle East, some of them think it was a very dangerous thing to do. With the exception of the forgoing incident, I think it was a safe thing to do. Most of the roads of the world are not like American freeways, where high-speed death is common.

I consider the above incident to have been our single brush with catastrophe on this trip; it happened because we were oblivious to the fact that we were dealing with a Muslim man unaccustomed to mixing unknown female companions with alcohol. We should have picked up on this when he started talking about those female nurses. Add guns, and authority, and I think it was a potentially explosive situation.

• • •

The farther east we traveled, the more there was to write about. When it became clear to JoAnne that I wasn't getting it all down, she started keeping a diary; she wanted to keep track of everything I was missing. That way I would be able to use her diary later on to help me write a few additional letters to Zerky. With so much to see, I was often too busy to write. Her diary also allowed me to keep track of whatever she found to be important. We didn't always agree on things and she liked having a record of her own.

Most of my memories of this trip have long ago departed, and those additional letters never got written. From here on, I have decided to include some of JoAnne's largely unedited notes in order to fill in some of the blanks between my letters.

From JoAnne's Diary
Baluchistan (Western West Pakistan)
Maps 3 & 4

November 26, 1967

Ran out of water this AM and had to take off unwashed, with dirty dishes. Stephanie is sick. We stopped for water at a vacant "Free Tourist Hut," but after hauling it up in a bucket with a primitive crank, we found out it was no good. Found some later at a "government rest house."

**Stephanie with Zerky and Bill and Eddie
trying to get water out of that well in Baluchistan**

Letter From Quetta

November 26, 1967
Quetta
West Pakistan
Map 4

Dear Zerky,

Tonight we are camped in the middle of the city of Quetta, in the yard behind the Pakistan Government Tourist Office. We stopped here to get information. We are rid of our hitchhikers, Eddie and Stephanie, and we miss them. Unfortunately, they did not want to go to Afghanistan—they wanted to go east, directly into India. Perhaps all that talk about working with Christian missionaries in India was not a scam after all. We came to consider them our friends. Because they had virtually no money at all, Stephanie and Eddie went to the tourist office this afternoon to ask where they might be able to spend the night. The government's response was for them to come back at closing time, at which point they would be welcome to spread their sleeping bags out on the office floor.

Thus it came to pass that in two different Islamic countries in the last three days—perhaps like Blanche in her streetcar named Desire—Stephanie and Eddie were able "to depend on the kindness of strangers." Neither of them, nor the people in either of these last two tourist offices, could have depended on me. Your mother asked the woman in the tourist office where might we be able to park our van for the night. Since it wouldn't fit into her office along with Stephanie and Eddie, the woman suggested we park it in the yard out back. I offered to pay, she said no, and I learned a painful lesson about hospitality, and about Islam.

I find this one-on-one attitude about helping people to be very refreshing. Why is it in America that if you need help you are expected to get it from the government, rather than from the individual? Why is it that charity has to be depersonalized, and anonymous, to the point where one's obligations can be expunged by some government bureaucrat's allocation of your tax money to some faceless agency you know nothing about? Why don't we give directly to people in need, instead of funding government programs?

Here in Quetta, and in Iran two days ago, two successive governments did not shove color brochures at Stephanie and Eddie, they gave them tangible help. My dictionary defines "help" as a transitive verb. Verbs are supposed to *do* something. They're supposed to denote *action*? Why is it then that in America we treat help as a noun—as a person, place or thing? We don't *do* help, we give money instead.

Like everywhere we go these days, we find the city of Quetta to be fascinating. It is much different from the cities of Iran; it has the feel of India about it. The buildings are low, usually single story, and generally of very flimsy construction. The streets are jammed with carts, donkeys, people, and bicycles. Everybody seems to be going shopping. The shops contain many strange items, but most noticeable is the absence of manufactured goods. It's beginning to look like their absence is an index of how far east we are.

Tonight we had curry. Tomorrow, Afghanistan!

Love,
Dad

From JoAnne's Diary
Quetta and Kandahar
Map 4

November 27, 1967

Got our tire fixed in Quetta, where Zerky was butted by a sheep, chased and pecked by a rooster, and fascinated by two caged parrots. Our front tire was slashed. Got it fixed again for two rupees. Canned goods are outrageously priced. We ran into the Swedish couple and four Americans while shopping. Lunched with the Swedes at the China Café. They almost got taken, too, in Tehran, at that same gas pump. Gave us some hash. Arrived Afghanistan at sunset prayer hour. A border official gave Zerk some raisins and wanted to know if Tarzan was a cat. Tonight Zerk has found four kids to play with at the Hotel Kandahar, and Tarzan is getting a lot of attention too. Good dinner at the hotel! Smoked the Swedes' goodie and fell in love with the heater.

November 28, 1967

Spent the morning wandering around Kandahar: shovel factory, shoe factories, blacksmiths, metalworkers, rug sellers, a painter of signs and mirrors, American canned goods, RAF World War II flak jacket, World War II Japanese flight jacket, armatures, springs, washers, a gal in purdah with nylons. A child kicked Tarzan.

Afghanistan

Letter From Kandahar

November 28, 1967
Kandahar, Afghanistan
Map 4

Dear Zerky,

I'm not quite sure I ever believed there really was an Afghanistan; it always seemed more mythological than geographical. Or maybe it's me that's mythological this morning, I keep wanting to pinch myself to make sure I'm really here. If I seem to be a bit befuddled today, Zerky, that's probably because your mother and I smoked a little hashish last night. It just seemed like the right thing to do.

Once more we have run into our friends the Swedes. They thought we should celebrate our arrivals in Afghanistan by partaking of a little of their stash. I declined the invitation on grounds that Afghanistan is already weird enough without any added stimulation. They understood, and gave us some for later. Before bedtime, after we had eaten our best meal since I can't remember when, and after we were settled for the night and you were sound asleep, your mother and I had our own little private Afghanistan arrival celebration. By then it was very cold outside, so we fired up the butane heater. It's funny, you know, how we never before paid much attention to that little heater's incredibly warm glow. Swimming around and around and around and around and around, in its shiny little reflector. I wonder how long we sat there staring at it?

For the last two nights we have been staying on the grounds of the Hotel Kandahar, a very old, once grand, now run-down hotel on the outskirts of the city of Kandahar, about sixty miles northwest of the border with West Pakistan. Kandahar is Afghanistan's second largest city and we approached it with great apprehension. After Tehran, I will never again be the same upon driving into a large Asian city. Although we almost never drive after dark, the road was nearly empty last night, and we were so excited about being in Afghanistan that we just couldn't bring ourselves to stop.

Shortly after dark, we finally saw some bright lights in the distance. Kandahar at last, we figured. It turned out to be Kandahar International Airport. A large, well-lighted sign proclaimed so in English to anyone who might be able to read English. It told them that Afghanistan's finest airport was built by Americans as a token of their everlasting friendship. Row upon row of silver mercury vapor lights lit up the runways. Other than that, everything was dark. The airport was totally deserted. It appeared to have no terminal at all, no buildings, nary an airplane, nothing but row upon row of extremely bright lights behind a chain-link fence with a locked gate and those two spotlights shining on that very lonely sign. We drove on, talking about how Kandahar International looked like a ghost ship adrift upon the ocean.

A half-hour later the desert gave way to a smattering of darkened mud houses. The outskirts of Kandahar, no doubt. But after driving for another fifteen minutes, we still couldn't find anything resembling the center of a town, let alone a number two city. All we could find were more scattered mud houses. We continued driving. Before long we were lost. We spotted some sort of military-looking guy in a uniform, standing in the middle of a crossroads. I drove up to him and stopped. "Where is Kandahar?" I asked. "Kandahar! Kan-da-har! KAN-DA-HAR!" I yelled.

"KAN-DA-HAR!" he yelled back, inscribing an expansive arc forcefully with his finger and outstretched arm. Confused, we looked around. Could this be the center of Kandahar? Not likely—just another mud village. After some more driving around, we finally had to admit that this place seemed to be a very *large* mud village. And then it dawned on me: Kandahar doesn't have electric lights. All the electricity is out at the airport. Where the people are not. Compliments of everlasting friendship, Afghanistan's number-two city is a city of candles and kerosene lanterns.

Now that eternal question: where are we going to stay tonight? We drove back and forth some more through the dark "downtown," looking for a hotel or at least somewhere to park for the night. We also looked for a bank to get money from the following morning. We found neither. Just as we were about to give up and head back out into the desert, we spotted a sign in English advertising the Kandahar Hotel, with an arrow pointing the direction. We followed it and soon ran into another arrow a few blocks away. And then another, and another, until, voilà: here we are at the Kandahar Hotel!

To our great surprise, the Kandahar has turned out to be an extremely interesting, western-style Victorian hotel left over from a previous era. I suspect it was built by the British when they were in control of nearby West Pakistan, then part of their colony of India. Although in crumbling condition, it remains one of those grand old dowager hotels that live forever off a once glorious past. The hotel has a wall around it with a very large gate, which we drove through, grandly, into the compound. Your mother, the most respectable-looking among the four of us, got out and went inside. When she returned, she was all smiles. We were welcome to camp in the courtyard, she said, inside the walls. Then she said we were even more welcome to have dinner in the hotel's very impressive-looking restaurant. What a stroke of luck! We would celebrate our arrival in Afghanistan with dinner at a very fancy hotel! Who would have ever thought? The food was excellent, I might add. There was even a fine bottle of wine. And then we went back to the bus, turned on the heater, and celebrated our arrival with the joint.

Love,
Dad

The Hotel Kandahar today

Letter From Ghazni

November 29, 1967
Ghazni, Afghanistan
Map 4

Dear Zerky,

Your mom has a lot of class. This morning as we were getting ready to leave Kandahar for Kabul, we remembered that we didn't have any Afghan money. Unable to find a bank in Kandahar, your mother decided to try to change money at the hotel where we were camped. "But they just won't let us do that," I told her. "We haven't even rented a room, and we look like a busload of hippies."

"I'll take care of it," she replied.

She spent the next hour getting all dolled up. Both of us brought along one set of good clothes, "just in case." Prior to arriving in the wilds of Afghanistan, neither of us has worn them. Your mom put on her white blouse and her brown suit. "Why not wear that cute little Tyrolean costume instead," I badgered, "the one that makes your boobs look like they're hanging out."

"Sure, that would be perfect for a Moslem country," she countered. Next came the nylons, then the high heels, then half an hour of doing her hair, nails and makeup.

"You look like a million bucks," I told her, begrudgingly.

"That's the idea," she replied, as she marched off to battle. Fifteen minutes later she was back with a big wad of weird-looking bills. "How did you talk them into it?" I asked.

Your mother then explained to me, as if to a child, that she hadn't talked them into anything—she just didn't give them the opportunity to say no. She had come to Afghanistan on business, she told the hotel manager. She explained that she was in the motion picture business in San Francisco. "San Francisco is near Hollywood, California. You've heard of Hollywood, California, haven't you?" Indeed he had. Then she explained that the price of making movies in Hollywood, California is exorbitant. "The cost of making movies in Afghanistan must be very reasonable in comparison, "don't you think?" He did. "And what with all your colorful tribesmen, beautiful deserts, and spectacular mountains," she larded it on, "I'm sure American audiences would love to see your faraway beautiful land."

Had he read the recent best-seller, James Michener's *Caravans?* she asked innocently. "It's all about Afghanistan." He didn't read English, of course. "Everybody's reading it in America," she went on. Finally she explained how she had arrived in Afghanistan only yesterday, and had not yet had the opportunity to exchange her American dollars. "Are there many such grand hotels as this in Afghanistan?" she flattered.

"Did you offer him the starring role?" I interjected.

"How much would you like to exchange?"

There's no business like show business.

Your mom out of mufti and loaded with dough, we set off for Kabul, about 250 difficult miles to the north. We were prepared for a rough four or five days of it. Previously, the roads had been terrible and we were expecting the worst. We were in for a surprise. Instead of a corrugated dirt track, we found a brand new superhighway—the best damn road since Italy. The story of this road between Kandahar and Kabul is an enlightening one. It's about what has been known now for a couple of centuries as "The Great Game": the Russians and the Americans are having a pissing match in Afghanistan.

For centuries Afghanistan was a point of rivalry between England and Russia. Up until a little over twenty years ago, Pakistan was part of India and India was part of England. That's called "imperialism," Zerky, when a big country steals a little country. Russia, too, was an imperial power, and war was the traditional solution when imperial powers clashed. But when England, or Great Britain as the British like to call it, and Imperial Russia collided here in Afghanistan, a standoff developed wherein both of them tacitly agreed that Afghanistan could be allowed to exist more or less independently, so long as neither of them tried to make it part of its empire.

This gentleman's agreement worked out well for more than a hundred years—for Great Britain and Russia, at least, if not for the tribes of Afghanistan. This is one of the reasons Afghanistan remains one of the poorest and most backward nations on earth. Someone once said that politics is war by other means. One of those "other means" has been going on here in Afghanistan for a long time. The English and the Russians never went to war over Afghanistan—they just politicked, intrigued, and skirmished on the margins, in the expectation that sooner or later one of them would get outmaneuvered and tire of the game.

This jockeying for position and power in Afghanistan was christened "The Great Game" by the oh-so-sporting British. But after World War II, it turned out that Great Britain wasn't so great at playing its great game after all, and was losing its empire to boot. So that the Russians would not prevail in this grand competition (read Cold War), the USA picked up the baton from the British. This ridiculous highway we've been driving on all day, Zerky, is America's latest chess move in our new, improved version of the great game. Your mother has doubts about how well we are playing it, however; one bad move could result in World War III. But so far, in return for lots of asphalt, concrete, technology, and engineering, we appear to be gaining increased influence and power vis-à-vis the USSR.

A few years back, the Russians announced a foreign aid package to help modernize Afghanistan. It was not an act of charity, just another strategic move. Part of Russia's new foreign aid program was a road-building project to connect Afghanistan with its more developed neighbors, Iran to the west, and the Soviet Union to the north. Check and checkmate. Our response was: "Nobody knows how to build roads like we do!" On a testosterone high, we decided to show the Russians how you *really* build a road. So to the highway the Russians were already building across the western half of Afghanistan— from Herat to Kandahar—the U.S. Army Corps of Engineers added an eastern half from Kandahar to Kabul. Compliments of the Great Game, Afghanistan now has a cross-country superhighway. The Afghans are learning how to play the game too. They are getting good at playing the great powers off against each other.

This crazy new highway project we've been driving on for most of the day was completed only last year. At first we couldn't believe it when we found ourselves zipping along, floor-boarded, at nearly seventy miles an hour. Between Kandahar and Ghazni we passed ten or fifteen vehicles, virtually all of them Pakistani trucks, none of which were going forty miles an hour. As for the Afghans, most of them were traveling their new freeway at about three miles an hour, walking speed. Their "ships of the desert"—their camels—do maybe five or six miles per hour; donkeys do about four. But most of the traffic on this new superhighway comes from people with herds of sheep, goats or cows, grazing along the sides of the highway as they munch their way onward. Let's say one mile an hour.

It is not safe to go fast on this brand new freeway—it's too easy to plow into livestock and pedestrians. In that unhappy event—the consensus from other travelers we have talked to about this seems to be—whatever you do, don't stop! You are likely to be killed by outraged tribesmen who don't take kindly to seventy miles an hour. The conventional wisdom here is to try and keep moving at all costs, until you come to the nearest police station or army cantonment where, supposedly, it should be safe to report an accident.

The problem with this new road is that we neglected to give the Afghans any cars to drive on it. Once again, it's the same situation as with that modern new airport outside Kandahar that I told you about, Zerky, the one that's all lit up at night like some New Guinea cargo cult trying to attract a wayward female airplane, while Afghanistan's second largest city remains dark.

All day long I've been wondering about some strange noises emanating from underneath our car. At first I thought maybe I'd just forgotten what a Volkswagen sounds like at seventy miles per hour. But unfortunately, the noise is getting worse. When I crawled under the engine this afternoon, I discovered that the differential and transmission housing are covered with black dripping oil. This is bad news. I'm not a mechanic, and there's not much I can do about it, other than wonder about whether my American Automobile Association Emergency Road Service card covers a seventy-mile tow into Kabul, by camel. We have seen nothing resembling an automotive repair garage since Kandahar, almost two hundred miles back. We haven't even seen a petrol pump yet, which is also beginning to worry me, because we are getting close to having to dip into the thirty-five-liter emergency reserve we carry up on top of the bus.

Late in the afternoon, we arrived at Ghazni, which our map shows to be Afghanistan's fourth-largest city, a city where one would surely think there ought to be a mechanic, wouldn't one? In the eleventh and twelfth centuries AD, according to our book, Ghazni was one of the most important cities in the world, a center of learning and the arts that was said to have been rivaled only by Baghdad. The book tells us that Ghazni's founder, Mahamud of Ghazni, once kept the cities of India "tethered like fat cows in the sun." Once a year he would swoop down through the Khyber Pass to "milk them," before returning to Ghazni with more riches, "to the glory of his empire." This sounded too good to miss.

When we finally got here, however, we were very disappointed. Only Ghazni's huge, crumbling walls make it appear much different from all the other ramshackle collections of mud buildings we've been passing through these last few days. As far as we can tell, Ghazni doesn't appear to have changed much since the twelfth century, except insofar as it has been continuously falling apart. Eight hundred years is a lot of wear and tear and depreciation. We decided we'd settle for a mechanic.

Ghazni is located just off the superhighway; surely all those beat-up Pakistani trucks we've seen rattling their way to and from Kabul must break down frequently and need the services of an automotive repair facility? But where might such a facility be?

We decided to drive back and forth through Ghazni on each of its streets until we spotted something. We might even get lucky and stumble across someone who speaks English. But we kept getting sidetracked at the bazaar by all the men in turbans, and by women covered head to foot in purdah. Your mother prefers to talk to women when it comes to finding out things. When you don't speak the language, you need to tune in to body language and facial expressions, neither of which work when you can't see bodies or faces. That, of course, is the purpose of covering up women in Moslem societies—to make them inaccessible to men. We decided to keep a sharp eye out for someone wearing a semblance of Western dress. We tried several men, but they just smiled, turned up their hands, and walked on.

Eventually, through an open gate I spied a large courtyard with what appeared to be the remnants of an old rusty truck chassis lying inside. Walking into the courtyard, I discovered the corpses of several old automobiles and trucks in various stages of rust and disassembly, carcasses in the process of being stripped of everything that might someday be useful. Someone's spare parts inventory. An ancient truck had its front end propped up on a couple of stumps, and was being worked on by a man underneath. He slithered out as I sidled up, trying to explain my problem.

Pointing to the differential in the center of a lonely nearby rear axle, I tried to get the point across that the differential on our car just outside the gate was leaking, leaking, leaking, and could he perhaps refill it with what my VW manual—here, look at it—calls "90 Weight Hypoid Gear Oil"? This drew a blank. I tried again, this time throwing in my best sign language. No contact. Then he motioned me to come with him into what turned out to be his workshop—a barn with a straw-covered, manure-covered floor, and some rusty old wrenches and a few other old tools lying in a corner. That and several five-gallon cans of oil lined up against one wall were all that appeared to make this barn any different from all the other barns in Afghanistan.

"Differential!" "Transmission!" "Gearbox!" "Drip, drip, drip!" "Very bad!" "Muy malo!" I said triumphantly, throwing in most of my Spanish, for good measure. "Oil. Oil. Gear oil!" I pointed to the row of oil cans along one wall. This got a response. The man started to smile. Well, if all I wanted was oil, why didn't I just say so? He picked up a five-gallon pail and brought it over to me. Upon examination it proved to be "Motor-Oil, 30 Weight."

"No, no, no!" I shook my head. "*Gear oil*, not motor oil!" So he brought me another pail of motor oil, which I again pushed away. And then another and another. I pushed them all away. He concluded I didn't like his oil. Now here I am again, the ugly American, demeaning a poor Third-World country. I tried hugging his bucket of oil. "Good, good! Afghanistan oil good!" I babbled on like some dumb Indian out of a "B" western. By now, I didn't know what to think he thought I thought; he probably thought I was crazy. It wasn't working. All was lost. I finally pushed away his last bucket of oil. It was much too thin, and with the wrong additive package. How do you explain that in Pashto or Dari?" In the end I paid homage to an old adage I find very inspiring at times like this: "Cowardice is the better part of valor." I beat a hasty retreat out the door. "That damn transmission will just have to make it to Kabul," I told JoAnne.

By the time nightfall overtook us, we had covered over three-fourths the distance from Kandahar to Kabul, and were having reservations about spending the night "camped wild" in such a wild, wild place. Throughout the day, we have been passing people wandering the freeway, many of whom appear to be nomads. They are a fierce and handsome people—women dressed in embroidered dresses, disdaining to cover their faces as we pass, their men in huge ragged white turbans and heavy, baggy pantaloons. Many carry rifles that appear to be left over from the nineteenth century. These are a people who know little of modern states, governments or laws. Their codes and loyalties are tribal. We are foreigners, intruders. Afghanistan has a long history of violence going back at least as far as when Genghis Khan's Mongol hordes ransacked the country. We've been reading about fierce tribesmen attacking tourists and foreign travelers—killing the men, raping the women, before carrying them off to be added to some tribal chieftain's collection of sequestered wives. We wonder how frequently such things still happen here in Afghanistan, in the middle of the twentieth century. And then we talked about how Afghanistan is not yet in the twentieth century. Such were our thoughts as we made camp for the night, just far enough off the road so as not to be stumbled over in the dark by a passing camel caravan. We had been reading too much James Michener's *Caravans*.

We spent an uneventful night beside the road. The next morning as we were preparing to leave, we heard drums. War drums! They seemed to be coming from over the hill. "Apaches!" I yelled to JoAnne as I started throwing all our junk into the back of the bus. And we were off on the next leg of our great adventure. Kabul was but an hour away.

Love,
Dad

From JoAnne's Diary

November 29, 1967

Cold as hell last night. We moved Zerky in with us, so nobody slept. As we were breaking camp, we heard the sound of drums coming from over the hill. We were "routed." Driving off, we came upon a wedding procession headed by dancing men with a veiled bride dressed completely in red, and her groom on horseback. Little girls in green dancing along with scarves. Plenty of drums and other instruments.

A roadside bazaar near Kabul

From JoAnne's Diary
Kabul
Map 4

November 30, 1967

Arrived Kabul, where we ran into the Swedes again. At the Khyber Restaurant. Had dinner together and after-dinner beer. They leave tomorrow for Faizabad, to go looking for snow leopards. This PM Zerky made friends with a turbaned old gent in the park; they were mutually intrigued with each other.

December 1, 1967

Cold and wintry out. We went to USSR Embassy today and decided that Samarkand, Tashkent, etc. are indeed feasible. Had lunch of duck and rice at Khyber Hotel. Spent the evening writing postcards and washing clothes. According to the *Kabul Times*, Ramadan begins either tonight or tomorrow.

December 2, 1967

Went to USSR Embassy again. We can't seem to get the point across that *we don't want to go to Moscow or Leningrad!* $75.00 per person to Tashkent, plus $10.00 per day for hotel, meals, and taxis. Visas and the necessary okay from Moscow will take at least ten days. Found a big bookstore!

December 4, 1967

Ice in the gutters.

December 5, 1967

Chapter 1 of *The Worming of Tarzan*: His medicine was given to him wrong, the result being that he threw up an ocean of bread and milk. As three kids and two adults were following us at the time, this was very unpleasant—but not nearly so unpleasant as his diarrhea a short time later when worms, worms and worms started coming out as a crowd of at least twenty people stood around us in a circle. Six inches of worm finally remained, hanging outside, the rest still inside. After a few embarrassing minutes I wound the six inches around a stick and pulled, until the worm broke.

Bill picked up the car, which now has the wrong kind of oil in its gearbox. And in the engine. They tell us there's no more of the right kind of oil in all of Kabul. We fear for our happy home.

Went window-shopping: earrings, amulet, necklaces, mirrored purses. Talked with a German woman at souvenir shop: how important is it, really, to keep Zerky's kidneys warm? My moneychanger in the bazaar no longer changes money. Back to the hotel.

December 6, 1967

Started the day determined that Tarzan shall be wormed right! A visit to the Pakistan Embassy for our road permit led us to the American Embassy, then to the Afghanistan Tourist Organization, both of which suggested we try the Afghanistan Ministry of Agriculture. Has anyone else ever gone to a government ministry to get their dog wormed? The ministry turned out to be next to the University of Kabul, where a Wyoming US Aider, Dr. Hoope, was teaching a class. No Dr. Hoope. Went to lunch, then back to university again. No Dr. Hoope again. He was in Farsi class, we were told. So we went to the zoo, where we saw our first yak, plus some leopards, hyenas, jackals, and various assorteds. Zerky was much impressed by a rabbit whose nose twitched. I enjoyed watching the German zoo director and his attendants chasing, but never catching, an ibex.

Letter From Kabul

December 11, 1967
Kabul, Afghanistan
Map 4

Dear Zerky,

We have been in Kabul for about two weeks now, and are having a good time. We've been staying in the Khyber Hotel, which is the only hotel in Kabul suitable for Westerners. It is a "luxury" hotel, luxury meaning *heat*. Except for the foreign embassies and the aid missions, the Khyber Hotel is the only building in Kabul that has heat—as far as we know. By Western standards, most Americans would consider it a dump, but to us it's our nice, warm luxury dump. It is snowing as I write. It would be impossible to keep warm in our bus. And besides, we need a john—that other luxury item we Westerners consider a necessity. The Hotel Khyber is our first hotel in more than eight months. You approve of this luxury lifestyle most heartily, Zerk. You love running back and forth in our room, and especially up and down the hallway. Running around seems to be your greatest pleasure these days. To us, living in luxury in the world's poorest country does seem inappropriate, but I'm afraid we just don't care; the lifestyle of the typical Afghan would be unbearable.

We find Kabul to be a stark and ancient city of rambling, single-story mud buildings thrown together with no planning for streets and sidewalks. You can wander around for days, picking your way through random passageways and alleyways that were left between buildings at the time of their construction. Since World War II, Afghanistan's government has been making an effort to guide the country out of the Middle Ages, by encouraging aid programs from the "developed countries" of the world. So far this appears to have resulted in only a few straight streets, an airport, a university, electricity, and—most important of all—a water purification plant. How nice it is to be able to drink tap water again. Ever since Tehran, we had been adding iodine to our bus water, which leaves a bitter taste.

Bringing change to Afghanistan is hard to accomplish; even the best aid programs—and ours is not one of them—cannot change in a few years what has been centuries in the making. On each side of Kabul's few modern streets, are open running sewers like that one I backed into in Tabriz—and got stuck in—do you remember, Zerky?

Most of our sightseeing consists of walking around getting lost in these back-street passageways. Commerce is everywhere, not just in the shops. Street vendors have their wares spread out upon the ground and the sidewalks, and your mother especially enjoys wandering through the bazaars, Asia's answer to American suburban shopping centers. In Kabul, you can find damn near anything in the bazaar—anything at all, that is, except anything you are likely to find in an American shopping center. Mass-produced goods are in short supply, which makes everything else seem new and interesting: piles of handmade pots and pans being pounded out one at a time on the ground; piles of beautiful handwoven Afghan carpets that bring warmth to the cold dirt floors of Afghan houses; piles of coiled rope for everything from lowering a bucket into a well to tying up your camel; mounds of unglazed pottery for all kinds of uses; stacks of handmade soap; bundles of tea; endless strings of pomegranates, eggplants, bananas, and fruits we don't recognize; random bits of shiny metal to be worn as jewelry; lambskin "sirs," those grey creased lambskin hats that seem to be replacing the turban on the well-groomed Afghan male. Throughout all the commotion run barefoot children, donkeys with bulging saddlebags, and newly purchased livestock on tether. And finally, there is the endless crowd of shoppers who are even more interesting to us than are the things they buy: nomads in beads and spangles; men in turbans; women ensconced head to foot in the *burkah* or *chador*, that pleated sheet they throw over Afghan women before they are allowed to venture into public view.

Islam is no easy taskmaster, Zerky. Last week was the beginning of Ramadan, a month-long reverse-holiday somewhat akin to Lent. I call Ramadan a "reverse-holiday" because Moslems seem to have holidays backward. Instead of having a good time, their holidays seem designed to make people feel miserable. This goal is accomplished by a number of austerity measures, the most basic of which is the prohibition against eating between sunrise and sunset. But if that doesn't make you miserable enough, you can still beat yourself with a whip and maybe even set yourself afire. Kabul doesn't cater to tourists in search of that Mardi Gras experience.

And even if you're not Moslem, you are still expected to join in all the fun, by starving yourself from sunrise to sunset. Throughout Ramadan the government makes mandatory the closing of restaurants during daylight hours. Our first two days here we barely made it to sunset, but we're doing better now, having discovered a speakeasy where they clandestinely sell westerners what a sign inside proclaims to be "The Best Damn Hamburger in Asia." Their clientele appears to be mostly westerners, most of them hippie-types. To get in, you have to knock on a locked door and wait for someone to open it.

Lest anyone get any bright ideas about other ways to while away the time before sunset, there is also a prohibition against sex. What I find most interesting about this weird state of affairs is how it stands our own idea of celebrating holidays on its head. But one good thing about this backward approach is that the ban on alcohol must make Moslem Monday mornings a lot less painful.

We are surprised at all the hippies here. Kabul is the major stop on the "Road to Katmandu." Both cities are said to be "pot paradise." Drugs of all kinds are openly available here. The other day our friend Mike was acting like a kid turned loose in a candy store. Already, he had tried two or three kinds of marijuana, plus hashish, opium, morphine, cocaine, and synthetic heroin. "The only thing you can't get here," he told us, "is LSD"; he's taking care of that by having some mailed to him from the United States.

It must be hard to smuggle drugs into Afghanistan. They're legal. Mike tells us he and Fiona are just trying them out, they're not interested in becoming addicts. He told us about their experience in Kandahar. Somehow they had managed to find a hotel there and were invited to light up by a couple across the hall. Those other two Americans have been living in Kandahar off and on for a couple of years now and, according to Mike, each weighed less than a hundred pounds. He told us their faces were ravaged by sores and disease, one had dysentery, both had lice, and they were covered with scabs. After the four of them lit up together, their talk became incoherent, Mike said. He told us that this other couple wants to return to the United States but can't; they would have no way to support their habits in America. Their life in Afghanistan now centers around making periodic trips back and forth between Kandahar and Quetta, in West Pakistan, in order to replenish their dope supply. So long as they don't go home, they can exist here on pennies a day. Opium is cheap, and if they have enough of it they don't need much in the way of food. Mike doesn't give either of them much longer to live.

Lars and Ula, "The Swedes," are in Kabul too. A week ago they managed to get special permission to travel up north into the Hindu Kush, a southern range of the Pamir Mountains. The Swedes are big on wildlife. They told us they went looking for snow leopards and Bactrian camels, that two-humped variety that originated in the ancient Greek kingdom of Bactria, which somehow is now part of northern Afghanistan. The Swedes didn't find any snow leopards, but they did make it almost to Faizabad, in Badakshan, north of Nuristan, on the edge of the Pamir Mountains, near the Wakhan Corridor, where Afghanistan, Russia, and China's Sinkiang Province all meet. Finally, they had to turn back because of the cold and the snow and because of the utter primitiveness of the towns, they said. It seems to us that going there in the winter is a very gutsy thing to do. We've got to hand it to the Swedes for having tried. We were also glad to learn that we are not the only ones in Kabul who find Afghanistan to be intimidating.

Each morning there is ice in the gutters. We bought you and your mother some furry sheepskin coats that cost $15.00 US each. I'm sure I could have bargained the price down further, but they are such grand coats! Even at $15.00, I felt we were taking advantage of the guy. Your coats do have a slight problem, however. Afghans cure their leather in sheep's urine, which makes the two of you smell like dead sheep.

A few days ago you had a very bad day, Zerky. It was time for your DPT booster shot, so we spent an entire day running around Kabul looking for one. Our travels took us first to the Afghan Tourist Office and then to the Ministry of Health, the United Nations World Health Organization's aid mission, the U.S. Embassy, and finally to US AID program headquarters, where you were set upon by a renegade American nurse. We thought you had forgotten all those sadistic nurses in Athens, but now you appear to have decided that people in white smocks are the same the world over. You fought like a true son of the prophet. We hope you'll not hold the needles against us. We managed to get you the last batch of DPT vaccine in all of Afghanistan, or so we were told; it was there for children of US AID workers. If you are an Afghan in Afghanistan, DPT vaccine is not available.

So you think you had it bad! You're lucky you're not Tarzan. He has worms! Our search for a veterinarian eventually led us to the Afghanistan Ministry of Agriculture, where we felt pretty stupid announcing to a high-up government official that our dog has worms. Fortunately, he was most helpful and understanding. No doubt Tarzan received more consideration here than he would have in Washington, D.C.

There are a lot of strange Westerners running around Kabul. We drove out to the Russian Embassy today, trying to get a visa to go to Tashkent and Samarkand, in the nearby Soviet Union. I was busy complaining to the Russian clerk there that their prepaid tours sponsored by Intourist, the Soviet government tourist agency, are much too expensive, when a stranger walked up and whispered in my ear: "Just remember," he told me, "what they tell you here isn't necessarily the truth. I'll be in the Khyber Restaurant at 5:00 tonight." Before I could answer, he was gone. We are in the market for a cheap way to get to Russia, so we arrived at the Khyber at 5:00 PM sharp, and quickly spotted "Secret Agent X" hunched over a table. We introduced ourselves, sat down, and I asked him what he'd been talking about at the Russian Embassy earlier. He said he was British and that he was leaving tomorrow for London via Tashkent and Moscow. He told us he wasn't spending anything near what they had been telling us at the embassy. He had worked it all out very carefully, and would be happy to give us the benefit of his research. "Here's how you do it." Whereupon he pulled out his pen and jotted down the following on a napkin.

1) Buy ticket for Kabul-Tashkent-Moscow-London with U.S. dollars.

2) Use ticket to obtain USSR transit visa.

3) Turn in ticket for refund in US dollars.

4) Buy new ticket Kabul-Tashkent only.

5) Use US dollars to buy Russian rubles in Kabul. Black market rate = 90 rubles to the dollar, official rate in USSR = 4 rubles to the dollar.

6) Fly to Tashkent with rubles and buy much cheaper ticket to Moscow at much lower internal rate using rubles bought in Kabul.

7) Fly on to Moscow and stay at (name illegible) Hotel.

8) Buy furs, vodka, cigarettes, diamonds, ticket to London.

9) Fly to London and sell the above, thereby gaining reimbursement for total outlay.

10) Net cost Kabul to London = Nil.

Before I had a chance to ask him whether this was legal, he jumped up. "Good luck. Got to run. My plane leaves early tomorrow morning. Hope to see you in Moscow." And he was gone. "Or maybe in Siberia," JoAnne murmured.

Until today, we had planned to fly to Tashkent and then on to Samarkand; now we aren't sure. Intourist makes you prepay all your hotels and meals, but how do you know where you want to stay, or what you want to eat, when you've never even been in the country before? We make such decisions *after* we arrive. The Russians don't make things easy for you—they try to make you travel first class so they know where you are. They tell us it will take ten days to two weeks to get visas, which have to come all the way from Moscow. That means more money for our hotel in Kabul, while we wait. And what if our visas arrive late?

We are at cross-purposes with ourselves. On the one hand, almost anything would seem reasonable for a once-in-a-life-time chance to visit Samarkand. We are so close! But then on the other hand, we are just as close to the Khyber Pass, and to Kashmir. And to the Punjab, all of which are cheaper, easier, and warmer. I suspect we will probably be giving up on the USSR—they make things too difficult. In any event, we will be leaving in a few days. Our hotel is extremely cheap by Western standards but still costs more than moving on.

Love,
Dad

From JoAnne's Diary

December 7, 1967

Tarzan still has worms. I gathered a stool sample this morning, much to the bewilderment of the eternally watching Afghans. Off to the university again, where we made contact with a vet with a pill. He is a US AID man. The USSR has a rival polytech school here.

Went to the bazaar: pomegranates, bananas, eggplants on strings; Soviet soap sold by vendors trying to keep warm with braziers burning; long striped quilted coats with overly long sleeves; children in bright colors with coins sewn into their headdresses; women in drab-colored burkahs with latticework eyes, and pleats around the backs of their heads; burros with saddlebags full of fruits and vegetables; carpet sellers on the riverbank; rope sellers behind the mosque; chickens having their necks wrung next to booksellers and jewelry sellers; turds along the wall next to the sidewalk.

December 8, 1967

Had a talk with _____ last night. After visiting with him for a while, he told me he was going home to take LSD and synthetic heroin. Says it's like a ten-minute "orgasmic flash." Says we, too, can buy cocaine here, legally, and that he can hardly wait. Opium too. He says anyone who didn't know him might think him a pothead.

Stayed home and read. Looked out the window. Fantastic view of the ancient walls of the city climbing up the mountains. A blue and white mosque with two minarets. Single-story mud buildings, mostly. People using the courtyard below as a public john. Children play in it.

December 10, 1967

Today we took the car to another garage to see about the leaky differential. We could not communicate with the mechanic, so we went to an office in town and had a man there write a note to the mechanic explaining what it is that Bill wants. The mechanic couldn't read.

December 11, 1967

The service is lousy in our supposedly modern hotel. The garbage hasn't been emptied for several days now and Zerk's dirty diapers were spilling out of the can in the hallway, until our "chambermaid," a man, pawed through them, stacked them up neatly, and left. It snowed a little this morning.

West Pakistan Again

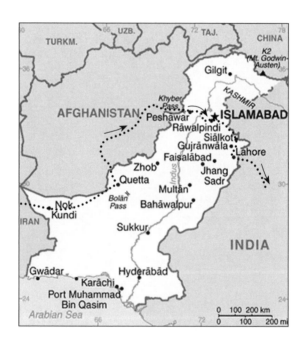

From JoAnne's Diary
The Khyber Pass
Map 4

December 12, 1967

Border officials are sadistic. Immigration told us our visas are no good because they have been already stamped at Nok Kundi. Customs told us our *carnet* is no good because it doesn't mention Pakistan on the cover. After watching our blood boil, they passed us on through, without comment.

The Khyber Pass. Wow!

We stayed in our first DAK bungalow tonight, 8½ rupees. The ceiling fan and the worn-out screen doors tell us we are nearly in India. Women beginning to show their faces!

Letter From the Khyber

December 13, 1967
Rawalpindi
West Pakistan
Map 4

Dear Zerky,

We are in West Pakistan again, this time three hundred miles northwest of where we left it on our way to Afghanistan. As soon as we crossed the border at Torkham, near the head of the Khyber Pass, we knew we were in Pakistan because of all the guns. Guns are everywhere, and are the defining image of Pakistan. This is no accident. We were greeted at the customs station by an official Pakistan Department of Tourism travel poster with a picture of a Pakistani soldier on it, holding an AK-47 across his chest. "Welcome to Pakistan," it said. This particular image was the choice of the Pakistani government. Everyone here appears to be counting the days until Pakistan is strong enough to march into Kashmir and seize it by force. Hatred for India seems to be the Pakistani obsession.

After crossing the border into West Pakistan, we approached the Khyber Pass with mounting excitement. Our first glimpse of the pass was a letdown, however. Where we had envisioned a formidable, snow-laden barrier astride lofty peaks, we found only an unimpressive notch in the hills. Approached from the west, the pass itself is hard to discern, due to its low vertical profile. On its eastern slope, this notch widens progressively as it falls off into an ever-deepening canyon, accelerating downward all the way to the city of Peshawar. Beyond there, the ever-widening valley is gradually absorbed by the oncoming Indian Plain. What is generally referred to as the Khyber Pass is barely a pass at all, but rather an inverted funnel down which violence has poured for many centuries. "The Khyber" is the general area where the barren highlands of Western Asia collide with the fertile lowlands of the Indian subcontinent. At the top of the pass, and in places along its eastern canyon, are ancient fortresses testifying to the many armies of invaders that have flooded down the Khyber, strewing death and destruction in their wake.

In the third century BC, down came the Aryans on their way to remaking the racial complexion of India. Alexander the Great's footsore legions also tramped down it, in 327 BC, on their empire-building march to redraw the maps of Europe and Asia. Between 1000 and 1024 AD, Mahamud of Ghazni's army came down it ten times, carrying the word of Mohammed to the Buddhist and Hindu infidels on the hot plains below. In 1220 AD, Genghis Khan sent his Golden Horde down the Khyber, in an orgy of slaughter that is perhaps the biggest bloodbath in history. Then in 1398 came Tamerlane, who also left India drenched in blood. Bahar Khan followed in 1518, conquering India and founding the Mogul Dynasty, which ruled India until the coming of the British.

Then in 1756, the Afghans themselves poured down the Khyber on their way to conquering Kashmir and converting it to Islam. And finally, throughout the nineteenth century, when the Khyber served as the British Empire's northwest frontier, the bloodletting continued. Stories of fierce, hard-riding Pathans, fanatically committed to the destruction of the British—sniping, ambushing, laying siege to their fortifications—

these are the images of the Khyber that were immortalized by Rudyard Kipling. And so it was very much to our surprise that we discovered that the excitement of the Khyber Pass exists more in the dimension of time than in space. Books! Without our books, the pass's puny physical dimensions would have been a great disappointment. It wasn't the power of the pass that drew us halfway around the world, it was the power of its *history*.

We did so want to get a picture of you, Zerky, standing there on the Khyber Pass, bravely. But what with all the soldiers and concrete tank barriers—and with our road permit forbidding us from stopping beside the road—all these things told us that taking photographs of you in such a sensitive area would be a mistake. So we didn't stop, not even to buy one of the famous Khyber rifles on display for sale along the road. Pathans hawk them to everyone who drives by. More than a century ago, they were hand-making them in nearby hidden factories under the noses of their British occupiers. Now they make them for tourists, adventurers, mercenaries, revolutionaries, and anyone else with money.

We are excited. Our descent through the northern part of West Pakistan marks the beginning of a new world. Crossing the Indus River, and all the way to the Pakistani capital of Rawalpindi, there is a big drop in elevation and a corresponding change in the environment. The climate is becoming warmer, the food hotter. The smell of curry is in the air. Already we sense the lush, semitropical vegetation of India. For months now, even though we have been farther south than the southernmost tip of Europe, elevation and season have conspired to rob us of the warmth we feel entitled to by virtue of our latitude.

And what colors! What a contrast from the grey-brown highlands we have been driving through ever since we crossed into Asia. Now we are beginning to see bright green landscapes with a rich assortment of people dressed in all kinds of intensely dyed clothing: burning vermilions, dripping magentas, flaming saffrons, dazzling chartreuse. Never before have we seen such colorful cloth as here in Pakistan. Saris are beginning to make their appearance—no more beautiful garment exists. And the Pakistani trucks! They are an art form in themselves, elaborate psychedelic works painted up into little blocks of bright colors, with bits of colored glass and fragments of mirror carefully inlaid as in a mosaic. And to cap it all off, women's faces are starting to emerge once again into the daylight—I hadn't realized how much I'd missed them. How barren the world without a little femininity. That is one of the reasons Afghanistan seems so unremittingly harsh.

We are spending one more day in Rawalpindi, picking up our mail at the American Embassy, eating hamburgers in the embassy basement, and trying as usual to get spare tires repaired. And to find the correct oils for our transmission and engine. We finally managed to find the correct gearbox oil, but so far no correct engine oil.

Before getting to Rawalpindi yesterday we saw a tire sign when we were passing through a village. The shop had a thatched roof and hundreds of worn-out tires piled around it; if they took all of them off and put new ones back on, they must really know their stuff, I figured. So we stopped, and within seconds a crowd began to gather. I dragged our flat tire out from behind the front seat, and rolled it to a man who appeared to be in charge of the shop. "Can you fix?" I inquired in my best pidgin English. "Is tubeless—T-U-B-E-L-E-S-S," my finger tracing the English letters on the side of the casing. "No tube!" I added emphatically. Tubeless tires are uncommon in this part of the world.

As the man began to examine our tire, carefully rotating it slowly through his fingers, the crowd started to multiply at an alarming rate. Our predicament seemed to be turning into a major event. They were all men, laughing and chatting amongst themselves. Soon, suggestions started flowing in Urdu, but I had not received a single word of English in response to my question, "Can you fix?" So I tried again and he smiled. I suppose a smile is better than a shrug? The tire examination continued. When the man I believed to be the owner finally finished looking at it, he passed it on to one of the older men in the crowd, who examined it further and, in turn, passed it on to the guy next to him, who examined it further. And further and further. In an atmosphere of somber intent sprinkled with joviality, my deflated tire slowly made the rounds. Each of the men examined it thoroughly in turn, and then discussed it thoroughly with the man next to him, before passing it on to the man next to him.

"If they can't fix it, why the hell don't they just say so, so we can get the hell out of here," I said to myself very quietly. A rapt, unintelligible discussion engaged the crowd. They seemed to be enjoying themselves, and I was reluctant to grab my tire and run; I didn't want to play spoilsport and pick up my ball and go home. Our reading about India stresses that *patience* is the key to traveling in this part of the world. It was time to start cultivating my attitude.

Eventually, after everyone in the crowd had had his opportunity to examine my tire, it finally found its way back to the man I had originally shown it to. More spirited discussion with the men around him. There seemed to be some difference of opinion, but gradually a consensus seemed to emerge. Finally, the man returned it to me and pronounced the well-considered judgment of the crowd: "No fix! Is tubeless." There was triumph in his voice. Greatly enlightened about this new land we are getting into, I was glad to be on my way. Throwing the flat tire into the back of the bus, I waved goodbye to the happy crowd. Somehow I was happy too.

Love,
Dad

From JoAnne's Diary
Rawalpindi & West Pakistan
Map 4

December 13, 1967

We have a beautiful campsite tonight outside a civil rest house beyond Rawalpindi. The toilet is a clean, wooden throne with a removable chamber pot.

It's great to see greenery and women's faces again. Saris! Along the road today we saw many monuments to the Pakistani army's various battalions and brigades.

Letter From Hussainiwala

December 14, 1967
West Pakistan
Maps 3 & 4

Dear Zerky,

We are camped tonight at a Pakistani government rest house, about a mile from the Indian border. When we spotted it late this afternoon, we decided to take advantage of it by putting off crossing the border until tomorrow morning. We asked the caretaker, could we please park our van inside the fence and spend the night? He readily agreed, but an hour later as we were cooking supper, we were approached by a Pakistani army officer who informed us we are not supposed to be here. This rest house is for military only, he told us. After questioning us thoroughly about who we were, where we had come from, and where we were going, and why, he finally told us we can remain here for one night only, but under no circumstances are we to leave the compound. So tonight we are both guests and prisoners, which comes as no surprise, because much of our reception in Pakistan has been this weird concoction of one part official government harassment mixed in with an equal portion of personal welcome on behalf of the Pakistani government's messengers.

It all started with our Road Permit, a special kind of permit for an automobile that you can only get from a Pakistani Embassy *outside* Pakistan, at the same time you get your entry visa. In no other country have we encountered such a document. On it, they write down your exact route and your entire itinerary inside the country. Any change in either, "whether voluntary or not, must be immediately reported to the police," it says on the permit, which goes on to say, "no photography of bridges, dams, headworks, communication centers, cantonments, etc., is permitted." This was obviously designed to thwart spies and saboteurs, and you—Zerky—you have been issued one too. So don't get any bright ideas—your permit has your picture on it and you have been designated a spy. Or maybe a saboteur. I should hasten to add that the same Pakistani government officials who threatened to shoot you also welcomed you into their country with all the delight and amusement reserved for small children everywhere.

All across this northeastern section of Pakistan, we get the impression that we are in an intensely militaristic nation. There seems to be tension everywhere. Here at Hussainiwala—the only border crossing between West Pakistan and India—nervousness is understandable. Four years ago, this was the scene of the India-Pakistan War over Kashmir, a war that neither country believes to be over. You are at one of the tensest, most dangerous borders in the world, Zerky.

As we came down from Rawalpindi today, population began to press in upon us. Our speed over the narrow one-lane highway, built in the days of the British, was gradually slowed by an increasing concentration of people, carts, bicycles, rickshaws, donkeys, horses, cattle, bullocks, water buffalo, and camels. By the end of the day it was rush-hour stop and go. Our speedometer never hit thirty. This crunch of humanity came to a mindboggling climax outside Lahore, our first major Pakistani city, population in excess of three million. I was determined to stay out of it at all costs. Entering the outskirts of Lahore, we watched intently for signs pointing the way to the Indian border a few miles away. We are on the only through road between India and the western world; surely there must be some kind of bypass around such a huge city. But there wasn't.

Inexorably, as into a black hole, we were sucked up in a flood of traffic, cascading us down into the center of the city. "Hang on to your hats," I yelled as we and a highway full of trucks, cars, and buses lurched our way down into the heart of Lahore, like icebergs down a series of rapids. There was nothing to do; we were caught up. Turning around in such a madhouse was out of the question. Fortunately, we were moving so slowly that it was impossible to run over anybody. Encased in our two and a half tons of good German steel, people and animals just thudded harmlessly off the sides of our van. Hopelessly, helplessly lost in a sea of chaos, we were squashed down onto the subcontinent. After three thousand miles of by-and-large deserted high desert, this new and bountiful concentration of sights, sounds, and smells serves as a harbinger of better things to come. After more than an hour of glorious abandon, we found ourselves washed up onto a narrow ribbon of crumbling asphalt, which in this part of the world goes by the name, "metaled road." Somehow we had accidentally stumbled back onto the "highway."

Tonight we are on the threshold of a new world, one in which time appears to be of little consequence and the space in people's lives very compressed. For most of the villagers we passed along the road today, a through route to Karachi or Bombay must seem as irrelevant as a rocket to the stars. When people go traveling here, it is probably to the next village, and probably on foot or by ox-cart. If you don't make it in one day, well, there's always the next, and, if not in this incarnation, then in the next. As we approach India, I am trying hard to gear myself up psychologically to not being in a hurry. I am trying to resign myself to lots of flat tires, and to twenty-five miles an hour. It isn't easy. Today we had our fourth flat tire in three days. Prior to that, we had had only one the entire trip.

Love,
Dad

From JoAnne's Diary
Final West Pakistan Entries
Map 4

December 14, 1967

Bill's total frustration at not being able to explain to the soft-drink vendor that he wanted to buy the two Coca-Colas he held in his hands, bottles and all. He ended up having to give them back. He left thirsty and empty-handed.

December 15, 1967

Upon leaving the rest house this morning, a grand old Pakistani presented me with a small bouquet of roses. He told me he'd been working at the rest house for forty years. Then, while going through Indian immigration, an Indian presented me with one more rose. The Indians and the Pakistanis: they are having a War of the Roses. What a fine way to arrive in India!

India

Note: The eastern part of India (south and east of Bhutan) was called Assam when we were there, and Bangladesh was called East Pakistan.

From JoAnne's Diary
Amritsar to Nepal, Assam and Calcutta
New Delhi, Taj Mahal, Shivpuri National Park
Map 4

December 16, 1967

While Bill was breaking camp this morning, I had a talk with a twelve-year-old girl who was staying at our rest house. She told me we should not be in Vietnam.

Arrived in New Delhi at dark, starving, no map, no idea where to stay. Finally ended up at the Ladhi Hotel, 23 rupees per day = $3.06 US at 7½ rupees to the dollar. Our snappy room bearer brought us dinner in our room!

That tire we had patched yesterday is starting to leak.

December 17, 1967

Made it to New Delhi via Amritsar, where we checked out the big temple. Bill is now checking out the feasibility of taking a boat to Africa. He is also checking on visas and automobile permit requirements for some of the countries we hope to visit there. He had to leave his passport with the Sudan Embassy.

Went down to Connaught Circle this morning to let Zerky play in the park. It was full of sacred cows. They have the keys to the city. In a half-hour we were approached by people trying to sell us grapefruit, shoeshine, massage (head or legs), peacock fan, money exchange, psychedelic windmill, fortuneteller.

December 19, 1967

Can't get visas into Sudan. Uganda has banned travel anywhere near the Sudan border. It should be possible to cross into Sudan farther north, from Ethiopia, they told Bill, but we would have to get our visa in Addis Ababa, in Ethiopia.

New Delhi: The Red Fort

Note: The following entries were written before Southern Rhodesia seceded from the British Commonwealth of Nations, during the period when the British were beginning to impose sanctions on Ian Smith's breakaway government in retaliation for Smith's unilateral declaration of independence. Southern Rhodesia became Zimbabwe.

December 19, 1967 (Bill's entry)

India no longer has formal diplomatic relations with Southern Rhodesia, so there is no chance of getting a visa from the Rhodesian consulate in India. My unsuccessful search for a representative of Ian Smith's government led me first to the British High Commission. The United Kingdom does admit to having relations with Smith's government, but its High Commission told me they don't know where I should go for a visa. Later they changed their story, telling me that the High Commission does sometimes issue visas—they just don't know whether or not Smith honors them. B. S.

Next stop U.S. Embassy, where I was told that we could, indeed, get a Rhodesian visa from the British High Commission in Nairobi, in Kenya. So I went back to the British High Commission in New Delhi and re-questioned one of their officials about this. He reluctantly admitted that we probably could get a visa from their High Commission in Nairobi. The British are issuing visas under the table—visas they themselves hold to be illegal.

Dear Zerky: When you were playing with some kids in the hotel's garden yesterday, you were acting shy, which got your mother and I into a conversation about returning to the United States. We have decided to stay for another six months, however, three for India and three more for Africa. But we may not make it all the way to South Africa after all. And then again, maybe we might!

Went to American Express. A boat that could take both our car and us leaves March 24, Bombay to Nairobi. This could work. The man at American Express is writing Cape Town to find out about connections from Africa to Colón, in Panama, six months from now. We hope to drive the Pan-American Highway back to San Francisco. The guy said he will forward the info on to us, at American Express, in Calcutta. He also called one airline, which told him that South Africa wants an import license for Tarzan. Rhodesia also says it wants some kind of special dog paper issued by their embassy (if they even have an embassy anymore). All this crap over dogs is why we never went to the UK or Scandinavia in the first place. It pisses me off.

December 20, 1967, JoAnne again
Bill got visas for Nepal and an application blank for an *East Pakistan* Road Permit.

Re: East Pakistan, West Pakistan, and Bengal

Under the British, on the subcontinent there was only India. Bengal was one of India's ancient kingdoms or princely states. After World War II, in preparation for India's partition upon independence, the British split Bengal into East Bengal and West Bengal, along religious lines. Predominantly Muslim East Bengal was renamed "East Pakistan" when it became the eastern unit of the newly created Islamic nation of Pakistan. Also created at that time was a western unit called "West Pakistan," which was cobbled together out of the former Indian states of Punjab, Kashmir, and Sind. Together, these two isolated units were supposed to make up the newly created nation of Pakistan. The problem was, they were a thousand miles apart, both geographically and psychologically. This was the situation when we were in West Pakistan in 1967 and in India in 1968. As they did in the Middle East and in Africa, the British loved to cut and paste.

After independence, West Bengal remained part of India. The city of Calcutta is in West Bengal. With its eleven million inhabitants, Calcutta is India's largest city and one of the largest cities in the world. Reassembly of the Indian subcontinent continued after we left there in 1968. East Pakistan and West Pakistan had little in common other than religion, and in 1970, in order to promote its interest in having a weaker Pakistan, India fostered East Pakistani dissidents in a revolt for independence. Thus, a new country was born out of the former East Pakistan, which had formerly been East Bengal, which had formerly been part of the British colony of India, which had formerly been independent and ruled by Muslim governors. The name of this latest British invention is Bangladesh.

When we were in India we planned to go on to East Pakistan, but we never made it—I don't remember why. I think it had something to do with the heat and the trots.

JoAnne's Notes from New Delhi Continued:

December 20, 1967

Went to Shri Lakshmmarayan temple with its magnificent orange, pink, yellow and white Hindu pagodas. The statues are gaudily dressed, especially Kali, who had live sparrows hopping about her shrine. There is a lovely white Buddha in the main temple and a gorgeous gold Buddha in a temple all its own. There is a wealth of animal statues, including monkeys, cobras, and elephants, elephants, elephants. Their heads are on the capitals of the columns, some of them docile, some of them proud. Two of them are fiercely angry. Panels of pastel paintings in black and ivory run along the ceilings. Numerous inscriptions of Hindu religious tenets in English as well as in Hindi. Bill was impressed by all the swastikas and by the explanations of how, over the centuries, they have become the symbol of the Aryan race. Inside the temple, it says, the written Aryan languages of Greek, Hindi, Chinese and Sanskrit were formed from the swastika. Also inside the temple grounds: a marvelously surrealistic park-playground where the three of us could walk into the jaws of a brightly painted tiger and between the paws of an equally brightly painted lion. Huge pink and white elephant sculptures guard the entrance. In the fountains and along the walks are representations of rhinos, stags, camels and cobras. We, alas, were barefoot, so Zerky couldn't run around. Upon leaving the temple we encountered a pathetic little dancing monkey and a snake charmer, who tried to force us into watching his mongoose kill an over-drugged snake. I refused.

Bill forgot to write about our visit to the circus yesterday. On our way to check out Old Delhi, we stumbled across one and impulsively decided to take Zerk—and ourselves—to it. For the first half-hour, Zerky was fascinated by the procession of animals, especially by the elephants, but also by the tiger, the lion tamer, and the acrobats. Bill was fascinated by the double-jointed female acrobat, and by all the positions he could fantasize getting her into. His erotic reverie was brought to a close when Zerky wet his pants on Daddy's lap. Afterward Zerk divided his attention alternately between the performers and the chocolate bar held by the sixteen-month-old girl seated next to him. He didn't even notice the man who let an elephant walk over his chest, and it took a bear riding a noisy motorcycle to return his eyes to the ring. When our excuse for going to the circus finally fell asleep, we decided to leave. Indian circus performers don't seem to have a sense of timing, drama, or plain-old show-biz razzmatazz. Their production was very flat.

Women's Clothing in New Delhi

1) The incomparable Sari.

2) A sophisticated version of "pajamas" like the ones worn in Pakistan and in the Indian countryside.

3) Gypsy full skirts. With scarves and ankle bangles.

Men's Clothing in New Delhi

1) Western-style dress clothes, with or without beard and turban.

2) Pajama tops with loose white trousers or *dhotis.*

3) Rags.

Overall, the people here are the best-dressed we have ever seen, Paris not excluded.

Traffic in New Delhi

1) Foot traffic, including people on foot carrying people in chairs.

2) Bicycles—Bill hit one with his side mirror.

3) Scooters, including scooter-drawn and bicycle-drawn cabs.

4) A few motorcycles driven by very brave men who hog the center line.

5) Dogs, cats, burros and, of course, sacred cows. With or without carts.

6) Slowest of all: oxen and water buffalo. Faster are camels, asses, donkeys, ponies and horses. Saw a bear today.

7) Buses and trucks, often without taillights or reflectors, and with burned-out headlights. This, along with all the bikes and carts that don't have lights at all, makes driving at night a fool's game.

8) Cars driving fast, honking their horns constantly. They pass on the right or on the left, over or inside of the center-line.

Ambassador Bowles is conducting a campaign at the U.S. Embassy "to make U.S. drivers the safest in India." His posters instruct embassy employees to "Give camels, water buffalo, bikes, cows, three-wheel cabs, horses, buses and cars the right of way."

It's Christmas season where we come from. I offered a hot buttered rum to our room bearer, who brought us the butter and sugar. "Will you join us for a Christmas drink?" Bill played the guitar for him. A 750-ml bottle of rum costs approximately 35 rupees—roughly a third of a month's salary of 50 to 100 rupees per month. In other words, alcohol is prohibitive for most Indians, because of its price. A few states are dry.

Forgot to mention: At the circus the other day, we saw an Indian Indian dressed-up like an American Indian—feathered headdress and all!

December 21, 1967

No dice getting diapers, milk or dog food at the American Embassy. Paper diapers and unsweetened condensed milk appear to be impossible to find.

Zerky had a good play with some Indian kids staying in the room below us. He was shy but eventually managed to overcome. We hope it is just a stage.

The newspaper reports more student-led riots in Calcutta, this time over the dismissal of some government officials. There are also riots in Uttar Pradesh, over the official languages bill.

December 22, 1967

Bill got road permit for East Pakistan. Also permission from India's Ministry of Foreign Affairs to visit Sikkim. For three days only.

Cleaned out the car today. Bill threw a bunch of garbage out onto a field, where it was snapped up by an eagle-eyed youth as soon as it hit the ground. He ran off with some shriveled-up oranges, two empty motor-oil cans, a plastic diaper bag and some empty baby-food jars. Earlier we saw a man picking soggy lettuce off a garbage heap. Ugh.

Zerky has made friends with a gang of Indian kids staying in our hotel. The oldest boy uses him as an excuse to play with Tarzan and, since Zerk is no longer the least bit shy, our little son is now very popular. The children of two of the mothers with caste marks are very well dressed and appear to have been very well brought up. The two families with children nearest Zerky's age, however, are of lower caste, I suspect. They are more poorly dressed and not so combed and clean. Their attitude toward Zerky is interesting: whereas the higher-caste kids treat him as an equal, these are shy. They take no liberties with him. But they are fascinated with his pale skin and fair hair, which they love to fondle. The oldest boy chased one of the younger children with Tarzan—laughing because the little one was crying out of fear of our dog. Tomorrow we leave.

December 23, 1967:

Left New Delhi in a light rain, which increased as we traveled south. After about six hours, the countryside turned into a morass. Everything is flat here, and there doesn't seem to be anywhere for rainwater to drain. It just collects on the road, which is barely higher than the surrounding countryside. Everywhere there is mud. If this can happen in a few hours during dry season, what must it be like during the monsoon?

Our room bearer's name is John Roberts. He is a Christian. He makes 112 rupees per month—$15.00 exactly, at the official rate. Forty-five rupees of it goes for upkeep of his younger sister—they are refugees from West Pakistan who came to India in 1947, at the time of partition. John is looking for a sponsor to emigrate to just about anywhere. He gave me three roses upon our departure.

JoAnne's take on the Taj Mahal

December 24, 1967

Sixteen outer walls and sixteen smaller sides surround the tomb. Standing in one room you can see two rooms to the right, two to the left, the tomb room, and the room beyond it, plus the view outside. With the aid of semi-translucent marble, this creates a feeling of being in a hall of mirrors without there being any mirrors. The effect is heightened by optical illusional patterns in some of the tile work on the columns, by the pools of water on three sides of the Taj, and by the river on its fourth side. The only colored ornamentations are a few simple floral

Zerky at the Taj Mahal

designs. So effective is all the white marble, that it makes the surrounding red sandstone buildings look garish. The landscaping of the Taj was done by people who understood show business. They knew how to wow an audience. You do not see much of the Taj until you step through the gated openings in the walls, and then, Whammo! That magnificent profile silhouetted against the sky!

Bravo!

Ghara, a bird sanctuary, is also near Agra. Along the road today we saw a fantastic variety of birds. With the omnipresent vultures and ravens, were some wonderful green birds of the brightest hue. There was also a gorgeous raven-sized, turquoise-feathered bird. Many sandpiper types. Some waterfowl with delicate pink-tinged wings and absurd long yellow bills. A funny limping bird. Fat grey quail-like birds. In Switzerland I collected wildflowers; here I shall collect birds.

JoAnne's Diary, Continued:

December 24, 1967

That "vulcanized" tubeless tire is leaking again. Bill finally had a wrong-sized tube put in it, in the bazaar, near the Red Fort.

On our way to Shivpuri National Park in the rain, we came across a truck lying on its side diagonally across the road. Nobody around. Don't know what happened.

The tilled countryside has gradually turned into a jungle-like mixture of underbrush, vines, thick-leaved bushes, and trees. In addition, the English language signs—our guideposts along the road—are more and more frequently covered over with paper, or painted out entirely. The Hindus want Hindi, rather than English, to be India's sole official language. There are riots going on in Lucknow over this, riots in which cars, trucks and buses bearing English language numbers are being burned. Car owners are covering their license plates with cardboard on which crude Hindi numbers have been hand-painted. In Madras, however, they are having riots protesting the use of Hindi. Most of the riots are in Calcutta, however, which appears to be the riot capital of the world.

Despite a lack of signs, we finally managed to find the DAK bungalow at Shivpuri National Park, where we have arranged to see the animals tomorrow at 6:30 AM. We are now settled in our bus and it is Christmas Eve. We gave Zerky a block set, which turned out to be too old for him, and very badly made to boot. Then, just as we had poured ourselves a Merry Christmas drink, he decided to make our silent night a smelly one, with an attack of diarrhea. Not knowing whether it was the tuna for lunch or dysentery, I hastily covered half an Intro-Viaform pill with sugar, told him it was a Christmas plum, and sighed with relief when he took it like a sucker.

We wonder how safe the water is. It comes from an open well and runs continually in the john nearby. The concept of maintenance doesn't seem to exist here in India. How many million leaking faucets might there be in this water-poor country? For lack of a washer a river was lost.

Letter From Shivpuri

Christmas Eve, 1967
Madhya Pradesh
Map 4

Dear Zerky,

You have been in India for a couple of weeks now, having spent most of your time in New Delhi, while I ran around to African Embassies in an attempt to get visas, car permits and Tarzan permits for our trip to Africa. I doubt that is going to work out, however; the multitude of countries in Africa makes planning nearly impossible. Never mind, there is more than enough to keep us happy here in Asia.

Your mother and I both find Hinduism almost incomprehensible. Religion seems to permeate everything here. What I find particularly strange is the strong sense of animalism that seems to pervade India. Invocations of animals are everywhere—they are part of the culture and of the religion. Hindu gods are often depicted in sculptures and paintings as the animals they once were in one or another of their many reincarnations. And those sacred cows of India? They do exist, thousands of them in the capital of New Delhi, wandering in and out among the city's eight million human residents. Cows are everywhere—in the parks, on the boulevards, on the sidewalks and in the streets—snarling traffic as they go. They act like they own the place, and in a way they do—cows always have the right of way, and it's a crime to hit one with a car, no matter how accidentally.

Last week one of the New Delhi newspapers carried a muck-raking exposé about the shameful condition at Bombay International Airport. Bombay International is supposed to be one of the most modern airports in the world, but lately a number of foreign pilots have been complaining about having to dodge cows on the runways during landing and takeoff. Because most of the airlines that have landing rights at Bombay International belong to foreign airlines, most of the pilots are not Hindus, the newspaper points out, and therefore cannot be depended upon to fully appreciate the privileged status of Indian cows.

It seems there once was a fence around the airport that has fallen into disrepair because of a dispute between the airport and the City of Bombay over whose responsibility it is to maintain the fence. Everyone involved, according to the newspaper, finds it a most vexing and wondrous problem. The dispute has been in the courts for many years now, and is being pursued diligently by people on all sides of this contentious issue. The newspaper is on a crusade to have the perplexities resolved once and for all, by the highest appellate court in the land. Meanwhile, newspaper readers all over India are following this trial with utter fascination and infinite patience, as complex legal arguments about culture, identity, history and religion are played out in a Bombay courtroom. Nobody seems to think this problem will be resolved anytime soon.

The cows and bulls of India are handsome beasts. They are of the Brahma bull variety seen in American rodeos. They are slick, white, and strong, with big humps, and large folds of skin dangling beneath their throats. Along the road today we passed many such cows—oxen really—some of them grazing peacefully beside the road, most of them drawing carts. It is a common practice here to dress animals up with jewelry and makeup. Their faces are often dyed with blues and with reds, with the tips of their horns encased in gold or silver caps. Often on top of their heads and between their horns are turban arrangements made out of wrappings of brightly colored cloths. Necklaces and beads often dangle beneath their necks. Makeup is used very liberally in India. Eye shadow is common on children and in the paintings of gods in their animal forms, which are typically very heavily made up in all manner of bright colors. India has a way with color. It is everywhere.

It has been raining here these last few days. It is frightening to see how the countryside seems to disintegrate in the rain. Yesterday we were on the major through-road going from India's capital, New Delhi, to its second largest city, Bombay. After a few days of only moderate rainfall the highway became nearly impassable. We saw where two large trucks traveling in opposite directions had each moved over partly off the pavement, in order to pass each other. The front ends of each were half buried in the bog that in dry weather constitutes opposite shoulders of the road.

Your mother is really enjoying the wildlife here in India. The countryside doesn't appear to be divided into civilized areas and semi-wilderness areas, as is commonly the case in our country. Here you find people living just about everywhere, and sometimes in places where wild animals intermingle with human society. Driving along, your mother has discovered a treasury of wild birds. There must be billions of them: flamingos, cranes, storks, parrots and countless others of all sizes and descriptions. Naturally, she has bought a book and is busy cataloging them all, just as she catalogued the mountain flowers in the Alps. Many of the birds here are as pretty as flowers. They hop from place to place, preening and strutting, and exploding into riots of color when you approach. We have also seen some very beautiful fish. And many orchids.

Yesterday morning we passed a mongoose and an elephant standing in the middle of the road. Later, while we were pulled over beside the road for our periodic liquid refreshment, a monkey wandered up. Tarzan spotted him first, and started going crazy! Snarling and barking, he began chasing the monkey as fast as his pathetic little dachshunds legs could carry him. The monkey, who had long, strong legs, and who was twice Tarzan's size, loped off at first. I'm sure he had never before come across such a noisy, stubby-legged, annoying little creature as Tarzan. Soon the monkey stopped backing off, and as Tarzan closed in for the kill, humped himself up like a cat, and bared his teeth, which were quite formidable. They made an instant impression on our hard-charging little dog and, as Tarzan slammed on his brakes and veered off at close range, the monkey reached out with his long, long arm and took a swipe at poor Tarzan, who yelped but never slowed down. Tail between his legs, he executed an amazing hundred-and-eighty-degree turn and, still going full-throttle, jumped back into the bus, with a thud. The victorious monkey did not bother to pursue his defeated opponent, especially after seeing your mother and me running like the posse to the rescue. Instead, he climbed a tree and sat there hurling profanity and abuse down upon the four of us. Now that Tarzan has been suitably chastised, I doubt he will ever chase monkeys again.

This morning we visited the Taj Mahal, in Agra, which is as lovely as it's cracked up to be. With its three Muslim domes flanked by four lovely minarets—all of them in white marble—the Taj is an architect's dream, a building designed and built for the sheer joy of looking at it. Its rooms are separated only by an open, delicately carved marble latticework. The exterior rooms converge onto a central tomb, like spokes radiating outward from the hub of a wheel. Unfortunately, someone has seen fit to fill the countless holes of the lattices with pieces of glass, in order to try to turn the latticework into a solid wall, which was a truly dumb idea if ever there was one. No doubt this cuts down on the breeze inside, but the glass is impossible to clean, and over the years has become so filthy that it is no longer possible to see through the latticework. This has done much to destroy the lacy openness of the interior. The dirty glass also has the unfortunate effect of cutting down on the interior light, which in turn makes it harder to see the interior of this world's most beautiful building.

The tombs—two of them instead of the one that the building was designed for—lie at the hub of the wheel. Both tombs are fakes; the real ones rest in an identical position inside a small room directly below. This was done so that visitors might pay their respects to the phony tombs above, while the Lady sleeps below, undisturbed. Muslim Empress Arjuman Bano Begum, beloved wife of Emperor Shah Jahan, 1627–1665, fourth in the line of the Mogul Dynasty, died in childbirth. They say the Taj is a monument to love.

Early tomorrow morning we are going to go hunting tigers in Shivpuri, a National Park, not far from where we are camped. Tonight is Christmas Eve. Your mother and I feel a whiff of nostalgia in the air. You, however, feel only the call of nature. The bug has got you and you are celebrating Christendom's most sacred holiday with a bout of diarrhea. Your mother, God bless her, gently cleanses you, with all the love and adoration of a virgin, while your father, convinced he is indeed in a stable, opens all the doors and windows and moves into the front seat of the bus in order to get as far away from you as possible. Your gentle Joseph then spins the dial on the radio, in search of a wayward Christmas carol. Not one. No Hallelujah Chorus, no snow, no pine trees, no jingle bells, only the warm Indian night, the buzz of mosquitoes, and some strange unknown sounds emanating from the forest. They must be elephants! Probably tigers, too! And cobras and worse!

I've got to wind up my hyperbole now, Zerky—it's late and time for bed. We have to be up by 5:30 tomorrow morning, in order to pick up our guide and be out on the game sanctuary at daybreak. That's when the tigers come down to the water hole to drink. But tigers, cobras and elephants are not the only things we are going to protect you from this fine night. One of the Indian tourists staying in the nearby guesthouse tells us that Shivpuri is notorious all over India for its *Dacoits*, a group of bandits who run around kidnapping people. He says not to worry, however; they never kill people, they just hold them for ransom. So tonight as we turn off the light, we are thankful there is nothing to worry about. Our magic boy will protect us in the night. This Christmas has been so rich, Zerky! Our senses are overloaded.

Love,
Dad

From JoAnne's Diary
Christmas Day at Shivpuri and Khajuraho
Map 4

December 25, 1967

Got up 5:00 AM to see the animals come to water. Unfortunately, our guide had so many keys for so many locks that he couldn't find the right one to let us in the proper gate, and we finally had to drive all the way around to the rear entrance. By the time we got to the waterhole, most of the animals had already come and gone. Saw no tigers or leopards, but did see a *cheetrai* (an elk-like deer), gazelles, peacocks, and a beautiful woodpecker. We gave our guide a ten-rupee tip and bade him Merry Christmas.

Upon leaving the rest house this morning, Bill got hit up by what he calls "a hustler." The man wanted a tip because he had cleaned the john. Bill said no. Later, we realized the man had probably provided us with a legitimate service, one that could not be performed by others, because of caste.

The land along the road between Shivpuri and Khajuraho is more jungle-like than the park itself. Saw several wild monkeys along the road. Also a fox and a mongoose. The sun came out. We are now in the state of Madhya Pradesh. Arrived Khajuraho 4:00 PM.

JoAnne's Diary, Continued:

A girl at dinner quizzed me about my comparative impressions of Pakistan and India. She was obviously fishing for me to say something bad about Pakistan. I pleaded ignorance. Justifiably. All three women at dinner were vegetarians—Brahmins smuggling rice back to Bombay.

One of the twenty-two temples at Khajuraho

December 26, 1967

We are a curiosity because we are living in a car, at this lovely Circuit House. We wash up each morning in public, without the help of servants. People think we are eccentric, but they are also quite curious. In this way we have met some interesting neighbors, including a twelve-year-old Indian boy whom Zerky has fallen in love with and who is showing him a wonderful time.

This morning we went to see the famous temples of Khajuraho, twenty-two of them in three groupings. Almost certainly they constitute the world's most extravagant display of erotica. The temples are noted for the way in which their individually sculptured blocks have been fitted together with neither cement nor mortar, thereby forming a three-dimensional jigsaw puzzle. A thousand years old and in extremely good preservation, they contain hundreds or thousands of sculptures ranging from wonderful animals (a marvelous carved boar, a huge bull, hundreds of small elephants, horses, camels, etc.) to lovely gods, goddesses, nymphs, demons, and erotic lovers fondling, feeding and reaching out passionately for one another.

The sculptures depict all the common sexual acts, plus some very uncommon ones that had Bill and me straining in an attempt to figure out which arms, legs, and whatevers belong to which of the you-know-whats. My favorite position has the man standing on his head while two servants are supporting the woman in a buttock-to-buttock union. There is also a bas-relief of a man screwing a horse, which takes one aback because it is exactly at eye level. Homosexuality was not unknown back then, nor was the French 69. Altogether, the temples, with their wealth of unabashed sexuality and imaginative representations of mythical beasts, give one the impression that they must have come from an age of luxurious, talented debauchery.

The nearby Jain temples, although not lacking in erotic sculptures and *aspanas* (dancing girls), show a calmer, more peaceful restraint, one emanating perhaps from the peaceful Buddhas who co-inhabit the Jain shrines. Bill got tired after the first thousand sculptures and sixth flight of stairs, so he and Zerk took a nap in the car while I wandered through the last of the temples alone. The two of them resurfaced, however, in time to see a large statue of Hanuman, the monkey god, painted tomato red.

After seeing the temples, we returned to the Circuit House, where Zerk had a wonderful time with the Dair and Patel children. But for Bill and me, the fun was marred by the behavior of the twelve-year-old Patel boy toward the servant's children. Zerky had brought out his jeep to induce them to play with him, whereupon the Patel boy became very upset and led Zerky back to us by the hand, after having taken the jeep away from the smaller children. One six-year-old youngster, better dressed than the rest, kept courageously coming back to retrieve the jeep, playing with it in front of us, and then taking it a few feet away so that the other children could play with it too. Each time, the Patel boy would take the jeep back again. He explained to us later that his "best toy" had once been stolen by some children like these, and that when his servant brought it back to him, his toy had been ruined.

Zerky at the Temples of Khajuraho

Later that evening the Patels and the Dairs joined us by bringing over a bottle of Johnny Walker. We got to talking about music, then Bill played some flamenco for them. Then Mrs. Dair, who has a lovely trained voice, sang Indian songs for us. Indian music is wonderful!

Then a political discussion about Vietnam:

Mrs. Dair: "We are glad you are there, otherwise all of Southeast Asia would be taken over by China."

Us: "But don't you think that maybe we are interfering in another nation's internal affairs?"

Mrs. Patel: "You must forgive us, India is a very young nation. We think first of our own self-interest. We have been governed by so many other countries for so long."

Mr. Dair: "What's bad for China is good for India."

Mr. Dair has been to America and likes many things about it. But all too often, he says, he finds us to be callous blunderers who are insensitive to the feelings and customs of those we profess to help. Mr. Dair is bitterly anti-Communist. He is rich, but still says the Russians have it all over us because they understand Indians better, and because they have tact. An example he gave us was Kennedy's trip to India when the U.S. State Department instructed Kennedy's entourage not to drink the water. "This was an insult," Mr. Dair explained. "Maybe we don't have good water in some of our villages, but in the cities we do—especially in New Delhi!" Mr. Dair finds Americans to be both "generous and insulting. It's not *what* they do, but *how* they do it," he says. All in all, a most entertaining and interesting evening.

Red-Hot Letter From Khajuraho
Rated X: 18 Years of Age and Over

December 27, 1967
Khajuraho
Madhya Pradesh
Map 4

Dear Zerky,

Khajuraho is where all the dirty statues are. In the United States, you can sometimes find pictures of them in expensive editions of the *Kama Sutra*. The temples at Khajuraho—all twenty-two of them—are a veritable cornucopia of perversion. Couples, triples, quadruples, and more, are depicted in countless acts of—as your mother so delicately puts it—"fondling, feeding and fucking." One's eyes ache after an hour of trying to disentangle all the limbs, in the course of trying to figure out who's doing what to whom. The place has been designated a national monument.

Ever since the movies were invented, there has been an ongoing cry in America to do something about the deleterious effects of pornography on adults and minors. The U.S. government should send a team of scientists here to study the long-term effects of pornography on the citizens of Khajuraho. For a thousand years now, these obscene temples have stood on the perimeter of Khajuraho village. More than fifty generations of children have grown up here using these temples as their playground. Not a single one of them has ever gone to Disneyland. In America, were you to show a child one of the postcards they sell in the kiosk here, you would be arrested. To the casual tourist, the people of this village might appear normal, but who knows what goes on behind grass walls in this village at night? Why hasn't the Indian government dynamited these obscene temples instead of going into the smut-peddling business and promoting them worldwide to tourists? Some of the tourists here are children and—and while I'm at it, Zerky, maybe they ought to study you too, you spent the better part of today wandering around in this paradise of perversion.

Tonight we are staying at a beautiful PWD Tourist Bungalow located right across the road from the main complex of temples. Because there are no campgrounds east of Tehran, these "PWD Bungalows," "Tourist Bungalows," "Inspection Bungalows," "DAK Bungalows," "Rest Houses" and "Circuit Houses," as they are variously called, have been a godsend. Until we arrived in India, the absence of campgrounds had created few serious problems, because most of the Middle East is very sparsely populated. With a little imagination, we always managed to find some nook or cranny to hide in for the night. But it's a different story here in India; I doubt there's a spot in the entire country that doesn't have people on it. As soon as we stop the car, even for a minute, we are quickly surrounded by a crowd that, so far as we can tell, gathers for no other reason than to satisfy their curiosity.

In this land without time, such concepts as "keeping busy" and "minding your own business" don't seem to exist. Too often we feel trapped in a fish bowl, with everyone staring at us. So we are very thankful for these PWD (Public Works Department) Bungalows. They are a godsend, even if we don't know which god sent them. Certainly not Shiva the Destroyer, or the black Kali, his terrifying wife. Maybe Brahma the Creator or Vishnu the Preserver, or Allah, or Buddha, or Jesus, or God knows who. All these friggin' people are getting on my nerves!

PWD Bungalows typically have a fenced-off section where the caretakers *(chowkidars)* will often allow us to park for the night and make use of "the sanitary facilities." Always, after a day of crowds, we crave privacy, and if it were not for these bungalows, I don't know what we would do. Back in colonial times, this network of bungalows was built by the British to house their traveling administrators. The European conquerors had an interesting problem on their hands. Because of their pasty white skins, there was a certain logic behind putting the British at the top of the caste system. Caste is a very complicated thing; your mother and I don't pretend to understand it. It has become apparent to us, however, that caste tends to fall along skin-color lines.

Along with the benefits that usually accrue to lighter-skinned Indians, who tend to be further up on the social and economic scales, there are also attendant obligations and restrictions. Certain actions are forbidden to higher caste Indians because some things are viewed as being "unclean." Having a relationships with lower caste people is one of these unclean things. So if you were a British administrator back in the good old days, traveling around this vast country in order to let people know who's in charge, you had a problem on your hands. Where were you going to stay at night when you were showing the flag in some place with no hotels? Going native with lower caste villagers was not an option, because making yourself dependent on people below you would undermine your authority.

This Public Works Department-Inspection Bungalow-Circuit House-Rest House network was the answer. It allowed the British—and later on their high-caste Indian cohorts—to travel the Indian countryside without losing face. Finally, when independence came at the end of World War II, the new Indian administrators knew better how to swim in its complicated social quagmire. Accordingly, there was less need for the far-flung bungalow network. Gradually, the bungalows fell into disuse and disrepair, until finally a new government began allowing them to be used as a substitute for an almost nonexistent Western-style tourist hotel industry. Often these bungalows are only the simplest of cabins, but in comparison with the mud and grass huts of the villagers, they are luxurious. They have chairs, tables, and beds, and—most important of all if you are a Westerner with diarrhea—toilets!

Being a curiosity sometimes has its advantages: it helps us meet people. The other tourists here (mostly well-to-do Indians) keep asking us questions. It appears they have never seen anybody living in a car. Who are we, why are we doing such a thing, what is this strange vehicle we appear to be living in? Virtually all upper-class Indians speak English, and twice now since arriving at Khajuraho we have been invited to dinner and treated as guests of honor. They all want to know our impressions of India. After having been cut off by the language barrier for so long, this is a great relief. In the villages, children often delight in using us to try out the English they have been learning in school.

But of course, it's only wealthy, educated Indians that one finds touring India by private car, and staying in PWD Bungalows. Last night two couples who were having dinner together invited us to join them. One is from Bombay—he, the chief photographer for *The Times of India* (probably India's best newspaper), and his wife, an artist. With them was an oil company executive and his wife, who is a nuclear physicist. All four of them have traveled the world extensively, so this made for a very interesting evening; we now have an invitation to stay with the photographer and his wife when we visit Bombay. Since they are wealthy, we have no hesitation about doing so. We look forward to looking them up when and if we get there. Our route is currently uncertain—we are thinking about going to southern India, too, but are worried about the heat. People tell us India is very different in the South.

We have also been seeing quite a bit of a second Indian family, the Patels. They lived most of their lives in Kenya, but were recently forced to return to India due to the new Kenyan government's "Africa for Africans" policy. You have taken a liking to the Patels' twelve-year-old son; you want to follow him everywhere. He in turn has taken it upon himself to act as your protector, and the two of you are becoming inseparable. I think he derives status from running around with you.

Almost everyone here has servants, except for the very poor. Labor is unbelievably cheap. Not only do servants make one's life easier, they also contribute to one's status. It appears not to be acceptable for upper-caste people to perform menial tasks for themselves. That sort of prohibition works out very oddly sometimes. Both of our upper-class dinner-host families have taken a shine to us, and all of them, especially the men, are fascinated by our camper. They keep asking us questions about it.

Yesterday I was on my back underneath the car, changing the oil, when Mr. Patel came over to chat, and to see what I was doing. When I crawled out from underneath the bus, he started peppering me with questions about car maintenance. Since he seemed very interested in such stuff, when I opened up the engine cowling to put the new oil in, I motioned him to come over and take a look at the engine. Getting the cap off the oil can and positioning the spout just right for the pouring never seems to work out very well for me, and by the time I was finished I had oil all over my shirt. Mr. Patel sat there watching me get oilier and dirtier, all the while asking silly questions I was sure he knew the answers to. I figured he was testing me.

Then he started asking me statistical questions about the car's performance. It could do *what to what* in how many seconds? That sort of thing. I had no idea. Then he started asking me how it handled. How did it corner in tight turns? I told him it was not a Ferrari, just a tin box on wheels, but that it did a good job of getting us from there to here. I was about to offer to let him take the van out for a spin, when he said something that hauled me up short.

I suddenly realized I was talking to a man who could not drive. He had a driver to do that. A man of his status is not allowed to drive his car, in India—that's what chauffeurs are for. Driving would be crossing a caste line. Here was a rich and powerful man, with a passion for cars, who was envious of some dirty guy in a VW hippie-bus. He wanted to crawl under his car, too, and get all down and dirty like me. Then he would have liked to take his car out by himself, and push it to the limit. But he would never be able to do that; his caste and culture had him in its ugly grip. It's not only the poor and the untouchable who suffer from this archaic custom, I suddenly realized. I was no longer mad at him for how he had raised his son. I felt sorry for them both.

I think I now have Mr. Patel very confused. Every morning your mother and I go through our household-chore routine. While she takes care of you and gets you squared away for the day, I do just about everything else. This includes sweeping out the car and doing the dishes. Mr. Patel is having trouble handling this. He just can't seem to accept the idea that a person of obvious wealth—and a man at that—could demean himself—in public—by performing such menial tasks. Twice he has offered to lend me one of his servants. Both times I tried to explain why I prefer doing things myself. But I don't think he understands what I am trying to tell him: that in America we take pride in independence and being able to take care of ourselves. Your mother and I are an affront to Indian social standards. Even though I like Mr. Patel, I must admit that I considerably enjoy his consternation.

We have met some other interesting people staying here in the Tourist Bungalow. There is a Polish couple with the Polish Embassy in New Delhi—the woman is nuts about Tarzan. Every time she sees him, she starts cooing endearments in Polish. She keeps calling him *shpitzie* or something like that. I think she's homesick. Then there's the *shikar* man. He is, or once was, German, having been interned in India by the British during World War II. When the war was over, there wasn't anything for him to go home to, he told us, so he has been here ever since. He has become addicted to the *shikar*. In America we call it "hunting." Year after year he drives his old La Salle all over India, searching for tigers, leopards, *cheetrai*, and *nelgai*—those latter two being a large species of Indian deer or elk. I doubt he has ever shot much of anything.

All in all, we are very much enjoying India. We plan to stick around here for a couple more days, and will then be heading for the Himalayas.

Love,
Dad

From JoAnne's Diary
Benares
Map 4

December 27, 1967

After many goodbyes in the rain, we left Khajuraho this morning. Less than an hour out, we slipped off the road while passing some water buffalo, and became stuck in the mud. Soon some kind Indian tourists stopped, then a whole busload of people, and finally our German shikar friend from Khajuraho. Together they all got us pushed up onto the road, and then, after some excellent advice about driving more slowly in the rain, we were off again.

Arrived late in Benares, where we finally found a tourist bungalow, and then, after having paid an "advance" totaling more than our anticipated bill, we had an excellent fourteen-rupee dinner and went to bed. Hit 20,000 miles on the speedometer!

December 28, 1967

LIFE IN THE STREETS OF BENARES: Eating, sleeping, working, shitting, pissing, and standing around. Cows, goats, horses, donkeys, monkeys, camels, hippies, dogs, chickens, pigs, mice. Brahma bulls. Narrow twisting streets studded with shrines built into the buildings. Kids playing in a coal heap. Hotels for pilgrims.

LIFE ALONG THE GHATS: Boats, bathers, yogis, fakirs with painted faces. Men selling colored paints and powders. Women washing clothes. Lepers. Kids with kites. Hawkers selling tourist junk. Naked men in loincloths. Drums, performers, holy men chanting. Kids jumping around through hoops. A goat ran off with a man's loincloth. An old woman asked us to come smoke dope with the hippies on her houseboat. Beggars and twisted trees.

Letter From Benares

December 29, 1967
Varanasi (Benares)
India
Map 4

Dear Zerky,

Benares blows your mind. Yesterday, walking down the street we passed a man with two heads; it didn't register immediately because there were too many other weird things going on. By the time I realized what I thought I had seen, and turned around in amazement, my two-headed phantom had vanished into the crowd. Benares is very disorienting; anything is possible here.

Wandering around in the warren of narrow streets today, we were nearly run over by a funeral procession. Four men carrying a corpse on a stretcher-like apparatus, draped in pink and purple satin, with bells, rounded a corner suddenly, jogging along to the rhythm of a drummer and to the bells. To the sound of the beat, all five of them were chanting a repetitive three-note melodic phrase. The procession moved rapidly through the crowd, which paid little attention—except for us. Noting it was headed towards the river, it was not without some apprehension that I picked you up and the three of us gave chase to a rapidly disappearing corpse. Our pursuit led us down to the ghats, a series of huge concrete steps going down into the Ganges. The ghats are the center of religious activity here in this holiest of Hindu cities. It is the ambition of many Hindus to be cremated here, and to have their ashes turned over to Ganga, the river goddess, who is the daughter of Himalaya, the mountain god. Both geographically and in terms of ancestral descent, the Ganges flows downwards from the top. Upon reaching the river, we were met with the following scene:

Burning on the riverbank, at the base of a cluster of Hindu temples, are several fires being fed from small piles of neatly stacked logs. There is an unlit fire waiting, with a structure of logs piled up in such a way as to leave little doubt as to its purpose. We are about to witness a cremation. With both fear and fascination we watch the ceremony unfold.

The bearers first lower the stretcher and place it beside the river. Two men remove the body from beneath its satin covering. It has been wrapped in a plain white cotton shroud and garlanded with fresh marigolds. Two of the bearers wade into the Ganges, and then, to the accompaniment of much prayer and ritual, they submerge the body, before laying it out on the sand. Except for the bearers, a priest, and ourselves, no one appears to be paying attention to what is happening here. Children run back and forth, playing games, and skillfully manipulating the strings of brightly colored kites that are darting and diving in the sky, in joyous abandon. Vendors hawk their wares to pilgrims. One approaches and tries to sell us on the idea of taking snapshots at five rupees each. I tell him no, we have our own camera. (I wish I had brought it.)

Along the ghats, old men are passing the time of day as they must have passed many a day: standing around in small groups, chatting. A few starving dogs pick their way in and out among the crowd, tails drooping, noses to the ground, looking for something to eat. A few white cows wander about, as contentedly as Elsie the Borden Cow, or as those Carnation cows. "Let's call them 'The Cremation Cows,'" I say to JoAnne. One ambles over to the corpse and proceeds to eat off the garlands. Is this part of the ritual?

In due time, and to the accompaniment of Indian drums and Scottish bagpipes, the still-shrouded body is hoisted atop the pyre and a salve rubbed ceremoniously over its head, face, and limbs. A brightly colored powder is then sprinkled on the corpse, to the accompaniment of more prayers and drums. Additional wood is then placed on top of the body, and then a priest—naked to the waist, except for a cord around his neck—bestows the traditional rituals. Collecting a small bundle, of dried reeds in one hand, he places a hot coal in the end of his bundle and gently waves it back and forth over the body, all the while chanting a prayer. Soon the smoking bundle leaps into flame. With his torch, he now ignites the pyre, which takes a half-hour to become fully involved in flame. Because the body was bathed in the river immediately prior to its cremation, we are spared the sight of the shroud quickly burning off.

Waiting for the corpse to be consumed, we begin to study the other fires. Various pyres are in various stages of cremation. Look over there. See? That one is nearly burned out. An ancient man—or is he a woman?—bent, toothless and shriveled, is sifting through a pile of hot ashes with a green wooden pole, picking out the last of the smoldering coals and placing them methodically into an earthen jar. They are the remains of someone who has just been cremated, someone whose ashes are soon to be sprinkled upon the Ganges, along with the ashes of all the other pyres. Each has its own stone pot and man in attendance, a man with a badge, his green wooden pole. They are collecting the souls of men about to be delivered over unto the river goddess. Look there. See that man using his pole to break up the remains of a body, in order to make it burn more efficiently? Now he's taking two-pound chunks of smoking carcass on the end of his pole and restacking them over still-flaming logs, so that they may be further reduced to ash.

At Benares, such cremations go on daily; we watch for another half-hour as two more corpses are delivered to the river in processions like the one we followed. Both are dipped into the river, and then the cycle begins again. Or ends, depending on how you look at death. We have just witnessed a drop in a river of cremations that has been flowing into the Ganges since the beginnings of Hinduism in a past more ancient than there are records. As always, life and death at the ghats goes on. Sacred cows wander unmolested through sweet grey smoke. From time to time a dog makes off with a still-smoking tidbit that appears to be a dog's due. "So that's why they call them 'pariah dogs,'" JoAnne exclaims.

Here at the Benares ghats, we are just two tourists and a child, watching the living lay the dead to rest. It's business as usual. No bereaved families, no tear-stained wives, no confused daughters, sons or husbands. As far as I could tell, Zerky, there were no next of kin there at all that day. No *American Way of Death*.

Death is no mystery at Benares. That fragile old man so painstakingly collecting remains in earthen jars—surely he must know that he, too, will soon be in one of those jars; that thought cannot have escaped him. And those children who are more interested in kites than in cremations: will not they grow up with a better understanding of their own mortality? In 1951, the average lifespan in India was twenty-seven years. In a country historically racked by disease and famine, your humbled father finds it comforting to have witnessed the Indian way of death.

Lovingly,
Your Dad

From JoAnne's Diary
Patna and Bihar to Nepal
Maps 4 & 5

December 29, 1967

Drove from Varanasi (Benares) to Patna today. Slowest going yet. Crowded narrow roads. Countryside tropical. Thatched huts. Rice paddies, palm trees, green tea.

This morning we pulled off the road to give Tarzan his worming medicine. As soon as we let him out of the car, he dashed off—this time after a little red-faced monkey. Tarzan will never learn. The monkey leapt into a tree and started chewing on a stick, whereupon Zerky, taking it all in, started imitating the little monkey by chewing on his own stick, a piece of sugar cane given to him by an Indian farmer. Tarzan finally lost interest in the monkey, and started sniffing around elsewhere.

Then the little monkey came down out of the tree and headed up the road, whereupon Tarzan gave chase once more. But this time the little monkey turned on him, and poor Tarzan was flabbergasted. How humiliating it must be for a dog to be chased by a monkey! I soon discovered the reason for the monkey's display of courage: in a nearby tree were two more monkeys, each of them with a tiny baby. When I approached, one of the mothers popped her baby onto her back and got ready to flee. The other one held her baby close to her chest, protecting him from our dumb dog.

Today on the road we met our first elephant. Yes, elephants do get the right-of-way, from us at least. Ambassador Bowles would be proud of us. Later on we saw two more elephants, one of them a baby with white flowers painted on its face and ears.

We passed a slow-moving, narrow-gauge train today, with people hanging outside onto all the doors and windows.

The DAK Bungalow is full tonight, so we don't have a john. A short while ago the Chowkidar grandly proclaimed to us: "The District Director of the Subdivisional Circuit so desires that you move this conveyance from the front of the premises." We call this "India-speak"—a combination of imitation, obfuscation, and lack of expertise in English. Translation: "The boss says to get your damn car off his front lawn!"

We have found a hotel with a restaurant nearby for tonight's dinner and piddle and for tomorrow's breakfast and shiddle. Dinner for two costs ten and a half rupees ($1.40 US).

Entered the state of Bihar. Later on we were passed by a man we had met in Tehran, who had hooked up with some Germans we had met in Tabriz. None of them knew about PWD Rest Houses, DAK Bungalows, Tourist Bungalows, or Circuit Houses, and had been sweating it out night after night.

The Ganges is immense. No bridge, no ferry, just some rickety junks.

December 30, 1967

We are in Patna, where we have been investigating the ferry. The stationmaster tells us it is impossible to take our car on his ferry, which is really a dilapidated junk. Looking for a bigger boat, we came across a clergyman who has been living in India for seventeen years. "Don't judge India by Bihar," he told us,

"Bihar is exceptionally poor." He advised us not to put our car on any of the boats around here—we would not be the first to end up at the bottom of the Ganges. So we drove back downriver to a bridge sixty miles south of Patna, and then sixty miles north again, just to get to the other side of the river. The going on the first half of this unplanned-for detour was extremely slow—much traffic, bad road, flat tire. A horseshoe punctured the rear one and somehow got caught inside, where it clunked around angrily and raised hell with the tube. Once across the river, however, we ran into our best road in India to date. Since the 1962 incursion into India by the Chinese Army, the Indian government has put in place a strategic new network of roads to enable it to better defend itself against a second attack. I think today was the first time our car has been in high gear since we left Benares three days ago.

Excited at the prospect of making such good time, we decided to drive late, still hoping to make New Year's Eve in Katmandu. We arrived at the Nepal border about 9:30 PM and considered crossing into Nepal, but the border guard told us that all travelers must be off the road and "settled" by 10:00 PM. So tonight we are staying at a DAK Bungalow in Raxaul, still in India.

December 31, 1967

The road we are on is named the "Tribhuban Raj Path." Steep, spectacular, and beautiful. We are excited. From the pass today we had our first view of the high Himalayan Range—a vast panorama of all the major peaks, including Mount Everest. Now it's downhill all the way to Katmandu.

Met an Australian on a motorcycle, whom we had previously met in Tehran.

Nepal

········· By car

---- ➤ By airplane

------ On foot

Letter From the Himalayas

New Year's Eve 1967
On the Road to Katmandu
Maps 4 & 5

Dear Zerky,

It's New Year's Eve and we are alone at last in the mountains. We have pulled off the road into a clearing, where we are going to spend the night. In the hour it has taken your mother to prepare dinner, only two trucks and a barefoot villager have passed by, on the road. Neither of them stopped. What a relief it is to be free from the crush. We have been in Nepal for only a few hours now, and already we love it.

Today in the car, reflecting back upon India, I tentatively reached the conclusion that the lack of privacy there is not simply a matter of population; I doubt the concept of privacy even exists in India. People there seemed to think it rude to ignore us and even ruder yet to leave us once contact has been established. This felt very strange at first—in the rest houses and bungalows we found it necessary to actively dismiss people. In the end we learned to just tell them to leave. Otherwise, we feared, they might move in with us permanently. It feels rude to tell people, "Go away," but as far as we could tell, we never bruised anybody's feelings.

Taking leave is a complicated thing in India. Everything is complicated in India; you don't get much feedback. It's hard to know what people are thinking. And here I always thought it was the Chinese who were supposed to be so inscrutable!

Benares has left us drained. After leaving there, we spent the next couple of days driving along the Ganges through the state of Bihar, probably the poorest and most heavily populated area in India. The Ganges draws people like flypaper. I suppose that's because it's so sacred, and because of all the fertility and death the Ganges bestows. Each summer, the wettest winds in the world blow in off the tropical Indian Ocean, to be blocked by the highest mountain range in the world. Here on its southern slope, most of the wetness falls as rain, and eventually finds its way back into the Indian Ocean via the meandering Ganges and Brahmaputra Rivers. Once these two giants leave the mountains, however, there is little to contain them. Each year, with the coming of the monsoon, they overflow their banks and turn the land in all directions into a shallow inland sea. People are often drowned in numbers that seem incomprehensible to us in the West.

And then each year, as the rivers recede, having laid down a fresh layer of silt, the living return once again to the fertile killing fields of the river goddess. Driving along the Ganges these last few days, I have been reflecting upon how it is that some of the most dangerous places on earth are the ones where people most like to live. The Indian government is currently working on an immense flood-control project meant to contain the mighty Ganges, but the forces of nature at work here are a match for even the most industrially developed of nations.

We ended up making the ultimate mistake in India: being in a hurry. We had hoped to spend Christmas in Katmandu, with the hippies, but when bad roads and the lack of a bridge at Patna made this impossible, we decided to make it New Year's Eve instead, which also turned out to be a bad idea because of all the people on the road. Your mother is terrified that I'm going to run over somebody and, indeed, that would be an easy thing to do. In India, pedestrians are not quick to leave the center of the road when cars approach. Many appear to be walking in a daze. Perhaps it is only indifference, or perhaps meditation, but sometimes I suspect this apparent lack of alertness has more to do with protein deficiency. Or maybe enlightenment. Contrary to widespread belief, starvation is uncommon in India. But in Bihar, potbellied kids still betray widespread malnutrition.

This morning we crossed into Nepal from the Indian border town of Raxaul. Beyond the Raxaul-Birgunj border crossing, virtually all traffic disappears. A sign bearing an American flag informs us that the first forty-seven miles of this road have been built with US AID funds. It slopes gently upward. Soon we are up off the Indian plain. A tangle of jungle begins to close in upon us from both sides. For the first time since Afghanistan, there is no one around. Hurray!

We are now in the *Terai*, a narrow band of dense forest at the foot of the Himalayas, separating the mountains from the Gangeatic Plain. The Terai is one of Asia's most extensive—and last—habitats for big game. Elephants, rhinos, buffalo, leopards and tigers run wild in this tropical rainforest. After another ten miles or so, the hills begin to close in on us. We are now headed up a canyon. Within minutes the road becomes a narrow sliver of asphalt, twisting its way ever higher. We are on the only substantial road in Nepal, which runs 138 miles to connect the capital of perhaps Asia's most undeveloped country with the outside world.

Now our road is no longer the work of Americans. This section was built by the Indians, who put up their own sign. The difference between these two sections of road reflects the different outlooks of the two cultures that created them. Whereas we Americans blasted out immense portions of earth in order to carve out, shore up, and build up a roadbed, the Indian engineers tried very carefully to carve their section of road into the existing nooks and crannies of the mountainsides, in accordance with the contours of the cliffs—so what if top speed is only fifteen miles an hour around continuous curves? Time is India's biggest commodity.

Continuing our climb higher, we pass several Nepali road crews improving new sections of existing road. Entire families are seated cross-legged on the road's surface, working. Each family member has a small metal hammer and is breaking larger stones into smaller stones. The smaller stones are then carefully pieced together so as to create a roadbed made of thousands of integrated rocks. Tons of gravel being made by hand. Could not the Nepali government have wrangled a rock crusher out of the rich Americans? But that would have put these Nepalis out of work. Their government is providing them with employment in a country without industries.

Our camper claws its way upward, in and out of more twisting canyons. We climb over a succession of forested ridges, each of them higher than the last. In a few hours we reach the top, where a sign announces we are at Simbhanjyang, a pass at an altitude of 8,200 feet. There is snow on the ground. The Himalayas at last!

Roughly speaking, the Himalayas of Nepal are divided into two more-or-less parallel mountain chains running east and west, fifty to a hundred miles apart. To the north, the inner Himalayan Range corresponds roughly to Nepal's border with Tibet. To the south, insulating the inner Himalaya from the Gangeatic Plain, runs a lesser parallel range, its peaks rising to around 15,000 feet. This is the range we are now crossing, and the view is fabulous! In front of us, beyond valleys and ridges, the horizon is formed by a glittering crescendo of glaciers and peaks culminating in Mount Everest, at 28,756 feet, the highest mountain in the world. Beyond Everest we can see the Tibetan Plain—the "Roof of the World." Our guidebook has a diagram profiling the Himalayan crests. All the major peaks are out of the clouds today: Dhaulagiri, Annapurna, Manaslu, Cho Oyu, Nuptse, Lhotse, Makalu, Kanchenjunga. Scarcely able to contain myself, I get back in the car and we continue on until shortly before nightfall.

What a relief it is not to have to be continually looking for rest houses and bungalows. Here we can stop almost anywhere, to spend the night. Tonight our clearing has all the makings of a first-class wilderness campground: quiet, scenic, and private. This afternoon, when our car started twisting its way through the mountains, Tarzan got so excited that we had to pull over to let him run. Tonight he is in heaven, scampering around in the brush, chasing who knows what? India was rough on him. Almost never did he have a chance to run loose, and he's making up for it now.

So here we are in the Himalayas, Zerky, on New Year's Eve. We never did make it to Katmandu, but instead we have our own private mountain stream flowing by, and our own private van, in which we are celebrating New Year's Eve with cupfuls of pure, cold, mountain water. For the first time in months, we no longer have to put iodine in our water tank. I think we shall be spending much time in Nepal!

Love,
Dad

From JoAnne's Diary
Katmandu
Maps 4 & 5

January 2, 2004

We have discovered a road to Tibet recently built by the Chinese. Unfortunately, it is closed to the likes of us.

Met a U.S. Peace Corps volunteer on his way back to the States after two years of working in the Philippines. His optimism about what we are accomplishing there has faded.

Saw some extremely phallic griffins on the corner roof supports of a pagoda.

The problem with letting Zerk run outside on the street is not so much the cars, which are few, but the shit, which is plentiful.

January 3, 1968

Talked with a German who sold his 1954 VW here for $300. Until recently, prices on used cars here were excellent, but now the word is out, and Katmandu is glutted with Land Rovers and VW buses. The Nepalese have learned to outwait the poor hippie, who typically needs to sell his car in order to fly home. Looks like we don't sell our van.

Went shopping. Bought two toy yaks and a Ganesa mask. Bill bought a handmade yak-hair jacket, which we have christened his "yaket." Hope it keeps him warm.

Took a tour this afternoon. Saw Singha Durbar, the largest palace in the world (1500 rooms); Krishna Mandir, a temple of stone with battle scenes carved on its walls; Hiranya Varna Mahaviha, the "golden temple of Buddha." Then we bought Zerky some cookies and, because he was so fussy, I gave him one in the store. Within thirty seconds, the entire box had been passed out to a crowd of previously unseen children.

Saw an erotic temple. Khajuraho had a bas-relief of a man screwing a horse; on this one the horse is screwing the man. There are also some lesbians, and two demons making it. All this seems to have been done with humor, if not with delicacy.

Letter From Katmandu

January 4, 1968
Katmandu, Nepal
Maps 4 & 5

Dear Zerky,

We are staying at the Paras Hotel, in downtown Katmandu. Our room costs fifty Nepali rupees a night, which at ten and a half to the dollar works to out to be $4.75 per night, including four meals a day for your mother and me. You get cold *Legume-Boeuf-Foie de Veau* out of a jar.

There is no heat in Katmandu, or at least so far we've not been able to find any. Our room drops below freezing each night and the days bring icy, hazeless blue skies filled with sunshine. Each morning we can barely wait for the sun to flood onto the tiny balcony outside our window, so we can go out and sit in the sun, which is our only source of heat except for the daily bath. Our room doesn't have a sit-down toilet, or a shower, or a bathtub, but for a few cents extra the room bearer will bring us up two buckets of luxurious warm water, both of them lovingly heated on the kitchen stove downstairs. Then, for a few delightful minutes, your mother and I get warm in turn, as our own private bucket is slowly poured over each of us by the other. This has become our daily get-warm ritual. But you, Zerky—you lucky dog—you fit in the bucket and get the only warm spot in the entire hotel! But then, unfortunately, like all good things that must come to an end, there comes that time when you need to get out of your bucket and get dried off. Teeth chattering, you cry and you wail, reminding us once again that, yes, your cold-hearted parents really should be taking better care of you, perhaps on some nice warm calm beach somewhere where the waves won't be knocking you down and your teeth won't be chattering. And—Oh, I almost forgot—you don't like the rats scampering about our room at night either. I have been trying to get Tarzan to do something about this problem, but he just keeps on telling me that's not his purpose.

Earlier today I went hunting for a better hotel. Unfortunately, the ones the tourists stay in cost four to six times what we are paying now, so we decided to try and get the guy at the desk to give us a kerosene heater instead, like the one he has downstairs. And to hell with the mice!

Mostly we keep warm by walking the city. There is much to see. Katmandu has the flavor of China about it, mixed in with the more predominant flavor of India. We read that pagodas originated here. Many of Katmandu's temples are built in the Chinese pagoda style, but the majority of them have roofs in the inverted U style of Indian Hindu temples. Downtown Katmandu, around Durbar Square, appears much as I imagine it must have appeared one hundred years ago. We walked there with Tarzan today. For 1.3 rupees apiece we got blessed, and now three of us have red spots on our foreheads—all of us, that is, except Tarzan. We tried to get him a red spot, too, but the guy with the spots couldn't put one on him, so this evening I had to give Tarzan a lecture about how lucky he is to have even been blessed at all. I told him about that preacher guy who told your mother her dog couldn't go to heaven with her, "because dogs don't have souls." Tarzan is now thinking about becoming a Buddhist.

You went to see Bodnath Stupa, a Buddhist temple built in the shape of an inverted half-grapefruit, which has a golden tower sticking up out of its center. At the base of the tower are two giant eyes looking at you like they're spying on you. Someone told us they're the all-seeing eyes of Buddha, but I think it's the Communists. Those eyes are pretty shifty and trippy and "hippiesque," even "Beardsleyesque"—all of which no doubt accounts for Katmandu's popularity among Western hippies.

Bodnath Stupa takes up nearly an entire city block. Around it, in the shape of a mandala, is a prayer wall with prayer wheels imbedded in it which you are supposed to spin as you walk by, thereby offering up your prayers to Buddha. But if you don't happen to be near a prayer wall, you can still haul out your own little portable wheel; they are for sale in many of the shops around here. You see people walking around with them everywhere, twirling away as they go. Your mother and I each bought one at a shop across the street from the stupa. The prayers are written on small pieces of paper rolled up inside their little cylinders which you spin with the help of a chain that goes round and round like a merry-go-round. I took both prayer wheels apart in order to try to figure out what makes them tick, but unfortunately the prayers are written in code, which your mother claims to be Tibetan. Our eight-rupee prayer is very short, while our prayer in the twenty-five-rupee wheel is more than ten times as long, all of which just goes to show you that if you plan to go to heaven it pays to buy the very best.

We also bought you a hand-carved rattle and a furry little yak. You don't much care for the rattle, but you sure do love your Jack the Yak! Whenever you are feeling down, Jack's tail scrunches up in your tight little fist and your thumb goes into your mouth, as you wander about, poor Jack dangling and swinging beneath your chin, until you feel better. Jack works better than prayer wheels.

On the street yesterday, we spent twenty minutes listening to a half-dozen musicians playing small, violin-like, four-stringed bowed instruments, each of them carved from a solid piece of wood, like Dutch wooden shoes. Over their hollowed-out sound boxes were stretched skins, to make them more resonant. The ends of the bows had cymbals attached, and were used to deliver a rhythmic beat to the accompaniment of the simultaneously bowed melody. One singer acted as a caller, calling out the refrain for the next verse, as the singers were about to conclude the preceding verse. His voice created a kind of counterpoint between him and the other singers, which made the music sound rather like a fugue, or a round. I found this music to be most agreeable and of surprising melodic and harmonic complexity. It had none of the driving *tabla* rhythms we have become accustomed to in India and the Middle East, but neither did it sound Chinese. I have no idea what kind of music it is. I suppose it's Nepali music.

Driving around today beyond the outskirts of Katmandu, we picked up three hippies and gave them a ride back into the city. They were totally stoned. There were only two of them when we stopped, but then one of them asked could we please wait a minute while he went off to find Frank. "Frank disappears a lot these days," he told us. "He wanders off into the hills with a copy of the *Tao Te Ching* under his arm, and then we don't see him for days." The guy also told us that there had recently been a hippie convention on top of a mountain eighteen miles outside Katmandu. "It was all very beautiful," he said, "until it was broken up by the fuzz." Two of our passengers appeared to be Americans, the other one said he was a Scot. All of them were covered with religious beads and jewelry, which is plentiful and cheap in the curio shops of Katmandu. Until the hippies started coming here a few years back, I doubt Nepal even had any tourists. Still, I do sometimes cringe when I think about what the Nepalis must think of us Westerners.

We ran into the Swedes again. Ever since Tehran, they have been following much the same route as we have. You and Tarzan were delighted to see them. In India, instead of going to Shivpuri National Park, they went to Corbett National Park, where they were almost run over by a wild elephant. Last night we had dinner together and swapped stories about Benares. They said they had taken a boat ride there, and seen a dead baby floating in the river, being eaten by birds. Their guide told them children don't need to be cremated because, until they are twelve, they already belong to Ganga.

Katmandu has a flourishing black market. The official rate of exchange here runs between fifty and seventy-five percent of the black market rate, which means that on the black market you can get nearly twice as much for your American dollars. Such transactions don't need to be carried out clandestinely, however, shady moneychangers congregate openly around the government tourist office and around American Express, their transactions being performed in full view of the police. The other day we went to a tourist hotel to change money at the desk—it's hard to change money in a bank because of the very long lines and because the banks are usually closed. When we attempted to change a hundred dollars, the desk clerk informed us he would have to give us the official rate, but that, since nobody exchanges money at the official rate, he was willing to sweeten the deal, as "a personal favor." So long as we didn't ask for a receipt.

And finally, I am very sorry to inform you, Zerky, you have not been having a very good time in Katmandu; you hate being cooped up in our dark, cold room, and so far we haven't been able to find you any kids to play with. Your mother and I had a long talk last night about going home. As you grow older, you are becoming more mobile and getting more interested in other people. We think you need more friends and stability in your life. Sometimes you are shy, and we don't know what to do about that. Your friend Tarzan doesn't like our hotel room either, and we've not found anywhere in Katmandu where we can let him run. Nothing has been decided yet for sure, and your mother and I are still having a very fine time, but we are beginning to think that maybe it's time for you to start doing some hard thinking about your future. After all, you can't bum around the world all your life.

Love,

Dad

From JoAnne's Diary
More Katmandu
Map 4

January 5, 1968

Our kerosene heater has run out of kerosene. The man at the desk says Katmandu has a kerosene shortage. Bill says the man at the desk has a money shortage.

Read and relaxed in the AM, walked around Katmandu in the PM. Met some interesting people at the Camp Hotel, which appears to be the center of organized trekking activity in Nepal. Sherpas cost 10 rupees a day, act as both cook and guide, and are also in charge of the porters, who cost five Nepali rupees

(50 cents) per day, per sixty pounds. The legal limit they can carry is one hundred kilos—220 pounds. Wow! Sherpas carry a twenty-pound load, less than Bill plans to carry. The flight to Pokhara costs seventy-nine rupees each way ($7.50) and is supposed to be one of the finest flights in the Himalayas. We are going hiking! Or "trekking" as they call it here.

We talked with three Englishmen who had just returned from a twenty-eight-day hike in to Thyangboche Monastery at the base of Mount Everest. They warned us to be very careful to get a good Sherpa. Theirs had cheated them in several ways, and especially on the price for food. They cautioned us that eggs should cost no more than three per rupee, and a handful of rice no more than one and a quarter rupees. Their porter turned out to be a drunk. The owner of the Camp Hotel offered to find us a good Sherpa, and we gladly accepted. We will have to pay his airfare from Katmandu to Pokhara and provide him with food and equipment for the trip. This is the "standard arrangement," we are told. We have decided to hike from the Pokhara airstrip to Tukuche, a village in the canyon of the Kali Gandaki River, which flows down out of Tibet.

Had dinner with the Swedes again. They will probably be coming with us. After dinner, they and Bill went off to the Camp Hotel to make final arrangements. There they met Brian, an Englishman, who asked if he, too, might come along with us. They tell me he seems like a very nice chap, so now it looks like there will be five of us going trekking together. Add in Zerky and Tarzan, plus the Sherpa and the two porters, and that makes ten of us. We shall be an expedition!

January 6, 1968

Zerk woke up early and decided to tantrum. At breakfast we had to remove him from the restaurant. Then Bill went off to Nepali Royal Airlines and returned with the news that he and I—and Lars, Ula, Brian and "Mr. Sherpa"—all have reservations on the Thursday morning flight to Pokhara!

January 7, 1968

Our Sherpa's name is Ang Lakbah. Along with Lars, Ula, and Brian, we went shopping for supplies.

January 8, 1968

Today we picked up our trekking permits. Then, more preparation. Tomorrow we fly to Pokhara to begin our 150-mile hike into the Annapurna region of Nepal. Tukuche is on the Kali Gandaki River between 22,653-foot Annapurna and 26,559-foot Dhaulagiri. Both are major Himalayan peaks, and Bill says the valley between them has the greatest vertical height differential of any place on earth.

From JoAnne's Diary
Trekking to Annapurna
Pokhara to Tukuche on Foot
Maps 4 & 5

January 9, 1968

Waited at the airport for the fog to lift. The Swedes were booked on another plane, which was diverted at the last minute due to the weather. So now they won't be coming with us after all. We shall miss them.

The view from our Fokker Friendship was disappointing because of the weather. The stewardess served us garlic for a snack.

Landed at Pokhara on a dirt runway with no terminal at all. Our porters were waiting for us at the end of the runway. Hiked a couple of miles to Tibetan Camp, where we put up our beloved little pup tent. This is the first time we have used it since Zermatt. Our Tibetan porters are quite friendly. Ang Lakbah, our Nepali Sherpa, is especially nice. Got our first view of Machapuchare today, also of Annapurna, far in the distance. We will have to climb around the base of it to the opposite side.

January 10, 1968

Our little troop of tenderfoots has blisters on its feet. Brian met a Gurkha who had been to Liverpool. An innkeeper wanted 3 rupees per head for a place to sleep, Ang Lakbah said no. We pushed on to Lumli, all six of us eventually staying together in a single small room. Climbed over our first pass today.

January 11, 1968

Marched all day in the rain. Ang Lakbah has taken it upon himself to be Zerky's protector and sole mode of transportation. Nepalis don't use backpacks like we have in the West; they use large wicker baskets with a strap around their forehead. Lakbah has rigged one up to carry Zerky in. First he stuffed his basket with sleeping bags, and then hollowed out a hole in the middle and plopped Zerky into it, unceremoniously. Now Zerk is warm and comfortable. Perched high on Lakbah's back, he looks like a bird in his nest, and enjoys the constant motion and ever-changing view.

Saw some red and yellow birds today. Lakbah calls them "tirkedunga." We slept in a village post office.

January 12, 1968

Clear and sunny this morning. Melting snow sliding off broad-leafed trees. Monkeys along the trail. It clouded over as we climbed to the top of the pass at Ghorapani. We had our first glimpse of Dhaulagiri. We also passed a mule train of between a hundred and two hundred mules carrying wool from Tibet down into India. They were gaudily decked out in red plumes and colored streamers, wore bells, and had bright carpets on their rumps. In charge at the head of the caravan was a Tibetan listening to a transistor radio.

**Sherpa Ang Lakbah with Zerky in a basket;
Annapurna in the background**

It is very cold at Ghorapani. Tough little girls with few clothes on have been sticking their feet in our fire. Snow is falling as we go to sleep. Five inches so far. Who's ever heard of a jungle with snow and poinsettias?

Ang Lakbah has rearranged Zerk's bag in the basket, and Tarzan is now riding in it too.

January 13, 1968

Woke up this morning to cold and clear. Three inches of fresh snow has made everything pristine. Our porters are slip-sliding their way down the trail, in Chinese tennis shoes. Slushy. Dropped below snowline by noon. Bought twenty-four tangerines for three rupees and watched women weaving carpets on hand looms. The people here are very self-sufficient.

January 14, 1968

Left tent, stove and half our baby food at Tatopani. Ang Lakbah tells us we don't need it, not until on the way back. Bill and I started out carrying most of our personal camping gear—pads, sleeping bags, tent, etc.—on our backs, but somehow most of it seems to have ended up on the backs of the porters. Now that we have less weight to carry, Lakbah is saving us money by discharging one of them. Bill paid him sixty rupees for five days. No matter; he's coming along with us anyway. He has a brother in Tukuche.

It was raining when we got up this morning. Steady rain most of the day. We are holed up in a typical Nepali house in Dana. Lakbah knows the people who live here and makes arrangements for his charges to stay here when he is taking them trekking into the Kali Gandaki region. By the time we got here we were very cold and wet and spent half the afternoon drying out our clothing and trying to get warm. The stoves in houses

Prayer wall along the trail to Tukuche

here don't have chimneys—most of the smoke finds its way out
through the leaks in the roof.

Bill told Ang Lakbah that he paid seventy rupees for his new
yak-wool "yaket." Lakbah told Bill he could have gotten it for
twenty rupees. Later on, a man in one of the villages reached
out and touched Bill's new jacket and nodded in approval. Bill
feels better now.

Our big Tibetan porter with the braided hair looks like an
Apache. This afternoon Bill made some imitation Kool-Aid out
of his "Fizzies"—he always carries them in his backpack. Fizzies

are dehydrated, weightless, sugarless instant pop. Bill swears by his little Alka-Seltzer-like tablets with artificial color and sweetening. When our Tibetan porters saw them fizzing away, they went into hysterics. Bill offered to share. They laughed harder.

The trail was very muddy today. Bill's ankle is sore and my knee hurts. Yesterday's long downhill slog from the pass took its toll. While cactus blooms red and yellow, and tangerines ripen, we are freezing. Bright red poinsettias on the hillsides. Palms and bamboo.

January 15, 1968

Sun's out again, but this morning we ran into snow on the trail. I have been penicillin-drunk all day. Bill fell and bruised his tailbone. Zerk is miserable. Not one of our better days.

Along the trail, we have been seeing a lot of "half-yaks," a cross between a yak and a cow. We have been meeting a lot of commercial traffic. Half-yaks appear to be the most popular beasts of burden.

Crossed into a new region of Nepal: Thakkhola. Tramped through our first Thakali village, Nye. We are now in the upper reaches of the Kali Gandaki River, a tributary of the Ganges, which we are following on up to Tukuche.

Ang Lakbah has found us a house for tonight. It is made out of stone and has a flat roof and a wooden floor, except for the foyer, which is mud. Our house has cupboards with dishes, brass cooking pots, and other household utensils neatly arranged on the wall. Zerky has fallen in love with a mean goat.

January 16, 1968

A grim cold wind pushing down the valley out of Tibet. Most of today's hike was directly into it, which slowed us down and made us feel like we were climbing a steep hill. Had lunch at a village before Tukuche, where we were tempted to turn back. Brian and Bill both have diarrhea. Ang Lakbah, however, not only talked us into going on, but also successfully challenged Brian into going beyond Tukuche, to Jomosom. As soon as we arrived in Tukuche, Ang Lakbah found Bill and me a marvelous room in a house, a room that has beds, pillows and hand-carved wooden shutters. Bill went to bed

Wind on JoAnne's Coat
Snow Plumes on Annapurna

immediately—he is really sick. Zerky had a good run around the village. We watched some kids playing with hand-carved wooden tops, which they spin expertly off the ends of strings. Tukuche is a Buddhist stronghold. Many prayer walls, and a Gompa. The landscape is no longer tropical. Much more like California. It is still full winter here.

Our porters are preparing our dinner for tonight: odd meat, onions, grapefruit, red pepper, rice, and something I don't recognize. A quotation from Chairman Mao is on the wall:

> *People of the world, unite and defeat the U.S. aggressors and all their running dogs. People of the world, be courageous, dare to fight, defy difficulties and advance wave upon wave. Then the whole world will belong to the people, and monsters of all kinds will be destroyed!*

This delightful little dog who sits up and shakes hands with me is *not* mistreated!

January 17, 1968

Bill collapsed again after morning tea. Zerk has diarrhea. While I was obeying an urgent call of nature, Zerky was blown over by the wind, repeatedly. Suicide is the only way out of these damn mountains!

Brian and Lakbah came back from Jomosom and got Bill out of bed after considerable prodding. Bill says he feels better now. We are heading back.

Going down that four-mile stretch of windy riverbed, this time there was no wind at all. Ang Lakbah ferried Bill and me across the Kali Gandaki River, on his back.

We have made it to upper Lete. That Terramycin Bill bought in Katmandu seems to have whipped his cold and diarrhea, but he still has a swollen tendon that is painful. He says he's just out of shape.

A village woman wants to know why I don't breast-feed Zerky—they do it here until three years old.

Saw a llama with an amulet around its neck, which is said to cure bad health. Both Ang Lakbah and our porter have red ribbons around their necks, "to protect them from harm," Lakbah tells us. That porter we left in Tukuche, with his brother, came from Tibet to Nepal eight years ago. The journey took them three years.

January 18, 1968

God, Lete is beautiful! Much more so than Tukuche. This would have been a worthy destination for our trek, had we only known. Two of Annapurna's several peaks are out to the northeast, while Dhaulagiri towers above us in the west. Both were hidden in the clouds when we came through here on the way up. They are two of the highest mountains in the world. Both have great plumes of snow blowing off their tops—the winds up there blow at hurricane force.

We had lunch in Ghasa, a Thakali town, where we put some "magic mercurochrome" on the badly burned foot of a baby who had fallen into a fire. Then a man with an inflamed eye wanted medicine from us. We had nothing to give him.

Managed to make it all the way to Tatopani today. This same stretch took us a day and a half on the way up.

Bill's feet are very sore. Now Ang Lakbah has given him his shoes! We rounded the corner of a ridge today, and, presto! Instant summer. Now we have oranges growing. On the other side of the ridge there is snow on the trail.

January 19, 1968

Tarzan was butted by a mean goat. I have taken my shoes off and am hiking in my stocking feet. Bill's feet are sore, too, but he is doing better now than Brian.

This morning we washed up in a hot spring at Tatopani, where Lakbah gave Zerky a warm bath. We are taking a different route back. This way is longer, but not so much climbing. So I am told. We are in Magar country now. Lower down than before. The people here look different, more Hindu, and they no longer have that Tibetan appearance. Some wear huge brooches and nose rings.

Had lunch in a straw hut and spent the night in a farmhouse far above the Kali Gandaki River, which now we are following once more. The trail went up and down all day as we climbed across a series of canyons. A fellow with a huge cyst under one of his eyes asked us for some medicine, but once again we had nothing to give him.

Crossed a hanging footbridge over the Kali Gandaki River. It was ready to collapse. One of its towers was bent and twisted to sixty degrees, and its cables were pulling out. Ang Lakbah insisted it was safe. Per usual, Ang Lakbah was right. The trail on the other side turned out to be a long staircase carved out of marble. Tarzan is out of biscuits.

January 20, 1968

We bypassed Baglung. I had been looking forward to seeing this big remote town with no road to it. Tarzan was attacked by a cow with a new calf.

My feet are better, and the valley is opening up as our trail along the Kali Gandaki descends into the Terai. Today, a long hard march yielded our best mileage to date—maybe fifteen miles. We are very tired.

Had lunch earlier today in Beni, just rice and dal, like the last two nights. Bought a green pineapple.

We are spending the night in a bamboo hut in the small village of Sorsadara. We have walked from Siberia to the South Seas in three days. It is warm again. Even the mornings are not bad. We had our last view of Annapurna today, high in the sky, and far away. No more snowy mountains. Some very big gorges, which reminded Bill of King's Canyon in the Sierras.

January 21, 1968

Left the Kali Gandaki River today. We cut back north up one of its tributaries, and now it is warm and tropical. Lakbah told us about a climbing expedition he had once been on. He thought it funny when he told us about one of the mountaineers who had to cut off his toes from frostbite.

**Phewa Lake near Pokhara
with 22,958-foot-high Machapuchare and
26,041-foot-high Annapurna II in the background**

Some goats followed Tarzan. I think they thought he was their baby.

Pitched our tent in a rice paddy.

January 22, 1968

Climbed for most of the day. Crossed a saddle into the Seti River valley, the same river that flows through Pokhara. We saw both the lake and the city from a notch on a ridge, about twenty miles away. We are spending the night on another ridgetop, twelve miles from Pokhara. Cold. Blisters. Had our last view of Annapurna, plus the classic fishtail view of Machapuchare, 22,740 feet. It reminds us of the Matterhorn.

A village woman fixed us rice for dinner, and a little meat curry. Water scarce: she did the dishes with hot coals and ashes. Ate the last of our food.

January 23, 1968

A twelve-mile very fast walk over level ground is getting us into Pokhara with *very sore feet*. Brian is now setting the pace. Ang Lakbah is in a hurry too.

Reached Pokhara about 2:00 PM and paid off our remaining porter. Much to our surprise, we score four seats on the 4:30 plane to Katmandu! There isn't another plane for the next four days. They were booked solid today, so they put on a second plane. This is marvelous luck; we are out of food and money, and are very tired.

We are back at the Paras Hotel in Katmandu and have paid off Ang Lakbah. One hundred forty rupees ($13.33 US), plus a seventy-five-rupee tip. He is happy. He is worth much more. Katmandu is cold. Again. We should have stayed in Pokhara, where it was warm.

January 24, 1968

Settled up with Brian and went back for another look at Bodnath Stupa. Read *Newsweek*.

**Machapuchare and Rhododendrons
near Pokhara, Nepal**

Bodnath Stupa near Katmandu
(Bill to the left of the man carrying a carpet)

Second Letter From Katmandu

January 24, 1968
Katmandu, Nepal
Maps 4 & 5

Dear Zerky,

Nepal has been the highlight of our trip. You just got back from a two-week hike from Pokhara into the village of Tukuche, which lies in the valley of the Kali Gandaki River, between the peaks of Annapurna and Dhaulagiri. Our feet are still sore, except for yours. You had it easy. You rode all the way in a basket on top of our Sherpa guide's back. My most memorable part of the trek was the close-up views of the mountains, two of them among the highest in the world, or perhaps it was our close-up look at village life and the opportunity to eat and sleep with people we would otherwise never have met. Our wonderful Sherpa guide, Ang Lakbah, made it all happen. He is a gem and a saint.

Katmandu is a fascinating city, but has little to do with the lives of most of the people in Nepal. Nepal is a rural agricultural society. Whenever we leave the Katmandu Valley, the centuries roll back, exposing a lifestyle that almost seems to exist out of time. Today, the larger towns of Nepal, such as Pokhara, have airports and radio communication with the outside world. This is the first step in the process of trying to bring Nepal into the twentieth century. Whether that is a good thing, I'm not sure, but I do know how inadequate your mother and I felt when we were pestered along the trail by people needing medicine for serious medical problems. Roads and airports will hopefully change that.

China is much in evidence. To our amazement, and to Tarzan's great delight, there are a lot of little Pekingese dogs running around Nepal. Most of them are purebreds, yapping, pompous little aristocrats whose lineage predates Tarzan's and mine. And yours. But Tarzan has a louder bark. I keep telling him to shape up and stop acting like the barbarian from the West that he is. Just how these little Pekingeses managed to escape the mongrelization that has produced the generic short-haired mutt of Asia, I do not know.

We are only about forty miles from the People's Republic of China. Walking down the street yesterday, we came across the Nepal-China Friendship Room, a library consisting almost exclusively of the thoughts of Chairman Mao. Then, right down the street, we ran into the Soviet-Nepalese Friendship Library, which was plastered with pictures of Russian factories and heavy industrial machinery. Finally, and most ostentatious of all, was the U.S. Information Service office, with its shiny glass and aluminum cases full of color displays of *The American Way of Life*. Space and medicine were the subjects. I find something obscene about touting heart transplants and spaceships to people who can't afford aspirin tablets and bicycles. American aid programs are notoriously unsuccessful in enlisting the respect and allegiance of people living in these kinds of undeveloped countries.

So near and yet so far. Our proximity to Tibet creates a longing. I always thought of Tibet as the most fabled land on earth, but now, here we are, forty miles away, with a car, and we have discovered a brand-new paved road to Lhasa that was recently completed by the Chinese, supposedly for the purpose of furthering trade relations between the two countries. I suspect it is more for the purpose of making India nervous. Talk about the Chinese water torture: we torture ourselves daily with imaginary schemes to get into Tibet.

We ran into our old friends the Swedes again. This is the fourth country where we have bumped into them. I suggested to them that since Sweden is a politically unaligned country, they might be able to wrangle a visa for Tibet. The next day they went out to the Chinese Embassy, but the gate was locked, as was the one I tried to visit in Kabul. How sweet it is, the forbidden fruit.

After nearly a month in Nepal, your mother and I are finding ourselves reminiscing all too often about the delightful subtropical climes of India, and I'm afraid the time has come for us to move on. This should make you happy, because you still don't like it here very much. You don't like the cold room, and you don't like the fact that we have not been able to find you a park to play in. Nevertheless, Nepal is a wonderful place and its people are extraordinarily friendly.

Love,
Dad

Back into
India

From JoAnne's Diary
Nepal to Kaziranga Wildlife Sanctuary in Assam
Map 4

January 27, 1968

A youngster waved us across the border into India without stopping. Today must be some kind of holiday. This would account for why we were turned away at a DAK Bungalow, and then again at a Circuit House. Drove late to Motihari, where Zerky is sick from eating oranges and is getting chewed up by mosquitoes.

January 28, 1968

Road excellent! Made Siliguri late afternoon. Had trouble finding accommodation. We stayed in a garage at a PWD Bungalow.

January 29, 1968

Royal fuck-up day! No mail for us at Bagdogra and then, when we were all set to leave for Sikkim, Bill discovered he had mailed our permit off to New Delhi by accident. Had to reapply for permission to go there. After much hassle, we finally managed to change some money in a bank. It took the usual forever. Replenished our supplies. Left for Assam. PWD Inspection Bungalow in Fal Kata. Nice room, no lights, rain. We saw a big-tusker elephant beside the road.

January 30, 1968

Made it into Assam. The countryside is beginning to look like Southeast Asia. Jungle-covered hills, thatched roofs, huts of intricate bamboo construction, bananas, coconuts, dates, rice paddies, women wearing sarongs. Beautiful red-blossomed trees. Wild storks with long yellow bills and black wings. Small

**JoAnne and Zerky with Mahout at Kaziranga
Feeding Bamboo "Tamales" to Raibhadu**

kingfisher-like birds, the males red and blue, the females black
and white spotted. Many eagles.

Stayed in PWD Bungalow in a small village, the water
filthy—no lights. We brought in our candles from the car.

Bill was bugged by the presence of six men last night who
"moved in on us," as he put it. When we left this morning, we
had an audience of seventeen. Ah, yes, back in India.

January 31, 1968

Went shopping in Gauhati. Found peanut butter, dog biscuits, unsweetened canned milk, hot achar, and other luxuries. But no film. We are out of color film. Also we can't find a map of Assam. Looks like they don't make any. No tourists to sell them to, I guess.

There were riots in Gauhati on January 26. Many buildings were burned, and martial law was declared. There is now a 2:00 PM curfew for Republic Day.

Stayed in a very comfortable circuit house in Nowgong, where we had a good Indian meal and electric lights.

Got up early, but had to stick around Nowgong until 10:00 AM, when the banks open. Then we spent nearly two hours in the bank, undergoing the usual frustrations. We finally cashed some traveler's checks and took off for Kaziranga Wildlife Sanctuary. Many monkeys along the road. We had an audience of eight of them for lunch. They all kept their distance, but did make answering the call of nature a problem.

Arrived Kaziranga 2:00 PM and got a room at the lodge. Lots of tame elephants around. Tarzan started barking at one, Mohan, the resident big-tusker. Tarzan the Elephant Hunter!

Our guide has problems with numbers. He tells us the Brahmaputra River is five miles wide, three miles deep, and twenty-five thousand miles long.

Tarzan piddled in the forest hut drawing room. Later, when he escaped from our room, someone warned us that the tigers might get him. Dinner and early to bed.

February 1, 1968

Eagles and beautiful blue jars.

February 2, 1968

After lunch, Zerky got taken off by the range officer's seven-year-old son. The father told me that his three-year-old daughter wanted to play with Zerk. Not knowing for sure whether it was the right time to visit, I went along too, thereby causing a total disruption of their household. The poor mother felt compelled to invite me in, even though I was completely unexpected. Then she sent her kids scattering, one to borrow sugar for tea, the other to go get her husband to come help with the English. In the midst of all the chaos, Zerky wet his pants. Fostering our son's social life can get very complicated. He thoroughly enjoyed his visit, however.

Towards the end of the afternoon, all the riding elephants were brought up to the grounds near the bungalows, where they were inspected, painted, and fed tamales made of grain-packed bamboo shoots.

February 3, 1968

Got up early to go wild elephant hunting. Tarzan was bitten by a dog, but we couldn't find any broken skin, so we left him alone in the room.

Our mahout and guide were both very surprised when we split our lunches with them; another caste prohibition violated, which elicited talk about the Americans who were here during the war for the building of the Burma Road.

We came back to find a very sick Tarzan. He had indeed been bitten. His back muscles are injured and he cannot walk. He can barely stand. He seems dazed and feverish. Poured mercurochrome and sulfanilamide into his puncture wound and went to bed, not sure he would survive the night.

February 4, 1968

Took Tarzan to the sanctuary vet today, who cleaned out his wound and put a permanganate-sulfa-boric acid mixture in it. When Tarzan screeched, a bunch of kids laughed, and then Tarzan ran away. He now seems somewhat improved from last night, however. On display in the vet's office, pickled in jars: Rhino Penis and Kidney of Leopard.

Bill spent the afternoon outraging the locals by washing our car, along with the menials, who were washing the sanctuary jeeps.

Zerky had another good play with the range officer's kids, but now, as soon as he goes visiting, the neighborhood kids are sent home. The range officer thanked us profusely; apparently all the other playmates are not to be similarly favored with Zerky's presence. Caste.

February 5, 1968

We really confused them today when we spent the entire day cleaning out the inside of our car and then waxing the outside. This really gets 'em!

Last night we were the guests of two Indian men who want to go to the United States but can't, "because of balance of payment problems," as they so artfully put it. Both were very friendly, but very anti-U.S. stand on Vietnam. Except for that, however, they seem to like Americans, or so it appears.

Last night we also enjoyed watching the elephants being brought up to the bungalows for their nightly feeding and grooming. Tarzan is a little better now, but stayed in bed all day.

February 6, 1968

A day to be forgotten! Zerky got me up early, and while Bill had diarrhea, I went back to bed. A madhouse, in the midst of which Tarzan's swelling burst like a balloon, spurting blood and pus all over the bedding. Then Bill went looking for a vet and finally found one, fortunately, just thirteen miles east of Kaziranga. This vet was very gentle with Tarzan, but suggested we take him to the veterinarian college back in Gauhati. When we finally got there, Bill collapsed at the Nowgong circuit house, with Montezuma's Revenge.

February 7, 1968

Woke up this morning with diarrhea and no john. During the night, someone occupied Room #9 next door. We'd been using its john. So now it's out to the woods or behind the garage.

Tarzan saw that vet in Gauhati and was brutally treated. The vet's probing opened his chest wound to the size of a quarter. Now, with all the hair shaved off the back of his neck, poor Tarzan is a mess. Even Bill was revolted. We decided not to leave him with the vet—after he asked us whether we had brought Tarzan's chain. As we were leaving the vet's office, a car turned over ahead of us, right in front of the veterinarian school. Bill stopped to see whether anybody was hurt, and within one minute, at least a hundred people gathered outside in the street: students from the school, laborers from the fields, and people on the road coming from all directions. I was appalled by all their excited grins. What ugly vampires! Later on Bill told me it wasn't the victims they were so excited about; it was the upsidedown smashed-up car. They all wanted to turn it back over, and pretty soon they did. Along with two vet school students, we drove the injured passenger to the hospital in Gauhati.

February 8, 1968

Bill has diarrhea again—thank goodness we had a john this time. Later on we took Tarzan back to the vet, who was much easier on him than last time. Afterward we went east towards NEFA while Bill went to sleep in the back of the bus and missed some bare-breasted beauties walking along the road. We finally stayed in a PWD Rest House with no electricity, where Bill went to sleep again while I read in bed with a flashlight.

**JoAnne, Zerky and Tarzan
with Indian family at Kaziranga**

Zerky and Friends at Kaziranga
JoAnne and her Elephant Friends in the Background

February 9, 1968

The rest house manager tried to charge us ten rupees but accepted four when that didn't work. We took Tarzan back to the gentle vet, who graciously gave us some medicine, and then showed us how to treat the wound. He would accept no money for the drugs, telling us that we were "guests of Assam." He suggested a paper collar to keep Tarzan from licking his wound. Tarzan is now sporting one of Zerky's bibs.

Had another flat tire. No tubes the right size. They don't know how to repair tubeless tires here. Fortunately, we had another spare on top of the bus, which Bill had had mounted on an extra rim. If that last tubeless tire gets punctured, we shall have no spare tire at all. Drove on through increasingly tropical scenery to a very nice tourist bungalow in Sibsagar, where we had dinner.

February 10, 1968

Bill is sick again, after eating European food at the bungalow. We suspect it's the water, which we have not been iodizing lately. I am less sick.

While Bill slept in, Zerky had fun playing with his ball and with the bungalow staff. Later a liberated staff member brought his little daughter over to play with him, and after some initial shyness, she and Zerky had a wonderful time.

Stopped to see two Ahom temples. The *Ahom* were the Burmese rulers of Assam from 1523 to 1786. These temples are still in use, but we were not allowed to enter the sanctum. The temples are very nicely shaped and have a few delicate bas-reliefs that are still in good condition. Bill is feeling rotten—I drove while he and Zerky and Tarzan slept in back. Through miles of tea estates. Coconuts, dates, bananas, orchids growing in trees. A lovely turquoise-backed bird with a yellow breast and a long beak. Many wild waterfowl.

Looked for a room in Digboi at the Assam Oil Company's guesthouse, but a sporting event had filled it to capacity for the weekend. There is oil production near Digboi. The town's name is said to have originated in colonial times, when a British commander exhorted his Indian charges to "Dig, Boy, Dig!"

Drove on to the little town of Margherita, where we found a lovely PWD Inspection Bungalow, again with no electricity.

One of the Ahom Temples

The white walls and dark stained studs remind me of where we used to live over The Movie, in San Francisco, at 1032½ Kearny St. Our room has a lovely verandah-balcony that we can gate off for Zerk. There is only one small bed, so Bill has decided to sleep on the floor tonight.

Unfinished Letter From JoAnne to Her Friends
February 10, 1968
Margherita, Assam
Map 4

Dear Mims, Bill and Bill,

I have long been meaning to write you a letter, but this trip has been so rich that trying to start one is more like starting a book—there is no telling when it will end.

Tonight we are staying in a small town on the eastern edge of Assam, just a few miles from the beginning of the Burma Road, which once connected Burma with China. I am writing this by kerosene lantern, and feel lucky to have one, because India is suffering from a kerosene shortage. We use candles, mostly. Although this coal-mining town does have electricity for industrial purposes, the electricity has never been hooked up to the houses. Most of Assam has no electricity at all, just as most of India does not have hot running water. These are the two luxuries we miss most.

A week ago, Tarzan was badly bitten by a dog. We have been to three vets since. Nearly every town has a government vet who treats animals free of charge, and there is only a small charge for medicines. Tarzan's penicillin shot cost the equivalent of twelve cents. Coincidentally, we also took a man to the hospital after witnessing a car accident on our way back from the vet. Medical facilities were available to him and they were free.

Assam is tropical. We sleep under mosquito netting, lianas and orchids often hanging from the trees. At dusk tonight, we had a skyline of date palms and coconut trees. The road we traveled on today was lined with tea plantations, and often with people wearing sarongs and saris. They live in mud huts, and/or in huts made of woven bamboo, with thatched roofs.

Their clothes, both the men's and the women's, are as bright as their lives appear to be uncomplicated. To the north of us is NEFA, the North-East Frontier Agency, which is not a state but rather an Indian-controlled buffer zone between India, Burma and China. In this complicated area live tribal peoples of various customs, some of whom were headhunters during the early part of this century. Eastern Assam is remote, and is an anthropologist's paradise.

We have been following a road just south of the Brahmaputra River, which is India's largest river. Every year it floods, keeping the standard of living here very low. As is the case with the Ganges, there is only one bridge across the Brahmaputra.

Last week we spent five days at Kaziranga Wildlife Sanctuary, probably the best animal sanctuary outside of Africa. We stayed at a tourist bungalow just outside the sanctuary, where they told us an irritable old tiger lived "just down the road, beyond our bungalow." Our two trips into the park have been on elephant back. Bill tells me that when he gets back to San Francisco he is going to turn in our four-wheel-drive International Scout for a four-legged-drive elephant—they go through elephant grass and brush too thick to get through in our Scout. Often the reeds are higher than our heads, when we are seated atop Raibhadu, our favorite elephant. He just plows through everything, like a bulldozer. Our guide told us that going in cars to look for elephants is dangerous, and that not long ago a Russian Trade Commission party had been chased by a rogue elephant and saved only by the timely arrival of an armed patrol.

On our two trips into the sanctuary we saw many Indian one-horned rhinos *(rhinoceros unicornus)*. Approximately five hundred of them—roughly half the estimated world's one-horned rhino population—live in Kaziranga. One of them kept trying to charge our elephant's side. Each time, our mahout would preempt the charge by turning Raibhadu ninety degrees, to face the threatening rhino. Each time when the rhino saw Raibhadu's superior firepower, he reconsidered.

We also saw many wild buffalo, reputedly the most dangerous of all animals because they will charge at virtually anything. We also saw wild boar, various Indian deer, and many birds, including pelicans. We did not see any leopards, tigers, or wild elephants, however, although there are many wild elephants in this area. We did see a tiger's lair, but once again no tiger. As we were leaving, our mahout lit fires behind us. Every year they burn off much of the elephant grass.

On our second trip into the sanctuary, we went through many more miles of elephant grass, to a group of little lakes. We had lunch in a clearing near one of them. The grass teemed with wildlife that was impossible to see, so our mahout had the elephant graze in between the reeds and us, for protection. After lunch, Raibhadu waded into the lake and the mahout proceeded to give him a bath. First Raibhadu lay down on one side, and then on the other side, head submerged, trunk waving in the air, like a plume, as the mahout scrubbed his immense body with a very stiff brush. Then he cleaned Raibhadu's tusks, and finally his mouth, which yielded a leech. All the tamed elephants working in the sanctuary are cared for in this way, daily. Their grooming includes painting their faces, shoulders, and rear ends.

Besides elephant grass, we also saw pockets of real jungle. Our mahout gave Zerky some branches of dried pods, which rattled musically when he shook them. We also ate a little "wheat"—a black dust inside the stem of a tall reed plant—and some tiny sour crabapples. My favorite tree growing alongside the road is the Indian cotton tree, which is covered with big red waxy-leaved flowers the way other trees are covered with leaves.

India is full of birds, the most common of which is the raven. Sometimes they nearly darken the sky. Eagles are often found in the big cities. Wherever an animal has died or been run over, huge vultures gather in sickening fashion. Yesterday, we saw a newly dead cow being torn apart by so many vultures that the cow jerked about as if it were still alive. My favorite common bird, however, even lovelier than the green parrot, is the blue jar, a turquoise-and-dark-blue-colored bird the size of a magpie. There is also a comic stork standing almost four feet tall, with a long yellow bill, a rusty head, and ungainly black wings. Beautiful white waterfowl—egrets, herons and cranes—all are very common here.

It is raining hard outside. This is not surprising, even though it is the dry season. Cherrapunji, in Assam, at five hundred inches per year, is said to be the wettest spot on earth.

We spent the last three nights at "tea gardens," in which we were invited to spend the night by three separate Indian tea estate managers. These tea gardens are fantastic, their former colonial owners having built huge bungalows with gorgeous tropical gardens for their managers to live in. They all have electricity, hot water, and—wonder of all wonders—bathtubs, the first we have seen in India. These tea gardens, or tea estates, are relics of Great Britain's imperial past. At the first one we stopped at—and were subsequently invited to spend the night at—there were nine servants taking care of the single bachelor who lived there. Our second estate had twelve servants to care for one young couple and their two children.

Our hosts were all very gracious but seemed rather lonely. Because "management" consists of so few people in this isolated pocket of the world, it appears to get pretty lonely up at the top. Enter us. We have never been so popular in our lives! Zerky especially is a hit, but so is Tarzan. Bill and I are enjoying the attention too. Our Indian hosts appear to lead the most luxurious of lives, living in exotic bungalows with beautiful gardens, verandahs, fireplaces, modern bathrooms, and lovely furnishings. And to top it all off, the company pays for the education of their children…

Perhaps as anticipated in her first sentence,
JoAnne never finished this letter, which was written
to a different Bill, to her friend Mims, and to me.

Letter From Assam

February 11, 1968
Margherita, Assam, India
Map 4

Dear Zerky,

Until recently, I never knew there was a place called Assam. Not long ago, during our relentless travels eastward, we began to notice we were running out of India. But there was still this funny-looking place on the map called Assam, which looked like the logical way to get to China. Assam is marginally an Indian state, but most of the native peoples here are reluctant or unwilling to concede their identity to their gargantuan neighbor next door. In some ways, the Assamese appear to have more in common with the Burmese than with the Indians. Assam has the smell of Burma about it, a certain wildness. Yesterday near Digboi we passed a wild man walking barefoot and carrying a bow and some arrows. He wore nothing but a colorful loincloth and was what English speakers here call "a tribal."

Besides Assam, there are four additional troublesome Indian states nearby, in which most of the inhabitants don't consider themselves to be Indians. The tribal peoples of Nagaland, Mizoram, Manipur and Tripura consider themselves to be members of their tribes or, at most, members of their above-mentioned ancient kingdoms. These are the "unruly hill people" who have existed for centuries in a world of their own—a world culturally and historically quite different from that of their "flatlander" neighbors. It is a world much feared by the leaders of India's still-budding democracy, because it embodies the face of Indian separatism, a force that is threatening to tear apart the world's largest democracy. My own opinion is that the hill people don't give a damn about India; they just want to be left alone.

So there is revolution in the air tonight, especially in nearby Nagaland, which has been set aside as a tribal reserve for the Nagas, and is closed to foreigners. Here in India, the Indian reservations are for non-Indians. Exclusively. Your mother and I wonder what they would do with an American Indian?

In spite of some difficulties, we find ourselves loving Assam, probably because we knew nothing about it beforehand, and therefore were without preconceptions. Someday you will go traveling on your own, Zerky, so let me suggest to you a paradox: that you will derive more pleasures from your travels if you confine them to places you know nothing about. Those are the places where you have the most to learn and it is the learning that makes discoveries exciting.

Assam is full of tea estates. Along with neighboring Darjeeling district, in India proper, Assam is responsible for much of the world's tea production. That is probably why the British glommed onto this remote piece of jungle in the first place. A few days ago we stopped at a tea plantation, to ask for directions, whereupon we were immediately invited into the house by its owner, Bahrid Chattopadhyay. After a little chitchat, Bahrid and his wife invited us to spend the night. We begged off, but promised to come back and stay with them later. The Chattopadhyays have a son named Deep, who is a couple of years older than you are, Zerky. The two of you had a good time playing with his toys. I suspect Deep is lonelier than you are.

Driving eastward into Assam, the countryside becomes less populated and more exotic. Increasingly there is the smell of jungle in the air. Monkeys, elephants, orchids, colorful tropical birds. Near the easternmost point of Assam, at Lekahpani, there is a sign marking the beginning of the Stilwell Road, a lesser-known wartime addition to the famous Burma Road. This leg was built by General "Vinegar Joe" Stilwell and his American troops, during World War II, after Vinegar Joe had been charged with creating a vital road link to connect India's rail system with Chiang Kai-shek's nationalist army near Kunming, in China. Earlier in the war, the American air force had been trying heroically to ease Chiang's desperate straits by means of a cobbled-together airlift over the Himalayas. This airlift became known as "flying the hump," the hump being the Himalayan Mountain Range. The completion of the Stilwell Road obviated this inadequate airlift.

From Lekahpani, it is only a few more miles to the end of the road, at Jairampur, where we ran into a military roadblock. Jairampur marks the "outer line" of NEFA, an acronym for India's North-East Frontier Agency, where India, the tribal states, Burma, and China all meet. Ever since China's border "incursion" a few years back, much of NEFA has been under control of the Indian Army. Their "outer line" has become our outer line, too, unfortunately. For us it is the end of the line. The Stilwell Road is impassible beyond the Burmese border and our hopes of driving all the way to China have been thwarted by an Indian army roadblock. At the barrier, we ran into two Indian families, both of which extended invitations to us to come and stay with them on their tea estates. One of the families lives on the Namdang Tea Estate, near Margherita, the other on the

Maran Tea Estate, near Dibrugarh, farther west. We took them both up on their offers.

We are delighted with our beautiful bungalow here in Margherita, which is located not far from the end of the road and from Burma. Our room costs one rupee per night (thirteen cents) plus fifty paisa (seven cents) for the sweeper, plus fifty more paisa for kerosene for the lanterns. That adds up to twenty-seven cents total per night. For all four of us. This is the life! We are meeting lots of people in Margherita. The other night a friendly neighbor loaned us one of his servants when he discovered that we wanted to drive to the Digboi Club to see an advertised showing of *Romeo and Juliet,* starring John Barrymore, Leslie Howard, and Norma Shearer. This is the kind of movie we showed in San Francisco. But in Assam? When we arrived at "the club," a little late, our "servant" stayed in the car to babysit you, while your mother and I went to the movies, only to discover that the show had been cancelled.

When we started asking questions, we were quickly referred to the man in charge of the Digboi Club's weekly film series, Simon Penny, who told us the film had simply not arrived. He said he had just announced that unhappy fact to his assembled audience, whereupon they all let out a great sigh of relief. It appears the peoples of Assam are not all that interested in John Barrymore, Leslie Howard, Norma Shearer, or Shakespeare. Simon's film showings are popular because they provide people around here with an excuse to get together weekly and socialize. They also provide Simon with the opportunity to indulge himself in his passion—movies. Having just cancelled his showing, to cheers from the audience, he betrayed the pride of a professional when he explained to us he had just given his audience what they had come for, the chance to get together and drink. Now nobody would have to sit through another boring movie. Everyone was happy, including Simon. Simon is a cinema buff in one of the most unlikely places on earth. When we told him we could relate to his problem of not having the film show up on time, because we had recently been running an art theatre in San Francisco, we became instant comrades-in-arms. On and off, we have spent much of the last two days with Simon. We find him to be a fascinating man.

Simon Penny has lived in Margherita for fifteen years now, working for the Namdang Tea Company. He loves India and is still a bachelor. He tells us that he left England in his early twenties, because of some vague dissatisfaction, but that in a few more years he fears he will have to leave India because of the deteriorating foreign exchange rate that is beginning to make remittance to Great Britain financially unrewarding. Simon seems lonely and, like so many of the people here, he enjoys the opportunity to talk with foreigners. He exemplifies a curious perplexity that seems to run rampant in Assam, one greatly inuring to our benefit.

Both the illegal, all-pervasive Hindu caste system, and the supposedly obsolete British Empire system, have left their ugly marks on the fabric of India's extremely complicated society. Once again, as was the case with that rich man at Khajuraho who was prevented from driving his own car, here on the tea plantations caste restrictions and social restrictions similarly prevent the British and upper-caste Indians from fraternizing with their labor force. Although I have not discussed this with India's poor, most of whom do not speak English, I find it very interesting to see the deleterious impact these two institutions have had on the rich. I view it as a kind of divine justice, except that we have somehow become the beneficiaries of it all. Almost everyone we meet is anxious to talk with us, and, I would imagine, with any other new blood that comes wandering down the road. Not very often, however, does a little blond angel come toddling down the road, nor a stumpy little dachshund on miniature legs. You and Tarzan are taking this place by storm!

Perhaps because of his wide-ranging interests, Simon does not appear to be quite so lonesome as most of his compatriots. His closest friends appear to be our young host Raj, who has invited us to stay with him, and Roy, a big Christian national from Kerala, whom Simon says is unique in that he possesses both "drive" and "a sense of urgency." We have been talked into staying another day, and into breaking our scheduled appointment with the Chattopadhyays. Everyone assures us that being a couple days late for dinner is totally acceptable in India.

This morning we went to visit Simon at his "bungalow," where he proudly showed us his magnificent oriental garden on a small hill at the edge of the forest. Then he took us on a jeep ride back into the tea estate. His plantation is currently in the process of expanding, as new land is cleared from the forest to plant tea on. Simon tells us there are leopards, tigers and snakes in the uncleared portions of the jungle, and that one of the planters' biggest problems is with wild elephants. They truly resent the clearing of the land, he says. Then he told us about an elephant that had recently come out of the jungle carrying a log, and used it to batter down Simon's new tea plants in such a systematic way that it left little doubt as to the elephants' anger at the clearing of the forest. We have decided that Simon is secretly on the side of the elephants.

Yesterday we took a short walk with Simon, down a trail dense with ferns, creepers and orchids. Along the way we met several groups of tribals with whom Simon conversed in a primitive local variation of Hindi, which he speaks fluently. He says the tribals come down out of the hills to exchange pan leaves, which are widely used in India for wrapping betel nuts. He says most tribals carry a long knife and a small grate to cook on. The ones we saw wore loincloths, cast-off shirts, and had hanks of bright cloth wrapped around their heads. Simon was positively delighted with them. They are very happy, he says, and lead simple lives. We suspect Simon wants to be a tribal too.

On the trail yesterday, we ran into a group of tribals who suggested we walk with them to the river. One of them had a safety pin through his ear—an earring—another carried a cigarette in a hole in one earlobe and two cigarettes in the hole in the other. Unfortunately, Simon had to go to work, so we had to decline the invitation. On the way back, he pointed out a village about a mile across the valley, on top of a small ridge. Nontribals are not allowed to go there, he said, because the village is in NEFA. He, however, has recently obtained special permission to go there during the village's next festival. He is fascinated by the hill country and by its tribal societies. Just last week he watched opium being smoked in one of the nearby villages. Simon tells us this is very common.

He also tells us he would never visit Benares because, to him, it symbolizes everything that is wrong with India. He is quite pessimistic about India's future. "Where do you think it will all lead?" I asked. "Probably to a military takeover," he replied. He believes democracy is not for India, "not at this time." Simon has spent nearly his entire adult life in India, but has no legal status here. We think of him as a man without a country. We told him he should get married.

Simon took us to an Indian friend's house, for lunch. There we met Ivan and Alfred and Rufus, a Christian from Ghazipur, in Uttar Pradesh. They told us stories about World War II. Rufus said there were 200,000 American GIs here, spread out between Dibrugarh and Lekahpani, during the construction of the Stilwell Road. He said many of the planes that flew the hump took off from a nearby airstrip, near Tinsukia. Back then, there were no towns in the area. The towns of Margherita and Ledo were built from the immense quantity of American junk that was left over after the war ended. Some of the old beat-up trucks we have been seeing hauling logs out of the jungle are leftover World War II U.S. Army trucks, Rufus explained. Alfred told us several of the U.S. Army's old DC-6s are still in use here. Ivan told us that the amount of material brought in on the railroad to the roadhead at Lekahpani was "a wonder," even to the GIs. To the local people, many of whom had never even seen an automobile, it must have been an awesome sight.

Simon told us that he tried driving over the Stilwell Road a few years back but that it is now impassable because the jungle has reclaimed most of the grade. Once the war was over, there was no maintenance. This seems to be the way everything unravels in India. But I suspect also that the Indian government has little interest in making far-flung Assam and its rebellious hill peoples easily accessible to India's traditional enemies, China, Pakistan and Burma. Simon told us that the last person to go over the Stilwell Road was Peter Townsend, who was given VIP treatment and help from the military. Peter Townsend is a large landowner-farmer here in Assam, who is said to have benefited very handsomely from U.S. Peace

Corps seed. Dashing Group Captain Peter Townsend, you may recall, was the love of Princess Margaret's life. And for those who don't keep up on this sort of stuff, Princess Margaret was Queen Elizabeth's sister.

Earlier this evening we had dinner at another big tea plantation where we had been invited to stay: the Ledo Tea Estate, near the beginning of the Ledo Road, the original name of the Stilwell Road, before it was renamed in honor of dear old Vinegar Joe. We had chicken tandouri and it was delicious! The tea people on that estate are very anti-Christian missionary; they blame the missionaries for stirring up trouble with the tribals, who, they say, are getting arms from China.

Once again it is getting late. We head back in the morning. I need to turn off the lantern now and go to bed. Assam has been an exceptionally memorable experience for your mother and me, and we are very glad to have come here. Perhaps we shall come back again some day to visit all the friends we have made.

There was a magnificent sky tonight, with spectacular cloud formations. Raj says there's a tropical storm brewing.

Love,
Dad

From JoAnne's Diary
West to Darjeeling and Assam
Map 4

February 13, 1968

Left Margherita and Namdang Tea Estates. Drove back to Moran Tea Estate to visit the Chattdopadhyays, who were delighted to see us. Bahrid is a Bengali from Calcutta who has

**Zerky at the Stilwell Road,
Extension of the Burma Road
Built by General Vinegar Joe Stilwell**

lived in Assam for seven years. His wife entertained us with a constant procession of food. For some reason, Bahrid didn't seem to be at ease. We had a fine evening nevertheless. Our presence seemed important to both of them, and Zerk had another marvelous time with their son Deep.

February 14, 1968

Left AM. Drove back to Kaziranga, where Zerk met his friends again. We are out of color film, so we had to take black and white pictures of him and the elephants.

Yesterday we heard that *khedda* is going on near Lekahpani, where the Stilwell Road begins. Khedda is a method of trapping wild elephants by driving them into a pit prior to training them to be used as work elephants, circus elephants, tourist elephants, etc. They are lucky I didn't run into any khedda when we were there a few days ago.

Many of the people we have been talking to lately are full of fascinating stories about their experiences with wild elephants, snakes, tigers, leopards, panthers and leeches. A man at Bahrid Chattopodhyay's told us about the time he tried to honk a tame elephant off the road, and it wouldn't move. He found out later that it wasn't a tame elephant at all, but a house-tearing-down wild one.

Bill thinks Bahrid was nervous about entertaining us. I think he was just tired. They have a one-month-old baby with 6:00-10:00 PM colic. Bill forgets how tired we both were when Zerky was that age and had colic and night feedings.

Bahrid also told us tales about Margherita. He said the last incident of tribal headhunting near there was in 1953. He also told us about a previously unknown eighty-year-old American missionary who was discovered near Margherita, after having worked in the bush for sixty years. Bahrid has studied and worked in both Germany and the UK, and was delighted to learn that we had heard of Tagore, Ravi Shankar, Vivekananda, and Satyajit Ray.

February 15, 1968

Saw another tribal with a bow and arrow today, near Digboi. When we were moving into our PWD Inspection Bungalow tonight, at Nalbari, we attracted a huge crowd of people standing around staring at us, as usual. We tried to get some of the kids to come and play with Zerky, but the adults told them not to. I tried handing Zerky's ball to various children, but none of them would touch it, even though you could see that they were sorely tempted. I tried hard for you, Zerk, but no go. Caste seems embryonic in kids as young as two.

February 16, 1968

Aralen Day. The jackals are howling tonight. They sound like a cross between a dog baying and a cat in love. There was a lot of yowling at the Chattopadhyays too.

Yesterday I commented to a mother: "What a beautiful little girl you have."

"Yes," she replied, looking at Zerky, "but she is a bit dark, don't you think?" Where does this come from? From the religion, the British, Alexander the Great? Or what?

Crossed back into West Bengal, where we shared a circuit house with the army, at Jalpaiguri.

February 17, 1968

In Siliguri today we got permission to drive to Darjeeling along a narrow one-lane road it shares with a narrow-gauge "toy train." As soon as we got into the foothills outside Siliguri, the people disappeared, just as they had disappeared in Nepal. We do not understand why they do this. It's cool in the mountains! Why do Indians insist on living in heat? We love this part of India.

Today we passed many fluttering prayer flags and streamers, and a small Buddhist shrine beside the road. Before arriving in Darjeeling we stopped to look at a Buddhist monastery.

Darjeeling has a serious parking problem, due to having almost no streets. This beautiful hill station, so beloved to the British, is held together by a network of paths and narrow, winding streets closed to vehicular traffic. I'll bet the British got the idea from their favorite mountain playground in Switzerland—Zermatt. Today brought us our first parking problem since Europe.

At 7,000 feet, Darjeeling is cold, but not as cold as Katmandu. We spent the night in our car outside a fancy tourist lodge, on the edge of town. This is a good deal for us; we can tramp into the lodge and use all the "facilities." Unfortunately, we are out of butane, and Zerk had croup last night, so we tried steam heat *à la JoAnne*. Zerk is better now but still has a cold. Tarzan's wound is healing. He will be okay, but with a scar.

February 18, 1968

Cold but bearable this morning. Gave all our dirty laundry to the government of West Bengal's tourist lodge, except for the filthy, ragged clothes we are dressed in. We are a semi-resident mess, parked outside a very posh lodge.

Walked around town. Tarzan was attacked by two different dogs, and his ear was bitten through. We don't think it too serious. We said the same thing last time.

There are lots of Tibetans wearing Chinese tennis shoes and Chinese caps, with earlaps that turn up and snap on top. Since 1959, 85,000 Tibetans have fled Tibet; 60,000 of them are in India.

Beggars again. We didn't miss them in Assam.

All day long we have been watching a spectacular show of immense cumulus clouds billowing up around Darjeeling. We had a few intermittent sunny periods lasting only one to five minutes, but could never catch a glimpse of Kanchenjunga. Nevertheless, this is a very scenic town, probably the most European-looking place we have seen since Connaught Place in New Delhi. Lots of coniferous trees. Lots of parks and playgrounds. Lots of expensive homes and churches, many of which have rusty red corrugated-iron roofs. The British call Darjeeling "Queen of the Hill Stations."

February 19, 1968

Another day in the clouds, with short sunny periods. Bill spent most of the day fighting tires. He had three of them repaired, one of them twice. He put a 700-15 tube inside a 700-14 tire—they don't have tubes for Volkswagen-sized tires in India, which has its own automobile industry. They make Ambassador cars here, but unfortunately their valve stems are too skinny, so Bill filed out a hole in the rim and stuffed a wrong-sized tube into a Volkswagen tire. Hope it works!

Found peanut butter, but no Kodak film. India won't import American film because the United States won't accept Indian rupees. Eastern European countries accept Indian rupees, so they sell Hungarian film and Czech film in India.

Bill got permission from the Deputy Commissioner of Darjeeling to visit Gangtok, Sikkim.

Kanchenjunga as seen from Darjeeling on a clear day

It really makes me sick not being able to see the orchids in flower. Unflowered as they are, they grow on the trees, between the stones of the walls, and even on the ground. I decided to visit the botanical gardens alone. Bill is having foot trouble from jacking up the car, and I've been out exploring. From the only automobile road in Darjeeling, you descend a long, steep staircase at the bazaar, down into the gardens below. The area is largely Tibetan, but there are also many Chinese-looking Indians, which makes for some very lovely girls. Going down the staircase, cement houses are built out from the cliff, their front ends supported by poles. At the bottom I found the gardens more exciting in their possibilities than in their realities. Let's face it: February just isn't the month for flowers! Nevertheless, I did see: 1) a living descendant of a fossil in China that dates back twenty million years; 2) a beautiful white Indian cotton tree with ten to twelve petals, each of them about three inches long; and 3) some grand cymbidicims *(insigne multiflorium)*, tiny green and purple sprays. On the way back I bought some yummy little mini-bananas in the bazaar.

NOTES ON PEOPLE'S DRESS: Many Tibetans and monks in red robes wearing Chinese caps or Nepalese-style balaclavas. Jodhpurs with baggy seats and tight-around-the-calf-style trousers. Moslem women dressed in stylish pink "pajamas." A young girl in pants, with a long shirt-and-scarf set. Beautiful saris. Lots of riding clothes. Rented horses are probably the most efficient way to get around this trendy, carless vacation spot.

The twisted bands looping through Tibetan men's braided hair makes them look like they are wearing halos!

Letter From Sikkim

February 21, 1968
Gangtok, Sikkim
Map 4 Inset

Dear Zerky,

Sikkim is a very little country tucked into the Himalayas between India, Tibet, Nepal and Bhutan. Its capital, Gangtok, is not far from Darjeeling as the crow flies. Upon leaving Darjeeling, we descended via a steep, narrow paved road, into the valley of the Teesta River. Ever since the days of Marco Polo, the Teesta has been an important trade route connecting the cold highlands of Tibet with the hot plains of India. Our descent was breathtaking. From a cold winter morning seven thousand feet in the clouds, we wound our way down through coniferous forests, into the tropical jungle of the Terai. While I was showing our papers at the Indian checkpoint, you and your mother wandered off to buy some tangerines and a bundle of those tiny little bananas we have all become so fond of.

Crossing the old stone bridge over the Teesta, we climbed back up the other side, following the ancient trade route. After a few miles, we were stopped at the Rangpo checkpoint and put through some additional passport formalities in order to enter Sikkim, which is a nominally independent country. Just how independent is open to question; its external affairs are administered by India. *(Note: Sikkim is now part of India, having been annexed by force of arms in 1973.)*

355

The first thing that impressed us about Sikkim was the beauty of its native people—the women especially. The indigenous inhabitants here are known as *Lepchas,* and are of different appearance than the Indian and Chinese populations. Lepchas are said to have originated eons ago in the area around Northern Burma, Eastern Assam and Southeastern Tibet. Their language derives not from Sanskrit, like Hindi, but from the "Tibeto-Burmese group of languages"—it says in my book. Lepchas resemble the peoples of northern Burma, and are physically small. They have big brown eyes framed by smooth oriental skin over an Indian bone structure, which creates, in the women especially, a petite femininity that your father finds most appealing.

Climbing into the Himalayas, we began to notice more and more Tibetans; they stand in magnificent contrast to the delicate Lepchas. The Tibetans are large-boned and have a Mongoloid appearance, with long foreheads, flat noses, and black braided hair. Their sculptured faces remind us of our American Indians.

Tibetans and Lepchas are not the only racial groups making up this diverse little country. Most numerous of all are the Nepalis, who have settled here in large numbers. Butias from Bhutan, too, constitute a sizeable minority. And finally, at least here in Gangtok, Indians are much in evidence, especially among the merchants. They are, however, Sikkim's smallest ethnic group. All told, the native Lepchas add up to only about 20 percent of the population, the result being that they have become a minority in their own country. This situation has led to considerable political unrest. The king and most of his government are Lepchas, but the king's wife is an American. Her name is Hope Cooke, and she is widely, if perhaps inaccurately, portrayed in the press as "the debutante who married a king and ran off to Shangri-La."

From Rangpo onwards, the road is paved. This is the only road in Sikkim, and has lots of problems. Each summer during the monsoon, portions of it disappear into giant mudslides that sweep everything before them into the torrent of the Teesta. The Sikkimese don't seem to bother trying to protect their lone road—that would be a hopeless task—there being no culverts running underneath the highway; they just let the water plunge on down the canyons and over the road. In some places the road crew has built concrete pads on top of the road, for the water to run over, but that doesn't appear to be working very well. Every year parts of the road are entirely washed away. Then, once the monsoon is over, these parts are rebuilt from scratch. In the meantime, since there is no railroad or airport in all of Sikkim, the country is cut off from the outside world, except by foot. Now, after the Chinese incursion into India, the Indian Army has recognized that they have a major problem supplying their troops along the Tibetan border and India has begun to reengineer parts of this critical road through Sikkim from China.

As we climb up the valley of the Teesta, jungle vegetation gives way to pine forests, which in turn give way to terraced rice paddies carved into the near-vertical mountainsides. In the mid-levels of the Himalayas, many of the mountains were long ago sculpted into terraces to grow rice on. In Asia, rice is the eternal giver of life. Rice paddies require flat ground. Ergo, when there is no flat ground, people make it themselves. They make terraces. For hundreds, perhaps thousands of years, the peoples of the Himalayas have been chopping away at these biggest mountains in the world, with hand tools, thereby creating rice paddies. I venture to say this is probably the biggest construction project in the history of the planet.

Having driven all day to complete a journey that the map had led us to believe would take only about two hours, we reached Gangtok about an hour before dark. As seems to be happening with increased frequency these days, you are not happy being cooped up in the car, Zerky, and you made your point very effectively by subjecting your mother and Tarzan and me to another one of your tantrums. Fortunately, we have found you a very fancy lodge-PWD Rest House tonight, complete with a white picket fence and a four-year-old little girl, the daughter of the *chowkidar*. The bathroom we get to use, even has a hot water heater! Which doesn't work.

I am writing this from the Deer Park, in Gangtok, the capital of Sikkim. The Deer Park is a city park where deer wander about, undisturbed. They are large, magnificent creatures, with very broad antlers. The park sits astride a sharp transverse ridge at an elevation of about a mile above sea level. In front of me, the ridge I am standing on falls off rapidly, into deep valleys on both sides, which merge into the Great Canyon of the Teesta, which I can see a few miles to the south. On our left is a massive grey ridge with a saddle of fresh snow along its top, and with streaks of white dripping down its sides, where snow is sticking in the cracks and crevices of otherwise windswept rock.

Beyond the ridge, the massive forehead of a snowy mountain is peeking at me and keeping its eye on Gangtok. That snowy mountain is in Tibet. The grey ridge in front of it forms the border between Sikkim and Tibet. The ridge I am standing on continues upward until it meets that grey ridge. Beyond is the Chumbi Valley, a dagger-like slice of Tibet thrust into the cleft between Sikkim and Bhutan. With the Chumbi, China has a toe-hold on the southern slope of the Himalayas, a toehold to serve as a reminder to India that China does not consider the present boundary between the Tsangpo River to the north and the Brahmaputra River to the south to be an acceptable border.

Gangtok, in short, is an exceptionally beautiful spot for finicky Western tourists; its scenic appeal far surpasses that of "Queen of the Hill Stations" Darjeeling. Unfortunately, this tiny kingdom is a touchy place politically—an almost unknown front of the Cold War. Until recently, like Nepal, Sikkim was closed to outsiders, and even now the authorities will not allow us to travel any further than Gangtok. The newly built North Sikkim Highway goes all the way to the Tibetan border, but is tightly controlled by the Indian Army, which has pledged itself to defend Sikkim, whether the Sikkimese want it to or not. India maintains that Sikkim is an integral part of India.

We have just returned from the lamasery at the top of the hill, near the palace. We tried to visit Hope Cooke. We thought she might be lonesome, but her palace—an expansive rambling bungalow, really—has a fence around it, with a locked gate. We had to settle for a visit to the lamasery, a huge, white, two-story pagoda with golden roofs flanked by two long rows of prayer flags. Its walls, both inside and out, are covered with intricate hand-painted floral designs, and with dragon designs reminiscent of the paintings on Chinese lacquer chests. Inside, is an altar and a place where strange, surrealistic clay figures of dragons and demons are being made by red-robed monks seated on the floor. They are skilled artisans, who contribute to the income of the lamasery by making these religious figures. As in Tibet, Lamaism is the religion here, an exotic mixture of Buddhism and animal worship that deifies the mountain peaks.

Although usually associated with Tibet, Lamaism is also the predominant religion of the mountain peoples of the higher regions of Nepal, Bhutan, and parts of northern India as well.

Tibetans are an extraordinary people. Unlike the stereotypical inscrutable oriental, they appear to be total extroverts, who always seem genuinely delighted to talk with us, as far as our language disability will allow. Whenever we meet Tibetans, their friendly, animated faces seem to light up, and whatever they are saying is continually being reflected on their faces. What a welcome change they are from the Indians, who have learned all too well how to hide their feelings from the white man. You are as fond of the Tibetans as we are, Zerky. Today one of them plucked you from our grasp and took you off to the rear of his shop, where he gave you some cookies, the exact nature of which your mother and I prefer not to contemplate.

This southern slope of the Himalayas—of which we have seen bits and pieces of all the way from Afghanistan to Assam—is probably the most interesting area of our entire trip. We wish we could spend more time here, but unfortunately, the authorities would give us only a permit for three days. And, once again, we are in the Himalayas at the wrong time of year. Tomorrow we head south. We shall be warm in Calcutta.

Love,
Dad

Zerky near Hope Cooke's Palace
Gangtok, Sikkim (a country that is no more)

India Again

From JoAnne's Diary
West Bengal to Calcutta
Map 4

February 22, 1968

Bright sunny morning. Left Sikkim about noon. Crossed down into West Bengal and made Siliguri by nightfall. Stayed in the same PWD garage as on the way up.

February 23, 1968

Drove south all day through northern West Bengal. The area between Kishanganj and Malda (Ingraj Bazaar) is the poorest place we have ever seen. The men wear simple loincloths, the women sarongs. Many of the children wear nothing at all, only their potbellies, which is a sign of malnourishment. Most of their houses are primitive bamboo huts. Today we saw people grubbing around in swamps and fishing with nets in a roadside pothole that has not yet completely dried up. In another place, we watched people using the side of the road as a platform for a homemade irrigation system that lifted small amounts of pothole water up onto the edge of the road, before allowing it to trickle back down into the potholes, a process that wetted but a few square meters of earth. These people live a marginal existence in a dirt-poor world. What happens to them when their potholes dry up?

Late in the afternoon, we were turned away at three government rest houses in Ingraj Bazaar, and have ended up in a "Tourist Abode," a private bungalow run in conjunction with a gas station. Twelve rupees. $1.60. Outrageous—how many fish must you catch in a pothole, to make twelve rupees?

February 24, 1968

God, things are difficult in India! Tonight we had to get special permission from the Public Works Department to stay in an inspection bungalow. It took us an hour and a half just to get an okay for a one-night stay. Then the *chowkidar* spent another hour and a half standing around putting up mosquito netting, making the beds, etc.

February 25, 1968

Made it to Calcutta, where we drove around in confusion until we finally stumbled across the Lytton Hotel. It has hot water, baths and good western food. There are lots of people living in the streets.

February 26, 1968

Picked up our mail today at American Express. Hurray! Money!

February 28, 1968

The hotel owner's Alsatian dog is terrorizing us. Tarzan was threatened and Zerky bitten on the lips. The wound isn't all that bad—just five small puncture scratches.

February 29, 1968

Oh, for the mountains again. The heat is really getting us. Walked around the city for an hour, and collapsed. There are lots of consumer goods in the stores, but they are very expensive. I bought a pair of shoes for 40 rupees ($5.30 US). A good shirt costs $10.00 US. Who can afford such prices? Overall, the people here appear better off than in the villages.

March 1, 1968

I shocked people today when I carried out our dirty laundry, instead of waiting for the room bearer to do it for me.

March 3, 1968

Walked around the bazaar. Hot! Came home and took a cool bath, which gave me enough pep to go out in the courtyard and sit down. I soon came back into the room, to lie on the bed underneath the ceiling fan. Our only antidote for this heat is ice water, lemon squash, and gin.

March 4, 1968

Miserable day. A real loser. Bill went to the Thai Consulate to find out about dogs. He says the people there don't have the slightest idea about their own regulations. Hong Kong and Japan have quarantine. Zerk has diarrhea. Earlier today he played with some kids in a park, and then I took him to a Jain temple with beautifully landscaped gardens and lots of windows, mirrors, mosaics, colored glass, silver, and light.

March 5, 1968

Zerky is learning to talk! Just since we arrived in Calcutta! Somehow he has picked up several words of English, and is using them constantly!

March 8, 1968

We all went to the zoo except for Tarzan, whom we left in the car. Zerk and I loved the children's zoo best. Bill wants to burn down American Express—they haven't done a thing about finding us a boat to Panama.

March 9, 1968

Dear Zerky: Calcutta is too hot! During the daytime we hardly move from our fans, which are always on at full speed. When Bill carries you half a block, his shirt is then soaked with sweat. They tell us it's cool now, compared to May.

March 10–15, 1968

Zerky has blood in his stool. We took him to a doctor next door, who is a "World-Famous Astro-Palmist," and who told us Zerky has liver trouble from the heat. We're not sure what to make of this diagnosis.

Today it was ninety-eight degrees and extremely humid. Our bowels have been loose lately. Tarzan sleeps a lot.

Lizards, rats, mice, cats, ants. Maggots on eggs. Vasectomies. Bus conductor vs. the police. Eugene McCarthy, New Hampshire primary. I am "Auntie" to Raju and Camar. When you ride in a rickshaw the passenger is in charge of ringing the bell!

Letter From Calcutta

March 18, 1968
Calcutta, India
Map 4

Dear Zerky,

We have been in Calcutta for about three weeks now, and have been staying at the Lytton Hotel, in a run-down part of the city. Everywhere in Calcutta is run-down. It is a very old city, but our room is cheap, comfortable, and reasonably clean. We have a 1933 hot water heater with a copper tank that sprinkles burning embers into our bathtub. Who needs hot water? It's sweltering here! Our room comes with five meals a day, two of which are morning and afternoon "tea." The tea in India comes loaded with milk and sugar, a kind of warm milk shake. They serve it with "biscuits," i.e., "cookies" where we come from.

For the first few days it seemed to us that Calcutta was seething with anger. You can't travel around this city without running into mobs of protestors. The giant oil company, Burma-Shell, seems to be the favorite target. Its workers are out on strike and there are pickets marching everywhere. The communists are on the march, and automation seems to be their big issue. Efficiency doesn't seem to be a priority. Nationalization of the banks is another big issue that fuels a lot of these demonstrations. Yesterday there was an article in the paper about a police van that had accidentally run over and killed a pedestrian. A mob quickly gathered and set the police van on fire. The entire state of West Bengal is currently under

"President's Rule," a provision in the Indian constitution that allows the federal government to nullify provincial governments and rule directly from New Delhi. Calcutta is a very unruly place. This bothered us at first, but after a while we began to notice how everyone else seems to take chaos for granted. And now we do too.

Last Thursday was a holiday, a festival commemorating Lord Krishna's frolics with the milkmaids. It is about fertility, and about spring. People paint their clothes and their faces, and go out into the streets, shooting colored powders and liquids at each other. After two days of this, parts of the city were put under curfew. Several people were stabbed. Three of them died. The paper attributes this to "too much drinking."

The streets of Calcutta are home to countless people inhabiting the vacant lots, the alleyways, and the narrow passageways between buildings. Not all people here without houses are beggars. However many of them are. Many are also deformed, some from accidents, some from leprosy, and others from a multitude of untreated illnesses. For some weird reason, we have been taking a shine to some beggars down the street from our hotel. Just as she did with her best customers at her movie theatre, your mother has started referring to them as "our regulars." There is an "our little beggar family" composed of a husband, a wife, a two-year-old boy and their tiny baby; an "our little boy leper;" a "mischievous little boy"; "our teen-age leper with the limp"; and "our pre-teen hunchback with the sweet smile." At first, we gave only "alms," but now we find ourselves having become proprietary about our beggars. This is getting out of hand. Your mother worries about them when they are not "at their stations." The other day she read in the newspaper that young babies are being sold in Calcutta while their bones are still soft and pliable, and can still be bent and twisted. The paper says these babies are much in demand because they can be marketed and sold as "investment income property."

The other day we were stopped on the street by two beggars. One was appropriately humble, the other inappropriately rude. Your mother dipped into her purse and gave some coins to the polite beggar, and then stiffed the rude one by giving him one paisa, essentially nothing. In retaliation, he rubbed his leprous shoulder against your mother's bare arm. Earlier that same day, I got brushed by a pickpocket near the bazaar. But he didn't get anything! We do have our little triumphs.

Today we went to a huge open-air market, where we bought your mother a beautiful sari. They are the loveliest garments in the world. Now if she could just figure out how to put it on!

It is with considerable misgivings, Zerky, that I tell you that we have finally made the decision to go back to the USA. Both China and Burma are closed to foreigners. We had hoped to drive to southern India and then put our car on a ship to the Panama Canal, but the American Express travel agent here tells us that he can't find any ships departing southern India. That leaves Calcutta the only other international seaport on India's east coast. We have located a freighter that will take our car to San Francisco. The stevedores will use a crane to pick up the bus in a sling and load it onto the ship. For the last week, I have been doing nothing but running around Calcutta getting signatures, permits, and other documentation, from all the various government bureaucracies whose blessings you need in order to export a vehicle. India thrives on mindless bureaucracy, abstract rules, and arbitrary regulations. The government wants us to drive our car back to Germany, just like we got it here.

Going home is an idea that strikes us as both appealing and appalling. We still have much of the world to see. At American Express the other day we collected our mail for the first time since New Delhi, two months ago. There was nothing in it to make us homesick. Our income taxes are higher than expected, our friend Francine is having problems with our car, and my beatnik friend Fred's wife, Lorraine, is lonely. No mention of Fred. All in all, it is not very inspiring. We felt very disconnected from America, reading Christmas cards in sweltering heat.

In a little more than a week we shall be flying to Bangkok, where we plan to stay for a few days, and then fly on to Hong Kong, to catch a boat to San Francisco via Japan. We are making reservations.

Two days ago, we had to visit the American Embassy in order to get them to add some more visa pages to our passports. We had used all the blank pages up. While we were there, we inquired about adopting an Indian baby so you could have a little brother or a sister, or whatever, Zerky. Unfortunately, there is too much red tape, most of it on the part of our government. When we get back to San Francisco we plan to start looking. No longer, then, will you need to keep making friends out of strangers. You have spent most of your life outside the country and we hope you enjoy the USA.

Love,
Dad

From JoAnne's Diary
Last Days in Calcutta
Map 4

Circa March 21, 1968

Thanks to Joan, I have now learned how to put on—and wear—my new sari. All I need is somewhere to go. Her Irish husband, Larry, is in the tea business, near Sibsagar, in Assam, and knows both Simon Penny and Raj. He tells me Raj quit two weeks ago and is immigrating to Canada.

This week we all have diarrhea. Zerk probably has it the worst, but on this last day before our departure, Bill, too, is *miserere sumus!* A true martyr, he did a beautiful job cleaning out the car, and he had to inventory everything inside that we are shipping back. We gave Zerky's outgrown shirts and remaining jars of baby food to our beggar family outside the hotel. They were delighted.

I took Zerk to the Temple of Kali. A Brahmin talking in a continuous chanting sort of shout latched onto me and showed me 1) The tree that bears neither fruit nor flower— barren women hang rocks upon its branches and pray to Kali for children. If in the next year they bear a child, it is dedicated to the Goddess. 2) The wild black face of Kali, her eyes and mouth bright red (atavistic). 3) A Brahmin prayer shawl with Brahma's own sacred thread. 4) The sacrificial yoke for the goats and buffalos that are slaughtered and then fed to the beggars around the temple. As I was about to leave, the heavens opened up with rain, thunder, lightning, and hailstones the size of ice cubes. Zerky and I sought shelter from the heavens in Brahmin's Cake Shop, next to a Shiva lingam. The leaky tin roof almost kept us dry.

Our trip is over. From zero in Munich, our odometer now reads 23,702 miles, about a thousand miles shy of the total distance around the world.

Thailand

Temple of the Emerald Buddha, Bangkok

From JoAnne's Diary
Bangkok
Maps 1 & 4

March 24, 1968

It simply never occurred to us that Bangkok might be hotter than Calcutta. We quickly found the nearest air-conditioned hotel, which turned out to be full of GIs on R & R from Vietnam, each of them accompanied by his own Thai bar girl. All the girls, and the GIs too, look like teenagers. Our hotel's Western-style bar-restaurant has beer for $1.00 a bottle, hamburgers for 75 cents, and a barbershop, a Turkish bath, a girlie magazine stand, and a nightclub featuring "tea-dancing"—whatever that is. Everything here is designed to separate a man from his money in the shortest possible time.

I find the GIs pathetic. On the jukebox last night someone was playing "Five-Hundred Miles Away from Home," "Oh I Want to Go Home," and "When You Come to San Francisco be Sure to Wear Some Flowers in your Hair." One of the GIs we talked to told us exactly how many days it had been since he'd left the States, and two of them knew exactly how many days it would be until they could go home. I suppose they all want to go home. Some won't.

Zerk is a smash hit in his jeans. The hotel staff has been lovely to him. In two days, they have given him two apples, two bananas, plus a little koala bear. They give him something each time he goes into the lobby. I suppose you don't encounter many children when you work in a whorehouse. Besides resident hookers, this place also has a resident adjutant stork, two doves, and a Buddhist shrine. Still, this can't be Bangkok? WE'VE GOT TO GET OUT OF THIS DAMN HOTEL!

March 24, 1968

Sunday we visited the Temple of the Emerald Buddha. It has several monasteries, huge pink, blue and green *chortens*, and an Emerald Buddha chapel guarded by two one-story-high demons. Around the courtyard are illustrations from the *Ramayana*; inside were priests pouring holy water over statues of cows. Lots of joss sticks and lotus offerings. A couple of stone lions covered with gold leaf.

This afternoon we went to the Phra Mane ground to watch people fly kites. On our way there, we came across an open-air market where Zerk and I got to look at some birds and animals. We saw everything from fledgling vultures to baby bunnies, puppies, monkeys, parrots and fish. Afterward, we drank pop and watched kites. One of them had a fifteen-foot red tail. Another was bright red with a big multicolored owl painted on it. There were also two large star-shaped kites, which took a son, a father and a grandfather to launch. On the way back, Bill bought a bottle of *Mekong*, a smooth, sweetish whisky that is supposed to have aphrodisiac qualities.

Zerky found a baby lizard on the floor of our room, and confidently dropped it into my hand.

Zerky at the Temple of the Emerald Buddha

Letter From a Bangkok Whorehouse

March 25, 1968
Bangkok, Thailand
Map 1 & 4

Dear Zerky,

Stepping out of the plane was like stepping into a blast furnace. We quickly booked a room in the nearest air-conditioned hotel. The Hotel Parliament is quite the place; it has about three hundred rooms, 90 percent of them occupied by American GIs on furlough from Vietnam, and by their "dates," the young Thai bar girls who are available at the bar downstairs. The restaurant specializes in such exotic dishes as hamburgers, southern-fried chicken, ham and eggs, milkshakes, and Coke. Its jukebox takes U.S. coins, exclusively. Everywhere we go in this part of town, the streets are packed with GIs and their bar girls. Servicing American troops appears to be Bangkok's number one industry. The merchants around here have found it good marketing strategy to dress up their neighborhood so as to make it look and feel as much like America as possible. The Thai business community and the U.S. Army are in a marriage of convenience.

The standard of living here in Bangkok appears to be higher than anywhere else we have been since Tehran. We have even found an American-style supermarket with disposable diapers and little jars of baby food! I hope someday you will appreciate how much the success of this trip has depended on diapers and baby food, Zerky. We almost cried when we saw them again; we were down to our last three packs of the diapers we loaded up on in Athens, and, in order to make them last, we had taken to cutting them into twos, and finally into threes.

Without a car anymore, we have a problem; we now have to get around town on foot and by taxi. It is too hot here to walk very far, and the taxi drivers all seem to be con men with techniques well honed from preying on young American GIs. As a result, we find ourselves spending far too much time in our room, watching American TV, in front of the air-conditioner. We are prisoners of the heat in this fascinating city with so much to see. I am afraid we are going to miss most of it.

We finally got up the courage to leave our beloved air-conditioner, and have moved into a Chinese hotel, a few blocks from the Parliament. Our new room is half the size for half the price, and comes fully equipped with two pairs of sandals and two sarongs. As soon as we get home, we get out of our damp, sweaty street clothes and into our sarongs. Your mother says your father looks cute. Your father says this is the first time he's worn a dress. And now he says, "Sarongs are the only way to fly!" Our new room also has an air-conditioner that works much better than the previous one, probably due to the smaller room.

We have managed to see a bit of Bangkok. We went to the most famous of the temples here, the Temple of the Emerald Buddha. In spite of all the churches, mosques and temples we have seen on this trip, this one is probably the most beautiful of them all. It consists of a complex of several brilliantly colored pagodas covered with extensive mosaics made out of colored glass and mother-of-pearl, and topped off with ornate golden roofs and spires. Gold is in abundance at this temple. Worshippers buy tiny squares of gold leaf at the door, to be used as offerings, which they rub onto the stone gods inside. Because this gold plating process is going on constantly and is being done by worshippers rather than by trained professionals, some of the gold leaf does not adhere to the statues very well, and, as you walk through the temple you find loose bits and pieces of gold tumbling along the floor, in the wind. I suddenly realized—belatedly—that we were walking quite literally in gold.

Yesterday, in order to escape the heat, we all went to see an air-conditioned Hollywood movie, *Far From the Madding Crowd*. You were sound asleep in my arms when we went in, and we expected you to sleep through the entire film, but as soon as we sat down you woke up and then stayed awake for the entire movie. This surprised us a lot. But what surprised us even more was how much you enjoyed the film. You chattered all the way through it. Had you insisted on doing so in your mother's theatre, we would have had to ask you to leave. You are just like your mother, Zerky, every time an animal came on screen you got all excited. This happened a lot. The story was set on a farm. When at one point a crazed sheepdog stampeded a herd of sheep over a cliff, you buried your head in my shoulder and began to cry. Yes, it was a very sad movie. But you stuck with it! How much you have changed in the thirteen months since we left San Francisco. You've spent most of your life in a car, dear boy, and you are growing up. It's time for a change.

Each night after dinner, on the way home from a Thai restaurant we've become enamored with, you have been having the time of your life playing with a gang of street kids on the sidewalk in front of the hotel. Once again, the children are intrigued with your blond hair. They compete with one another for a chance to play with you. You seem to enjoy Bangkok more than India, where caste restrictions all too often got in your way.

Poor Tarzan is having a rough time of it. Not only is the heat very hard on him (he's panting and sleeping a lot), but he also keeps finding himself being stalked by Siamese cats. For no apparent reason, walking down the street he's been attacked by them twice. They come at him out of nowhere. Since leaving San Francisco, Tarzan has tangled with dogs, goats, chickens, toads and monkeys, but never before with cats. I'm sure he will be very happy to get away from here, when we leave for Hong Kong tomorrow. Little does he know they eat dogs in China.

Love,
Dad

From JoAnne's Diary
More Bangkok
Maps 1 & 4

March 29, 1968
Went to see some Siamese dancers at a clip joint hotel. Bad dancers, good costumes. Zerky watched the entire show without getting restless. He enjoyed the bright colors and elaborate headdresses. But he didn't like the demon.

Hearing we were from San Francisco, a young Thai girl approached us on the street, wanting to know all about "hippies." She told us Thais don't like them because they are dirty—but she kind of thinks they're okay. She was very interested in learning about the Summer of Love. We suspect she is thinking of running away.

Bangkok is very modern. We would like to see some of the countryside. We miss our car. We are watching too much TV. My sarong measures 34 by 56 inches. Another cat attacked Tarzan. We haven't seen any beggars or people sleeping in the streets, but we do have a couple of uninvited guests sleeping in our room: Leslie and Lester, the Lizards.

China at Last

Letter From Hong Kong

April 2, 1968
Hong Kong, China
Maps 1 & 4

Dear Zerky,

We smuggled Tarzan into Hong Kong because the government wanted to lock him up in quarantine, and now he is terrorizing the city. When we walk down the street with him on a leash, people stand on the edge of the sidewalk to let him pass. Once, Tarzan got all excited and started to bark and the crowd instantly scattered into the street. How do you say "his bark is worse than his bite," in Chinese?

Our hotel room is as tiny as it is depressing. The opposite wall is but 4 feet away; Hong Kong is a vertical city without room to spread sideways, so everything has been compacted. It is a city of show windows and glass display cases—one big tax-free department store. I suspect Hong Kong has more consumer goods per square inch than anywhere else on earth; we haven't seen stuff like this since we left Athens. Somewhere in Turkey we started leaving a trail of little glass baby food jars all the way

381

across Asia. They were not litter; they were gifts. We started washing them out when we realized how much people liked them. I now know that the world is round, because here on the far edge of the Far East we have come full circle and found ourselves back in the wasteful West. Having learned how to get along without most of this stuff, we now realize how much of what drives the economy is junk.

You can probably buy anything in Hong Kong—perhaps anybody. And if you're in the market for flesh, there is plenty available in the many bars in this neon nighttime jungle. Just as in San Francisco's North Beach district, where you used to live, Zerky, erotic nightlife is a prime tourist attraction. Your mother and I wanted to take a peek, so we dirty-worked you last night and turned you over to a Chinese babysitter at the hotel, who I doubt had ever before taken care of a cute little Caucasian kid. She adored you, but you didn't like her one bit. She told us you had a tantrum after we left. Mommy and Daddy, however, had one fine evening, barhopping between such sterling establishments as the Fuji Club, the Hanoi Club, the Bunny Club, and the Playboy Bar. From the safety of your mother's company, I found it most enlightening to study the various techniques of the Hong Kong bar girls, as they fed like piranhas off the flesh of foreigners.

Yesterday brought us the best news of our entire trip: President Lyndon Johnson has just announced that he will not seek reelection! In addition, he promised to de-escalate the war. We don't know whether to cheer or to cry. The prospect of an end to this idiotic war has met with a curious reaction in the Hong Kong press. The newspaper here tells people not to be overly concerned about the future; while peace will no doubt bring a slowdown in business, initially, in time the reduction in American armed forces personnel will be more than offset by the increase in tourism resulting from greater stability in Southeast Asia. "The dominos will have fallen," they seem to be saying. War is bad for business. Why couldn't they have figured this out before?

The best thing about Hong Kong is the temperature. Cool at last! For the first time since Sikkim, we can walk around without being bathed in sweat. For the last three days, we have been hustling all over town, getting ready for our departure. Like most people who come here, we are having some clothes made by those "legendary Hong Kong tailors." Suits are extremely cheap, and when I get back to the United States I am going to have to get all dressed up and go looking for a job. I am having two suits made here, plus some dress shirts. We are also busy getting boat tickets for our homeward journey via Yokohama.

Our carefree days are coming to an end, I'm afraid. It's funny how here on the mainland of China we feel as if we are already home. Part of it, I suppose, is that we used to live on the edge of San Francisco's Chinatown. Still...that clock-tower on the Hong Kong Star ferry terminal sure looks like San Francisco's Ferry Building, and ferry boats are continually crisscrossing Hong Kong Harbor on their way to and from Hong Kong Island. We could just as well be in Oakland. Hong Kong and San Francisco seem to have merged.

Now that our trip is over, I am beginning to feel cheated by that plane ride we took from Calcutta to Bangkok. It seems to me that in order to get to Hong Kong from India, you should drive through China, and/or Burma, Laos and Vietnam. Unfortunately, both Burma and China are closed to foreigners. The other night in Bangkok I got my map out, and within half an hour I had figured out how we could cash in the remainder of our airplane tickets and use the refund to take the train down to Singapore. From there we would island-hop through my dreams, to Indonesia and New Guinea, and then on to Australia, where it would be easy to catch a boat back to San Francisco, or to the Panama Canal. If it weren't for the bloody heat! It keeps beating us back from the equator. I am afraid Southeast Asia is just too damn hot in April. And furthermore, WE HADN'T PLANNED ON YOUR GROWING UP SO SOON! So to hell with it—we're going home. Maybe someday this stupid Cold War will be over and you will be able to drive through Burma, Laos, Vietnam and China for us, Zerky. Or maybe by then you will not even be able to drive through France. What will your world be like? We can only wonder.

Love,
Dad

The Final Entry in JoAnne's Diary

First day out on the ocean. Many junks and sampans. Our ship has Japanese passengers, Chinese crew.

Zerky and JoAnne
Coming Home on the *President Cleveland*

The Real World

NOT LONG AWFTER WE ADOPTED ZERKY, WE DECIDED TO adopt a second child, as soon as we figured out where we wanted to live. In India, we had been fascinated by the beauty of the Indian children. They were everywhere, staring at you through immense dark eyes, sometimes made even darker with makeup. Might not one of them be in need of a big blond brother? Adopting a child in India made sense, but a trip to the U.S. Embassy in New Delhi disabused us of that notion: the necessary clearances were too hard to obtain and no one knew how much time it might take. A second child would have to wait until we got back into the real world, which turned out to be San Francisco again. It was time to get on with our lives.

The "real world" meant a job for me and a second baby for JoAnne. I still wanted to be in show business. I was addicted. But what about kids? Raising them in the confines of a big city was not attractive to either of us. What to do? We found a small flat out in the Noe Valley district of San Francisco and lost no time looking up old friends and business acquaintances. One of them was Chan, JoAnne's former film booker. "You ought to go to Santa Cruz," Chan advised. "Santa Cruz would be perfect for your kind of theatre."

JoAnne chimed in and changed my life: "Yes, Santa Cruz would be perfect—perfect for kids!" But if I wanted to get back into theatre business, I was going to have to find a new business partner. She had a new job planned out for herself. This Santa Cruz business would require the backing of a bank, she explained.

"Why do you think I bought those two new suits in Hong Kong?" I replied. "Why do you think I shaved off my beard?"

In the summer of 1968, a few days after they shot Bobby Kennedy, we moved 80 miles down the coast to Santa Cruz, California. The County Bank there had told me they liked my idea of an art theatre in their little town, and would probably finance it, provided I could jump through all their hoops. That would require being on the scene.

I spent the year 1968–69 in thrall to the bank. I also came across two other couples who liked the idea of an art theatre in Santa Cruz: Phil and Patricia Chamberlin, and Dick and Casey Daniel. Phil had been a professor at the then partially constructed new campus of the University of California at Santa Cruz; Dick and Casey were friends of his, and of his wife Pat. The six of us founded the Nickelodeon Corporation in October of 1968.

Most of my first year in Santa Cruz was spent looking for a suitable site for the theatre, finding a suitable architect, and getting all the necessary governmental permits and clearances—all the while trying to keep all six of us on the same page while still placating the bank. JoAnne's time was consumed by Zerky, and by the process of finding him a baby brother—or sister, I hoped. After a private adoption fell through at the last minute, when the mother changed her mind, we decided to try an adoption agency.

Excavation for the Nickelodeon began in the fall of 1968, only to come to a halt a few days later when the rainy season turned our construction site into a lake. Our frustration was salved in early December of 1968 when the adoption agency came through with a six-week-old baby, whom we promptly named Zachary Alexander Raney The Great. Now we had us a Zak and a Zerk, and nearly a Nick. Construction began once more in the spring of 1969.

**Zerky, JoAnne, Zachary, and Tarzan, in 1969, at
214 Lincoln Street, where the Nickelodeon stands today**

**JoAnne, Tarzan, Zachary, Bill and Zerky
at 214 Lincoln Street, Santa Cruz, 1969**

**March 23, 1969, Nickelodeon Theatre
Under Construction**

The first screen of the Nickelodeon opened on July 2, 1969, and over the years the Nickelodeon has grown and prospered. In 1992, I sold the business to Jim Schwenterley, who has since made it stronger and better. JoAnne and I started this now forty-one-year-old Santa Cruz institution, with considerable anxiety and downright fear, because of what had happened to her dreams of an art theatre in San Francisco. Oh, how I wish she might have lived to see how well it all worked out.

Between the arrival of our six-week-old Zachary and the impending birth of our little Nickel Odeon ("two-bit music hall," in French), our lives changed once again. JoAnne threw herself into motherhood while I tried to learn how to act like a CEO. It was an exciting time for both of us.

A few weeks after Zachary arrived on our doorstep, JoAnne took a trip to the doctor. She was pregnant. We already had two boys, this one just *had* to be a girl. I needed a replacement for my lost sister, I told JoAnne, who promised to do her best. Would I like to call her Penny? That was my sister's name. To do it seemed a bit weird to me, but we had recently been

NICKELODEON THEATRE

Feb. 28, 1969

214 Lincoln St. Santa Cruz, California 95060 — Telephone (408) 426-7500

Greetings from the growing Raney family. Our big news is a new adopted son, Zachary Alexander, born Dec. 2, 1968, alert, lively, and running mother ragged. Zachary is 5/8 Negro, 1/8 American Indian, and the rest more or less Caucasian. "He is," says mother "adorable--with big black almond eyes, silky wavy black hair, light brown skin, and double chins that just don't stop." "He looks," says daddy, "like a cross between Stokely Carmichel & Mayor Daley."

Xerky, who will be three the end of May, is taking Zachary well, but has decided I am not to be allowed out of his sight. Since he is in nursery school, this does create problems. Our little dachshund, Tarzan, is very jealous and sits on the end of the couch crying whenever I feed Zachary. The parakeets and seahorses, which complete our menagery, are not impressed.

To further keep life interesting it would seem that we are expecting another baby sometime in August. This one we are having the hard way, with no choice of sex, age, or color.

For those not up on our recent history, after selling THE MOVIE in San Francisco, we then took a one year's trip around the world driving from Germany to Calcutta. We are now living about 75 miles south of San Francisco where, thanks to the new campus of the University of California at Santa Cruz, Bill is building a new art-theatre. . . if the rain ever lets up. Bill has two partners in the enterprise.

Bill bought a new flamenco guitar recently, & between meetings with architects, contractors, equipment salesmen, film distributors, etc. he escapes to memories of sunny Spain.

As for me, my hands are more than full with the kids. I'm scheming how to get back to India, where the average $400/mo. income family maintains eight or nine servants, including cook, nursemaids, chauffeur, and someone who just sets the tea and/or drinks in front of one throughout the day.

Best wishes,

JoAnne & Bill Raney

playing an Ingmar Bergman film, *Through a Glass Darkly,* about a woman named "Karin," and I remembered how much I had liked the way they pronounced her name in Swedish—not "Care-in," but "Karr-reen," with a little roll of the "r." But I'd had my fill of Scandinavian angst when I was a kid in North Dakota, so I put an "a" on the end of it to give it a little sunnier, more Mediterranean flavor. Soon "Kar-ree-na, Kar-ree-na, Kar-ree-na" came rolling off both our tongues, in some barbaric mixture of English, Swedish, and Spanish. *Viva La Karina!*

On July 30, 1969, when the Nickelodeon had been open less than a month, I came home from work one night around 1:00 AM, to find everyone asleep. At times like this, I would sometimes tiptoe quietly up to my office to do a little work, and then sack out on the bed upstairs so as not to awaken anyone. JoAnne would have to get up early the next morning when the kids woke up. What with me back on the night shift now that the theatre was up and running, I had made her the promise that as soon as it looked like this Santa Cruz idea wasn't going to be a flop, I would hire a union projectionist to replace me on the night shift so I could spend more time with her and our newly expanded family.

The following morning I was awakened by a crying Zachary downstairs. I rolled over and tried to get back to sleep, knowing JoAnne would deal with him soon. But the crying didn't stop. I went downstairs to see what was up.

Zerky was still in his pajamas and the house was a mess. JoAnne was asleep. While fixing Zachary's bottle, I noticed that Zerky had gotten into his finger paints. He had them on his hands, on his pajamas, and on the bricks around the fireplace. This was going to be a project—getting all that paint off those porous bricks—and I wondered why JoAnne hadn't been keeping a better eye on things. I decided to wake her, even though it made me feel guilty. In the little alcove off the living room where we normally slept, I noticed that she seemed to be getting out of bed. Her covers were thrown back, one heel was on the floor, and her head was on the pillow, resting awkwardly. "Time to get up," I said, grabbing her by the shoulder and shaking her gently. I shook harder. Her shoulder was cool. She wasn't breathing.

JoAnne was over eight months pregnant at the time. Because she could have gone into labor at any time, we had her doctor's phone number pasted on the telephone. "I think JoAnne's dead," I told the doctor. "She doesn't seem to be breathing and when I grabbed her by the arm, to wake her up, she felt cool to my touch. Please come quickly, maybe you can still save the baby!" The doctor explained to me that a fetus can live only a short time, once the mother's heart stops beating. He told me to call the police.

The police station was two blocks away. The cops came quickly. "Were there any indications of impending death?" one of them asked. No. An efficient, well-organized crew soon arrived to carry away JoAnne's body. Zerky spent the episode silently receding into the far corner of the living room, thumb in his mouth.

JoAnne had bought Zerky those finger paints for a homework assignment from his new preschool. After the policemen and body crew had gone, I discovered additional traces of finger paint scattered about the house. Zerky had been up for awhile; his mother had been dead for hours. We kept the bedroom door open so we could hear crying in the night. My new wife, Nancy, reminds me that there was finger paint on JoAnne's nightie.

JoAnne's death came out of nowhere, a gratuitous insult to everyone who loved her. The autopsy found she had died of a cerebral aneurism, a hemorrhage caused by a burst blood vessel in the brain. It had been quick, the doctor assured me. The proverbial "good death." Karina's death was much more problematic.

Just who was she anyway, this Karina? Another phantom like my lost little sister Penny? A few days earlier, I had felt Karina kicking inside JoAnne's belly, as if trying to get out to join the living instead of staying inside and joining the dead. But according to JoAnne's official death certificate issued by the state of California, Karina never existed. No such death certificate was ever issued in Karina's name, nor does JoAnne's death certificate bear any indication that she was pregnant at the time of her death, even though Karina would have easily been capable of surviving her premature birth. Notwithstanding all of the above, it is the official determination of the state of California that my daughter Karina never existed. So here we are, unexpectedly, at the threshold of the abortion controversy. Perhaps it is fitting that Karina's existence be denied by the state of California, just as my sister Penny's existence is still denied by the state of North Dakota. Penny was secretly adopted. Karina was my lost Penny.

How do you handle the death of a spouse? I can only speak for myself: I think you don't handle it, it handles you. That is a blessing. I think it is proper that you to be miserable; it is your misery that will drive you to accept your fate. "Why me?" may be a suitable subject for philosophical reflection someday, but you first need to be miserable for quite some time. Why should you be otherwise upon the death of a loved one?

My biggest problem was that everything reminded me of JoAnne. I couldn't get her out of my mind. She had become an appendage, to the point where our lives were so intertwined in so many ways that it was no longer clear who each of us were. When half of you gets ripped away, shreds still remain, and they will haunt you at every turn. Where's the sugar? "JoAnne always kept it in the cupboard over the stove," replies the voice in my head. Or maybe I'm thinking about going next door to watch the movie. "JoAnne would have loved it," the voice replies. Or maybe I'm thinking about taking the day off and taking the kids to the beach. "Half as much fun for twice as much work," the voice squawks at me again. "Maybe I'll go out to dinner?" "With whom?" it mocks.

Cleaning out JoAnne's closet was the worst part of it. What to do with all her stuff? There was that sexy little dirndl we bought her in Austria—the traditional Tyrolean "St. Pauli Girl" costume with the frilly white blouse underneath and the embroidered green dress up on top, with the neckline cut so low that it looks like your boobs are falling out. And that beautiful embroidered green sari we bought her in the bazaar in Calcutta—the sari, the most elegant garment in the world. And how about that slinky jade-green silk brocade dress we had made for her in Hong Kong? The one I almost had to pour her into, and zip up. Everything reminded me she was no longer there. There is no way out. Not for a while.

But there's light. Eventually. And it's not forgetfulness either, or "closure." Closure is a newly invented product sold by the psychiatry industry. Our culture teaches us to honor our dead, not to forget them, because memories are what remain after death. And because diminishing them, diminishes us too. The dead are locked in time and can no longer follow us on our journey through life. We must give them a hand. There is a certain beauty and logic to it all. Our brains come with built-in automatic survival mechanisms that repair us slowly, by growing new associations and linkages in our minds. Once you've done your laundry fifty times on your own, doing it will no longer remind you of who once did it for you. One by one, the old associations start breaking down, as bit by bit you are forced into doing things differently. Slowly and inexorably will come the day when everything no longer reminds you of he or she who is no longer there. What more would you ask? A lobotomy?

• • •

About two blocks up and over from where the Nickelodeon stands today, was a "little black neighborhood" that JoAnne and I used to refer to facetiously as "the ghetto." Except for a few black faces, it was indistinguishable from the rest of Santa Cruz, which is a lily-white community. Having told the adoption agency about our attempt to adopt a child in India, we hit the jackpot when they gave us a black child. Now we wanted both brothers raised in a place where Zerky would not be the only kid on the block with a black brother. This little black neighborhood, then, was a welcome addition to our little white neighborhood.

A few months after JoAnne died, Zerky made his first neighborhood friend. He was Zerky's age and he lived up on Chestnut and Taylor Streets, and he was black. Both of them were four years old. Since Zerky had been acting shy in school lately, I saw this as an opportunity for him to have his own special friend, one not artificially created for him by grown-ups. I met with the mother and got permission for her son to come over to our house to play with Zerky after school. Our two four-year-olds enjoyed each other handsomely, and soon they were riding their trikes together up and down the sidewalk, hell bent for leather, like most of us used to do.

One afternoon I was working in my office when suddenly there came a pounding on the front door. It was Zerky's new friend's mother. There were tears in her eyes. "Zerky," she stammered, motioning me with her hand to come with her. We started running up Lincoln Street until she got winded; she motioned me to run on alone. Two or three minutes later when I arrived at her house, I spotted a policeman a block further up the street, near the end of what turned out to be no cul-de-sac after all. Running up to him as fast as I could, I spotted a small white blanket spread out upon the sidewalk. Next to Zerky's flattened tricycle. His little blue tennis shoes, the ones with the white laces, sticking out from beneath the blanket. When I got down on one knee to pull the blanket back, the policeman grabbed my hand gently. "You don't want to do that," he said.

The previous year when I had received JoAnne's ashes back from the crematorium, I didn't know what to do with them; they sat on the mantlepiece for several months. One sunny day I took a drive up into the Bonny Doon area north of Santa Cruz, where JoAnne and I had hoped to buy a house someday, "as soon as it looks like the theatre isn't going to be a flop," I had told her. But I couldn't find the right spot, and pretty soon her ashes and I found ourselves headed up Highway 1 towards San Francisco. Passing the turnoff on the right, to the little town of Pescadero, I remembered the lovely beach off to the left where the four of us had had a picnic a few months earlier. We had spent a few delightful hours there, watching the waves break out on the rocks and their remnants come lapping on

**Zerky at the church
across the street from the Nickelodeon**

into a peaceful little cove, where Zerky chased them back out
into the ocean by throwing sand at them, and yelling at them,
while Zachary crawled around on the blanket trying to eat all
the sand. It was there I sprinkled JoAnne's ashes.

When I returned to Santa Cruz and started telling people
what I had done, I soon realized I had overlooked something—
people wanted to be included. They expected a funeral; some
kind of ceremony; an opportunity to pay their respects. They
wanted resolution. They would have similar expectations now.
Here was an opportunity to make amends.

Sept. 8, 1970
214 Lincoln Street
Santa Cruz, California
95060

To Whom it May Concern:

The cremated remains of Erik Xerxes Raney have been
deposited along with those of his mother, Frances
JoAnne Raney, on a beach near Pescadero, California.
It is a pleasant place, ideal for children to play
and for adults to be pensive. Xerky and his mother
both enjoyed it during their brief lives. Others
might enjoy it, too.

It is my desire that the spot not remain anonymous--
that Xerky and JoAnne not become forgotten. Perhaps
people would like to visit their beach occasionally
while traveling to San Francisco. Children need not
know its significance--only its pleasures, and that
it was a very special spot for Xerky.

On ~~Saturday~~ Sun. September 13, at 1:00 P.M., I will be
leaving my home to pay a brief visit to this spot.
Anyone who is interested in knowing where it is
located, is invited to follow me. There will be no
ceremony. I wish simply to point out the location.

Sincerely,

William V. Raney

Exactly three-tenths of a mile north of the Highway 1 turnoff
to the quaint little town of Pescadero (approximately a third of
the way from Santa Cruz to San Francisco), lies Zerky's Beach.
If you turn left into the first small parking lot, three-tenths of a
mile north of that Pescadero intersection, you will immediately

come to a small sign marking a trail down to the beach. From the level of the parking lot, eight steps have been cut into the hillside, which will take you down onto a lumpy landing looking out upon the ocean below. Descending onto that eighth and final step, you will be facing Zerky's Beach, at the head of the small rocky cove directly in front of you. Where the trail forks sharply to the left, a second set of steps will then take you down onto the beach below, where we had our picnic that day.

Should you not wish to descend to the beach, a hundred yards or so farther out on that lumpy landing there is a stake in the ground at the edge of the cliff, overlooking the ocean. On it is a small brass medallion marking Zerky's Beach below, and slightly off to the left. As I said ineptly in that letter I wrote thirty-eight years ago, "It is my desire that the spot not remain anonymous, that Xerky and JoAnne not become forgotten."

Zerky's Beach disappears each winter because of storms. Best go there on a warm sunny day in the summertime, when there is no fog and you can see sailboats going up and down the California coast, as my wife Nancy and I were to do many years later. I don't know where God puts all his sand and ashes in the wintertime, but I do know he puts them somewhere safe from the winter storms, because the sand on Zerky's Beach returns each summer.

A month or so after Zerky died, Tarzan threw up all over the floor. There was meat in his vomit. We only fed him dried dog food. Later that day, I found meat on the ground in our backyard. It had been thrown over the fence—meat laced with rat poison. A week or two later, Tarzan was nowhere to be found. I asked around. I put an ad in the paper. A day or so later the phone rang. A male voice was telling me that he thought he had my dog. "Is he a very small brown dachshund male, with a shiny coat?" I asked. The voice told me it looked like my dog, but that I needed to come and see it to make sure. I wrote down the address carefully, and told him I would be there to identify Tarzan within half an hour. I already knew where the street was, but when I got there, I couldn't find the house. The street ended a block before where the address should have been. I asked a man working in his yard where that number might be. He assured me no such number existed.

How stupid of me not to have asked the caller for his name and telephone number. Now I could not call him back. When I got home, I decided to call the police. It was a long shot, but there just might be some kind soul there at the PD who might remember me from JoAnne or from Zerky, and who might be persuaded into trying to trace that call. I soon had a cop on the phone who sounded like he liked dogs, and I told him my tale of woe. When I got to the phone call part of the story, he dragged me up short, telling me that sort of thing happens all the time. He'd heard it before. "Why do people do things like that?" I asked. "People are funny that way," he replied.

Main Street, Consumers, Utah, 1936
Library of Congress Photo by Dorothea Lange

Company Store in Coal Town, Consumers, Utah, 1936
Library of Congress Photo by Dorothea Lange

Epilogue

SOMETIMES WHEN FILLING OUT FORMS ASKING "PLACE OF birth," a curious clerk would ask JoAnne where Consumers, Utah, was. "It doesn't exist anymore," she would tell them. "It wasn't really a town at all, just a mining camp up in the mountains. I think maybe it was somewhere near Helper, Utah, or maybe near Price. I like Helper the best, don't you?" This would usually get a laugh, or at least a nod, and then she would go on to explain that her father had once been the doctor in that little mining camp up in the mountains, and that he had told her Consumers became a ghost town when the mine closed down after World War II.

JoAnne was the kind of person who loved things like ghost towns and old mining camps up in the mountains, but by the time she started thinking about it seriously her parents had died. "Consumers is not on the map," she told me.

"But I'm very good at maps," I told her back. "It's got to be on some map somewhere—we've just got to find the right map." Someday I would do some research, I promised. Someday we would go looking for her ghost town together.

"Perhaps when we go looking for the ghost of your little sister," she replied. We thought we had all the time in the world.

On November 10, 1933, JoAnne was born in the tiny coal camp hospital in Consumers, Utah, then run by her father, the coal camp's doctor. Three years later, famous photographer Dorothea Lange, then working for the Farm Security

Administration, did a series of photographs depicting the lives and living conditions of migrant and rural families in Utah, several of which were taken at Consumers.

All my life I've been a camping nut. In the 1980s, long after JoAnne died, I fell in love with the deserts, mountains, and canyonlands of southern Utah. Often on my trips back and forth between California and North Dakota, when I finally went looking for that ghost of my little sister who had disappeared into the night, I would take roundabout routes through Utah and the other arid parts of the Great American Southwest. Once I found myself gassing up in Price, Utah, and I asked the station attendant if he had ever heard of Consumers. He said no, but I needed to buy a new roadmap anyway. Unfolding it on the hood of my pickup, there on the highway less than ten miles in front of me was Helper, Utah! I'd always thought Helper was

Consumers, Utah, today

just the punch line to JoAnne's silly joke. And then, off to the west of Helper, at the end of an unpaved road, was Consumers, Utah.

What remains of Consumers today is barely a ghost town; it's hardly any town at all. There is scarcely a building still standing, only broken concrete foundations and weathered piles of wreckage. I suspect the mining company probably dynamited the concrete buildings when it abandoned the mine after the war, when the price of coal came down. Unoccupied buildings would have been an "attractive nuisance," their lawyers would have told them. Or perhaps it was only the wind and the winter and the weight of the snow.

Poking my way through the rubble, I came across the ruins of a large building full of smashed-up chunks of porcelain. The hospital where JoAnne was born! I suddenly realized. All that porcelain was the remains of the old sinks, bathtubs and toilets.

JoAnne's Ghost Town

Stuffing a few chunks in my pocket, I wandered on, snapping pictures as I climbed through the rubble.

She was end of the line, my JoAnne. There were no blood relatives to notify of her death, only friends. Standing there contemplating the wreckage of this place that must have been so special to her and to her parents, I found it hard to hold back my tears. Why this rush from the past, I wondered? Why so sad about parents I never even met? Because there really are ghosts, I decided. I was being haunted by those well-known ghosts of the past.

What is it about ghosts, anyway? Why do they haunt us so, if they don't exist? Why do they flit and flicker about the very graveyards we build for them so that they might rest in peace? Why do we contemplate the dead when we first go back to the place where we were born? I think there is more to all this than nostalgia—I think there really are ghosts, tugging at us, pulling us backward in time and space, back into the mysteries of our childhoods. Ghosts are creatures of the fourth dimension, the dimension of time. Only the present exists in conventional three-dimensional space. And only for an instant. All else is in time.

Time is where our longings lie and our aspirations to the future. Notice how it's always "once upon a time," never "once upon a space." The fourth dimension is the repository for the detritus of our lives—all that stuff that got sloughed off during our breathtaking lifelong rush into a future that kept receding from us as soon as we got there. The joke's on us. The future is an illusion that precipitates instantly into the present, only to vanish again into the past, which is where our lives reside. Our pasts exist forever, all flimsy and tantalizing and just out of reach. They are those shimmering shadows we catch glimpses of in old graveyards, photo albums, ghost towns, and mining camps up in the mountains. Ghosts are our footprints marking the trajectories of our lives. They shimmer and shine because they are the beacons that beckon us back, lest we forget who we are. Ghosts are ourselves. It's our history that haunts us.

After the passage of nearly forty years, Zerky's death haunts me more than JoAnne's, even though hers hurt more at the time. But JoAnne had thirty-five years to explore her world, while Zerky barely got started. Who knows what his accomplishments might have been? The death of a child would seem to violate one of the fundamental laws of the universe, that law written down by Einstein which supposedly governs the interchange between matter and energy. Zerky was our little bit of energy that never got a chance to grow into matter. He was potential. He was magic. It was he who made our trip what it was. Zerky opened doors for us, doors that were to welcome us into the far corners of the world. Time after time we saw people's eyes light up as they encountered our little blond magician. Because childhood is what we all have in common. Zerky was the common denominator that brought us together with the peoples and cultures of the world during this thirteen-month-long adventure between the Atlantic and the Pacific Oceans. He was our passport to the world.

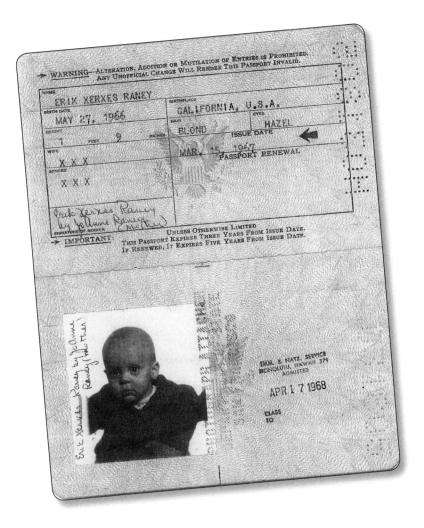

In Memoriam

I HAZARD TO GUESS THAT THE PART ABOUT DYING THAT most of us find most unacceptable, is not so much the pain, as the annihilation. It's that big black hole we're afraid of—that endless void. Let us then remember that after our deaths we survive in the memories of others, and that we are not gone until they are gone too.

So let us now remember the brave Tarzan, who protected us from the little monkey, who was protecting its baby from us.

And let us remember the gentle JoAnne, who loved all living things, and who remembered to say goodbye to her friends the bears, in the zoo at Bern.

And let us remember the little blond Zerky who brought peace to the Middle East one snowy night near Mount Ararat, where Noah's Ark finally came to rest.

Acknowledgments

ACKNOWLEDGMENTS, ACKNOWLEDGMENTS, ACKNOWLEDGMENTS.
How do you thank all the people who've helped you?

To my first wife, JoAnne, who got me into movie business
and gave me a job I loved. I hereby return the favor by making
her a posthumous author. JoAnne would have loved this!

To Zerky, who made this book what it is.

To Tarzan, who is in heaven with JoAnne.

To my new wife, Nancy, who throughout the course of writing this book helped me with much proofreading, good advice,
and valuable criticism.

To my aunt and uncle, Pearl and Allen Divine, who bailed
me out of an institution once upon a time long ago. He taught
me how to camp, hike and fish; she, what it is to be a lady.

To Mr. Lund, who was kind to me in that institution.

To my Port Angeles High School world history teacher,
Conner Reed, who taught me how to think.

To Dan Bessie, who saved me from myself more than once,
who was unstinting with good advice, and who helped edit this
book. And to Jeanne Johnson, who helped too.

To Helen Garvey, who helped too.

To W7RTU, Ron Floyd, who got me into ham radio when
I was in high school, whereupon I began traveling the world
at an early age. He also helped edit this book. And to Jane, his
widow.

To Lisa Jensen, who encouraged me to finish this book when I wasn't sure it was worth finishing. She held my hand when the going got rough, and also helped edit this book.

To my son Zachary, who is part of my story and who became a baseball player and a teacher in later life. He pitched for the Granada Sharks in Nicaragua, and for the Brasschaat Braves in Belgium. He is now a teacher in San Diego.

To my stepdaughter, Julie Atkinson, who spent a summer in Ghana, went to school for a year at Cambridge, lived in England for three years, and returned to America sporting a British accent. She is my caretaker at Zerky's Beach.

To my stepson Ken Atkinson, who lived in Paris for ten years, where he met his wife, Miwako. They now live in Japan, with Hiro and Hannah.

To my stepson Kevin Atkinson, DP, who studied in Avignon, France, in Japan, and in Argentina, and who is now a cinematographer living in Los Angeles. Kevin, too, has carried on the family tradition, by shooting films in Cameroon, the Maldives, and even in Louisiana.

To our grandchildren, Aubrey, Brianna, Isaac, Hiro, and Hannah, who are adorable.

To Capt. J.S.M. Vloemans, my fellow bullshitero and friend for so many years.

To Stan Stevens and the crew at the University of California, Santa Cruz Map Room, who turned me on to CIA maps in the public domain.

To Santa Cruz Mayor Emily Reilly, who helped me with Zerky's "Park"; to Santa Cruz Parks and Recreation Director Dannettee Shoemaker, who helped with it too; to Santa Cruz City School District Superintendent Alan Pagano, who also went to bat for me over Zerky's "Park."

To Dave Seawell, who sang tenor in the barbershop quartet I once sang bass in during my high school days long ago. We brought down the house at the old folks' home, at the local hospital, and especially at the school for the deaf and the blind. Dave was an American Legionnaire who got me a scholarship to Reed College in 1954, during the McCarthy era. Reed, which had recently been forced into firing a professor for allegedly teaching communism. And to the American Legion, who gave me money to go to a "communist university."

To my good friend Harry Clarke and his wife Lynne, who owned La Bodega, the Spanish bar where I first met JoAnne when I was both a beatnik and a bullshitero. They took good care of their bullshiteros by giving them leftover paella from time to time, not to mention many a glass of Manzanilla on the house.

To Hobie Hobart, who guided me through the complicated process of getting this book into print; and to Kathi Dunn, who worked magic with Zerky on the cover.

To Esqui Torres, who, unlike JoAnne, likes Price better than Helper, Utah. He rescued me one day when my truck broke down outside Helper, Utah, and spent the rest of the day driving me around in the mountains, looking for the remains of Consumers, Utah.

To book designer Sue Knopf, who magically turns manuscript pages into book pages, who designed this book, and who worked with me patiently.

To Dave Ebert at EbertsVWRepair.com, 2670 17th Ave., Santa Cruz, CA 95065, 931-476-8214, who has promised to keep my Zerky-Mobile in good repair.

To Christopher Reich, who read an earlier version of my manuscript and gave me some good advice.

To Jay Mayer of Delta Communications, who put up with me during the design of my website at www.letterstozerky.com.

To Jan Noto, current owner of "Zerky's House," at 616 Washington Street, Santa Cruz, about two blocks up and over from where the Nickelodeon stands today. Very early one morning in 1976, my wife Nancy and the kids and I went cruising up Lincoln Street in this two-story Victorian, popping a champagne cork along the way, looking cool. On Page 389 of this book are three pictures of it, taken in 1969, before it was extensively remodeled and fixed up.

And to Otis Coen, who was invaluable in doing the mix for "Zerky's Waltz," and its accompaniment, and who also invites you to join Zerky, JoAnne, Tarzan and me on our musical journey, as we "Waltz You Around the World. Come get the feel of a Zerky-Mobile!"

About the Author

BILL REMARRIED TWO YEARS AFTER JOANNE'S DEATH. Fortunately, Nancy is a traveler too and better with people than Bill ever was. She came to work at the Nickelodeon, doing publicity and public relations work. From time to time we would run off together for a few weeks, and pop into places like Papua New Guinea, Namibia, the Arctic and Mount Kailash in Tibet.

After selling the Nickelodeon Theatre in 1992, Bill and Nancy moved to Potes (see photo in color section) in Northern Spain, where Bill once wanted to live for the rest of his life. But the cultural barriers and language barriers were more than they could handle, so they returned to Santa Cruz six months later. Even though he now knows better, Bill still believes the grass is always greener on the other side.

In 1997 Bill and Nancy bought an old 42-foot trawler, on which they lived for the next eight years, cruising the Pacific Coast from Santa Cruz north to Alaska. They spent most of their time in Canadian waters, but today live in a redwood forest outside of Santa Cruz, California, with the deer, no antelope to play with them, but too damn many coyotes, and one remaining cat. Bill's wanderlust still grips him, although his seventy-three years have slowed him down. He suspects he spends too much time railing against the Iraq War. He hopes you enjoyed his book.

Sometimes it's weird how life works out. Sometimes the harder you try, the more you fail, and sometimes things fall into your lap, as if by magic. For example, we set out to take an extended European vacation and ended up trying to drive a car around the world. It just seemed like the right thing to do. This book was an accident too—I set out to write some letters to my son and ended up an author. As did JoAnne, who only set out to keep a diary. And now there's a Zerky's "Park" and a "Zerky's Waltz."

About Zerky's "Park"

After Zerky's death, I had no desire to revisit the place where he died, which was on high school property at the entrance to the Santa Cruz High athletic field. Several years later, Zerky's brother, Zachary, went to that same high school and, good little-league parents that Nancy and I tried to be, one night we inadvertently ended up at that field when we went to see Zachary play football. Upon leaving, I realized we were very near where Zerky died.

Years later, when I started editing and putting together these letters so that they might be a book, I returned to that athletic field once again, to refresh my memory so I could write about what had happened. I noticed that the field had been changed, and that where the accident had happened a building had been torn down. In its place was a small patch of grass, and a wall. On the wall were two brass plaques commemorating former students who had died in World War I. And then

I noticed that the playing field was named "Memorial Field." So why not a plaque for Zerky? Why not spruce things up a bit, haul in a few benches, and call it Zerky's "Park," as a memorial to Zerky. Too. I approached the school administration and they said yes. So now there will be a Zerky's "Park" at the corner of Taylor and Myrtle Streets in Santa Cruz, California. Perhaps I should call it a "minipark." Why not visit it anyway sometime, and try out the new benches and perhaps muse a little, about Zerky?

About "Zerky's Waltz"

One thing I learned in the process of doing this book is that once you've put your blood, sweat, and tears into such a project, you want people to read it. Which presents one with a different sort of problem. They call it "marketing." Ugh. And then one day a catchy little one-two-three, one-two-three tune popped into my head, and I realized it needed some words. So why not a "Zerky's Waltz" to help tell the story of our trip around the world? Hear it at www.LetterstoZerky.com.

Zerky's Waltz

William Raney

Come get the feel of the Zer-ky-mo-bile, it will waltz you 'round the world.

Eur-ope and As-ia and France, where they dance when they're

waltz-ing a - round ___ the world. Pa - ris and Lis - bon and Mu - nich and

Prague with Zer-ky, Jo - Anne, and with Tar-zan, our dog, we will take you to Tur-key, I-

ran, Pak-i-stan and Af - ghan-i-stan, too. And there's

Kan - da-har, Ka-bul, Za-he-dan, Is-fa-han, and there's Kat - man - du.

In - di - a, Thai-land, Bang - kok, and Hong Kong, we shall waltz you a - round ___ the

world. Do not stand there out - side. Come in - side! Take a ride. We've got pride in our

Zer - ky - Mo - bile

1

Come get the feel, of the Zerky mobile, it will
Waltz you 'round, the world.
Europe and Asia and France, where they dance, when they're
Waltzing around the world.
Paris and Lisbon and Munich and Prague, with
Zerky, JoAnne, and with Tarzan our dog, we will
Take you to Turkey, Iran, Pakistan, and Af-
Ghanistan too. And there's
Kandahar, Kabul, Zahedan, Isfahan, and there's
Katmandu...
India, Thailand, Bangkok, and Hong Kong, we shall
Waltz you around the world. Do not stand there out-
Side, come inside, take a ride, we've got
Pride in our Zerky-Mobile.

2

Come take a ride, put your troubles aside, as we
Waltz you around the world...
Come see the sights, all the big city lights, all the
Flags of the nations unfurled...
Zerky and Tarzan will take you away,
Tarzan, the dog, always just wants you to play. Hey
We got-a run, 'cuz we got to have fun in our
Zerky-Mobile...
Singing and dancing and driving around in our
Zerky-Mobile...
Singing and dancing and driving all day, we are
Waltzing around the world, get the feel, get the
Feel of a Zerky-Mobile, get the feel of a
Zerky-Mobile...

3

Now put some soul in it, let's rock 'n' roll with it,
Rockin' and rollin' along...
Pluckin' and cluckin' and keepin' on truckin' and
Singing, and dancing our song...
Standing around, put your ear to the ground, hear that
Sound, it's the sound of a Volkswagen bus going
Round, and around and around and around and a-
Round, and around on the ground... If you're
Happy and goofy and crazy then go, we will
Let you join in with our show...
Zerky, JoAnne, have a plan for their van, it's to
Waltz you around the world. So get on with it
Now, you're not hooked to a plow, you're a king in a
Zerky-Mobile...

4

Now we are cookin' and bookin' and lookin' and
Looking for good stuff to see...
Seeing the people and places we've been, all that
Good stuff for you and for me...
Come along with us, just take my hand,
We're gona travel all over this land and it's
One two three, one two three, driving along, in our
Zerky-Mobile... We'll be
Hootin' and hollerin' and singing our song, in our
Zerky-Mobile...
Strummin' and hummin' lookout, we're a comin', we'll
Dance you from night until dawn, get it on with a
Girl or a guy or a bird in the sky, or a
Zerky-Mobile...

5

One two three, one two three, now sing along with me
One two three, one two three, one...
Let yourself go, and get into the flow of it—
Come sing along with me now...
This is the time for to dance and to rhyme, to be
Thinking of going somewhere... To be
Singing and dancing and maybe romancing now
Get right up out of your chair... and start
Swinging and swaying and really conveying the
Feeling you're going somewhere...
Now is the time for to dance and to rhyme and be
Happy and merry and gay, in a land far a-
Way, where they dance and they play, in their
Wonderful Volkswagen Zerky-Mobiles...

6

One two three, one two three, come sing along with me
One two three, driving along...
One two three, one two three, one two three, one two three
Singing and dancing our song...
One two three, one two three, one two three, one...
One two three, one two three, son of a gun, it's just
One two three, one two three, one two three, one two three
Over and over again... Singing
One two three, one two three, one two three, one two a-
Gain and again and again...
Come get the feel, of our Zerky-Mobile, it will
Waltz you around the world... in a
Volkswagen bus, filled with people like us, singing
One two three, one two three singing our song...

7

Let your self go, we'll put on quite a show with our
Zerky show song, sing along with me long with me
Strummin' and a-hummin' and a-drummin' we're a-comin' and a-
Drivin' and a dancing, along…
Rockin' away, all the night and the day with our
Zerky show song, sing along with me now it's just
One two three, one two three, one two three, one two three
One two three, one two three, one… Let us
Rock and we'll roll, and get out of control, in our
Merry old Zerky-Mobile… It is
Never a thrill, to be just standing still, to be
Working and going nowhere… So just
Let yourself go, come join in with our show, in our
Merry old rock and roll Zerky-Mobile…

8

Come get the feel, of a Zerky-Mobile, it will
Waltz you around the world…
Europe and Asia and France, where they dance, when they're
Waltzing around the world…
Paris and Lisbon and Munich and Prague, with
Zerky, JoAnne, and with Tarzan our dog. We will
Take you to Turkey, Iran, Pakistan, and Af-
Ghanistan too… And there's
Kandahar, Kabul, Zahedan, Isfahan, and there's
Katmandu…
India, Thailand, Bangkok, and Hong Kong, we shall
Waltz you around the world. Get the feel get the
Feel of a Zerky-Mobile, get the feel, of a
Zerky-Mobile…

Index

Ordering Information

Yes, I want to order my copy of Letters to Zerky today!

Bill to (billing name and address)		
Name		
Address		
City	State	Zip
Daytime phone (for order questions only)		
E-mail address		

Ship to (if different from billing address)		
Name		
Address		
City	State	Zip

Description	Quantity	Price	Total
Autographed Dust Jacket		$27.00	
Dust Jacket		$27.00	
Autographed Soft Cover		$16.00	
Soft Cover		$16.00	
Shipping/handling per book		$5.75	
		Subtotal	
California residents please add 8.5% sales tax			
		Total	

Payment Options
☐ Check made payable to *Nickelodeon Press*
☐ Credit card: ☐ Visa ☐ Mastercard ☐ American Express
Number_____ Expiration Date _____ / _____
Signature (required on credit card orders) _____

Mail to: Nickelodeon Press   **Order online:** www.LetterstoZerky.com
PO Box 3573
Santa Cruz, CA 95063-3573

Ordered by: ☐ Postal mail   ☐ E-mail   ☐ Phone   ☐ Other

"Zerky's Waltz" and Bill's flamenco are available at www.LettersToZerky.com